*The Films of George Roy Hill*

George Roy Hill with the author on location for *The World According to Garp*. (Photo by Peter Britton)

# The Films of
# GEORGE ROY HILL

*Andrew Horton*

*Foreword by Paul Newman*

COLUMBIA UNIVERSITY PRESS
NEW YORK   1984

*Unless otherwise indicated, film stills are courtesy of the Films Stills Collection of the Museum of Modern Art, New York. Used by permission.*

*Designed by Ken Venezio.*


*Library of Congress Cataloging in Publication Data*

*Horton, Andrew.*
  *The films of George Roy Hill.*

  *Filmography: p.*
  *Includes index.*
  *1. Hill, George Roy, 1922–        I. Title.*
*PN1998.A3H484   1984     791.43'028'0924     84-5834*
*ISBN 0-231-05904-3 (alk. paper)*


*Columbia University Press*
*New York   Guildford, Surrey*
*Copyright © 1984 Columbia University Press*
*All rights reserved*

*Printed in the United States of America*


*Clothbound editions of Columbia University Press Books are*
*Smyth-sewn and printed on permanent and durable acid-free paper*

*for Odette*

# Contents

*Photographs appear in a group following p. 76*

# Foreword

## *Paul Newman*

*January 2, 1984, New York*

A hurried phone call:

"George, some yo-yo from your office just bullied me into writing some kind of Foreword for a book about you. I'm supposed to describe you in ten words or less."

"That should just about do it," replied George and hung up. George is like that. He is a very private person.

I am a very private person.

Now then, what can a very private person write about another very private person?

*January 10, 1984, Bernie's Grill, Austin, Texas*

"George, I've taken about six runs at this Foreword thing."

GEORGE: "What have you come up with?"

"It's just a start, you understand."

"Start," he said.

"George Roy Hill conducts his rehearsals like a ritual Prussian War Game. His chairs have legs four feet long to give him the advantage of height in case he's short on logic. If Olivier is an actor's actor, George is a curmudgeon's curmudgeon."

Silence—

GEORGE: "Run up that flagpole again, kid, and see what you come up with."

George and I have been friends for a long time.

I think.

It's hard to know if a very private person is your friend or if he's just less private with you than he is with his motorcycle. Tennessee

Williams wrote, "If I seem distant and wary, it's not because your arms are too long, it's because mine are so short." I don't know whether that fits George, but he wears a 15½, 33 shirt if that's any help.

*January 14, 1984, Gambier, Ohio*
  "George, I'm writing ten hours a day on this Foreword thing."
  "Spit it out, kid."
  "Well, the only fresh thing I've come up with is there's evidence you may be a clone of Tonio Kroeger."
  "Is that some kind of sandwich?"
  "No. Thomas Mann's *Tonio Kroeger*." A 'bourgeois manqué' is what you are."
  "Come again?"
  "An imperfect bourgeois is what you are."
  Silence.
  "Let's go short on this clone stuff and whip up something rakish."
  "Like what?"
  "Like George Roy Hill embodies the best of Fellini, Bergman, Truffaut, Reinhardt, René Clair, John McEnroe. . . ."
  "McEnroe's a tennis player."
  "That too."
  And hung up.

*January 20, 1984, Mombasa*
  George Roy Hill and Tonio Kroeger. I pondered the connection. Kroeger says of himself, "The artist must be unhuman; must be extra human; he must stand in a queer aloof relationship to our humanity; only so he is in a position, I ought to say only so would he be tempted, to represent it, to present it, to portray it to good effect. The very gift of style, of form and expression, is nothing else than this cool and fastidious attitude toward humanity."
  By George, I thought, there's a lot of George in that.
  But, what about the rest of him?

*January 25, 1984, Okinawa*
  "George, I did about thirty pages on you and Fellini and you didn't come out so hot. I'm back to Tonio Kroeger."

"What about me and McEnroe?"

"Thomas Mann says that Kroeger is also a softie; that he watches the 'blue-eyed people' with gentle envy."

"You write that about me and I'll chop your gonads off."

". . . that he lives between two worlds and is at home in neither and suffers in consequence. It's the suffering and the anguish splattered all over the sidewalk that is the wellspring of all your humanity."

I could hear George weeping on the other end of the line. He makes lightning transitions.

Actually, George does Tonio one better. George lives between two worlds and is *accepted* by neither one of them. The artsie fartsies in the film world despise him because he is bathed in success. The bourgeois grow silent when he enters a room because they see him as an eccentric, infallible loner who exudes pure POWER.

*January 29, Lourdes, France*

What is George's special allure? Why do performers tickle his soft underbelly with affection and pick up all the dinner tabs which he never sees. Because they know that they will never be better; that George's "detached" eye will spot a successful mannerism, an irrelevant gesture, an irresolute intention, a personal comment, stomp it underfoot and politely ask for something original.

In the largest sense, he is insurance (not always "no fault" insurance), but the sweetest coverage around. In the environment of film, where there is so much bad taste, so many berserkers, amateurs, executives and people "puttin' on airs," George is truly a straight arrow. He assumes the title of "professional artist in residence" and gives it a good name.

# Preface

As late as 1976, George Roy Hill was the first and only director to have two films on the all-time top ten box office hits: *Butch Cassidy and the Sundance Kid* and *The Sting* (both starring Robert Redford and Paul Newman). A filmmaker with a diverse background in music, drama, and television, Hill has proven to be a master and popular story teller in a variety of genres. His films, directed with a flair for style, are tied to important American themes. They reflect an ironic, bittersweet vision of life.

Erwin Panofsky has suggested the double nature of all art: "While it is true that commercial art is always in danger of ending up as a prostitute, it is equally true that non-commercial art is always in danger of ending up an old maid." Between prostitutes and old maids, there are movies like those made by George Roy Hill, which are worldly women with a flair for adventure and independent action who nevertheless maintain a tough innocence.

While Edward Shores' book on Hill has recently appeared, the limited scope of his work makes it necessary to study Hill's entire career if we are to better understand the accomplishment of his films.

Hill's films deserve close attention for another reason. His films have been popular, yet they have often been lambasted by critics. Andrew Sarris, writing on *Slaughterhouse Five*, states that, "The ease with which Hill slides back and forth between reality and fantasy, between objectivity and subjectivity, goes beyond conventional slickness into idiosyncratically odious oiliness," a line that inspired Susan Sarandon to embroider the last three words on a sofa pillow as a gift to Hill. Pauline Kael labels Hill as "implacably impersonal." The general consensus of many New York critics is that his films are stylish but empty, and that he rushes from genre to genre for no apparent reason. He has, so they argue, thus failed to establish himself in one consistent (predictable) pattern.

The split of opinion between the public and the critics is of course due in part to the deep-rooted suspicion by many critics that "popular" implies a lack of artistic value. There is also the fact that Hill has not played the role of a director in the public eye. He has given few interviews, has avoided fashionable circles in Hollywood, and has often kept the press off his sets. In an age of the director as superstar, Hill has elected to remain virtually anonymous.

Furthermore, critics have tended to attack Hill for being what he is not. He is not John Ford carving out the Western as his niche nor Hitchcock branding the thriller with his name. And though he frequently deals with social issues directly and indirectly, as in his treatment of World War II in his television version of *Judgment at Nuremberg* and in *Slaughterhouse Five*, he is not a social crusader, political revolutionary, or even in Voltaire's sense, a moral *philosophe* attempting to educate a superstitious public. Nor is he like younger directors who can be carried away by the technical wizardry of cinema.

I wish to suggest what George Roy Hill is and has been: an American director unaligned with any particular movements or trends who has worked within the Hollywood commercial framework, drawing upon a richly diverse background to make an equally diverse series of films that are surprisingly consistent in characterization, theme, and tone. Furthermore his movies are a celebration and a critique of America, past and present. His characters are wanderers, but their roots are of a general American culture; and the form of his films is often a variation on American film genres. Finally, instead of being "implacably impersonal," Hill has put much of himself in his work. But unlike more self-indulgent directors, Hill chooses to keep us at a far enough distance from his characters that our response to his films is never purely emotional.

Hill the man, on the other hand, is perhaps best known by those who have worked with him. Robert Redford describes Hill as, "bright, tight, fun, talented, untrusting, and demanding." He smiles as he thinks of Hill and concludes, "And I like him." Redford feels Hill is one of the smartest people he knows and that Hill's insight comes out in unexpected ways. "Some people read the funny papers in the newspaper because that's as far as they can get, but George reads them because for him they speak of something very much of this country. He recognizes that the way comics are constructed has a lot to do with a comic view of life."

Paul Newman finds Hill unique among Hollywood directors. "Hollywood tends to corrupt," says Newman, "but one of the least corrupted is George. More and more films tend to be designed for the lowest common denominator, but George has come through all of this with an ethical perspective. He doesn't simply do things to have a job. He has a thirst to complete something of merit."

Hill's closest associate for over fourteen years has been producer Robert Crawford. Crawford notes the special touch Hill has with bringing a screenplay, a scene, a moment, a character to life. "What George is able to bring to most scenes is a *resonance,* an obliqueness that rivets an audience and makes them ask questions about what will happen."

Screenwriter Steve Tesich *(The World According to Garp)* feels that much of Hill's sense of privacy comes from his earlier career as a writer. "When George makes a film, it is George's film. He does not talk a lot about what he is going to do with others, which is how a writer thinks."

Casting director Marion Dougherty, who has worked on most of Hill's films since *Hawaii,* sums up the feelings of many who work for Hill: "He is very demanding and very exciting." Part of being demanding, Redford feels, is a positive sense of paranoia. "Like any good general, you have to have a certain amount of paranoia to succeed and to keep the troops together." But Redford is quick to point out that the qualities that make Hill a general do not include rigidity of mind. "People who are militaristic in their style," Redford observes, "tend to be shut off in their minds, but the thing I respect about George is that with all of his control and discipline that he demands from the people who work for him, he manages to keep an open and inviting mind, to challenge himself and others. I should know, because I feel I am very much like that myself."

Finally, Hill is one of the few directors who can bring a film in on budget. His tight control of the purse strings has earned him the reputation of being, as one studio head said, "cosmically cheap." Screenwriter William Goldman, who has done *Butch Cassidy and the Sundance Kid* and *The Great Waldo Pepper* with Hill, puts it this way: "I think George is one of the most gifted film directors in the world. But he is also unbelievably cheap when it comes to money. He's the cheapest person I've ever known!" he says with a smile. Newman admits that Hill is "severely cheap" but that he is getting better. He is also quick to point out that Hill can be very generous with his time and advice. When Newman was in Oregon shooting *Sometimes A Great Notion*, he found himself in a great muddle as he tried to direct and star in the film at the same time. "When George heard I was in trouble," Newman remembers, "he fueled up his own plane and flew up to Newport, Oregon. He arrived on the set, locked himself in the editing room for two days and came out and showed me what was needed to save the film."

In short, Hill is as eclectic as his films. He loves classical music and plays the piano well, is obsessed with flying and addicted to crossword puzzles. A tall trim man in late middle age, Hill has rugged good looks. Depending on his dress, he can look like a Kansas farmer (as one critic has noted), or a Marine officer when he crops his hair (he was a Marine pilot), or an Ivy League businessman complete with button-down collar and class tie (he is a Yale graduate). He has the Irish gift of storytelling, a hearty Midwestern laugh that borders on a guffaw, and a grim frown that sends those who work with him scurrying for cover. He lives in a spacious apartment on Fifth Avenue but his life style is simple to the point of austerity. Above all, he is a private person, a loner who avoids the social scene though he is sociable and outgoing with those he knows.

# Acknowledgments

I am grateful to those I interviewed, most especially to Marion Dougherty, Robert Crawford, Henry Bumstead, Jim Appleby, David S. Ward, Steve Tesich, William Goldman, Robert Redford, Paul Newman, and John Irving. The whole project would have been far more demanding without the generous help of Camille De Mave, Hill's assistant for many years. Warner Communications was helpful in arranging screenings of Hill's films, and the Brooklyn College Film Department and staff were supportive in numerous ways. I owe special thanks to those who have read all or parts of the manuscript and made useful comments: John Belton, Ken Hey, Michael Goodwin, Dan Georgakis, Jim Holte, Frank McConnell, Srdjan Karanovic, Stanley Hochman, Eileen Lottman, and Peter Biskind. Barbara Brady deserves special thanks for typing the manuscript. My wife, Odette, has been a sympathetic companion and a keen critic throughout the time I have spent viewing, reviewing, interviewing, and writing. William F. Bernhardt and Leslie Bialler, my editors at Columbia University Press, have been both kind and firm in their faith in the manuscript.

Finally, I appreciate George Roy Hill's patience and good humor in his three-year cooperation with me on every aspect of this study that required his attention. He has consented to be thoroughly interviewed for this book.

*The Films of George Roy Hill*

# 1

## "Creating an Environment"

I'm a woman of experience, and I know the world. Just for the sake of amusement, ask each passenger to tell you his story, and if you find a single one who hasn't often cursed his life, who hasn't often told himself he was the most miserable man in the world, you can throw me overboard head first.—The old woman in Voltaire's *Candide*

Bruno Bettelheim has devoted much attention to the importance storytelling and myth have for the healthy development of children. Most recently, he has turned his attention to cinema: "One thing great art does is to provide a *myth*—a shared fantasy of mankind."[1] Bettelheim does not mean that myths must be moral fables working didactically on the surface level. Instead he points out that fairy tales, myths, and fantasies often make their most important statements indirectly, on a *subtextual* level.

George Roy Hill's films function on the same principle. The story entertains, but the subtext is often disturbing, contradictory, unresolved. The tension between story and subtext is a measure of Hill's art. It is no accident that producer Robert Evans credits Hill with helping to restore the primacy of a strong story line to American film after years of seemingly plotless "improvisations by other directors."[2]

Hill's films reflect an ironic double vision much like Voltaire's old woman. While not a cynic, Hill, like the old woman, does not believe that this is the best of all possible worlds. His movies reflect a wry amusement, concern, and finally, acceptance of man with his fears, folly, and fantasies. Like Voltaire, Hill is a master storyteller who frames a serious view of life in a comic-ironic vein, manipulating genres for his own purposes.

Hill is fond of quoting George Bernard Shaw's remark that "Tears are the natural expression of happiness and laughter is the natural voice of despair." His films begin on a light note and become progressively more serious. "Nothing ever ends happily," he comments. He refers to Garp's line in *The World According to Garp:* "Sometimes you can have a whole lifetime in a day and not notice that this is as beautiful as life gets. I had a beautiful life today." The same bittersweet view and the need to celebrate fleeting happiness permeate all of Hill's work.

A study of any artist's work will reveal some sense of unity. Thematic and formalistic continuity and repetition do not in and of themselves mark the quality of a filmmaker's production. Rather, as Robin Wood has said of Alfred Hitchcock, "This steady development and deepening seems to me the mark of an important artist."[3] To review George Roy Hill's films from *Period of Adjustment* to *The World According to Garp* is to trace an ever-deepening sense of sympathy and scorn for the human condition. Technically and artistically his broadening awareness of the possibilities of film as a medium for storytelling, in the widest sense that Bettelheim suggests, has made Hill's films increasingly worthy of discussion.

I shall make no attempt to rank Hill among the Pantheon of American directors. Instead I wish to suggest through a study of his films that he is an important director whose work is deserving of a much closer look than it has received until now. Edward Shores has written that, "the overtly commercial surface of . . . [Hill's] work masks but does not obliterate the intelligence of his films."[4] I would alter such an evaluation to state that the entertainment value of his work is in fact one indication of the intelligence of his films.

Hill feels that all of his major characters "create an environment, a fantasy, an illusion, and then go on to make it happen." We shall trace the thematic characteristics that are consistent with Hill's depiction of protagonists who create their own environments and then attempt to inhabit them. Then, in individual chapters, we shall study in detail the art, craft, and style of each of his films.

*What Are Heroes?* Figures may be turned into myth or legend by rumor, the press, books, or films. *Butch Cassidy and the Sundance Kid,* for example, opens with an old silent film based on their lives. But larger-than-life heroes do not exist in Hill's universe: his characters remain human beings with lively imaginations.

In A *Little Romance*, Laurence Olivier plays a civilized old rogue who pretends to be what he is not—a retired diplomat with an equally fabricated past—in order to entertain the young protagonist-lovers of the story. When he is exposed by the young boy, Olivier—with all the wisdom of age—attempts to explain himself: his actions have been an effort to bring "a little romance" into his and their lives. He then asks them, "What are heroes but ordinary people doing extraordinary things?" Once Olivier explains the importance of illusions to the young lovers, they proceed to make his "lie" come true by rushing to Venice to kiss under the Bridge of Sighs at sunset and thus, according to Olivier, to be united forever.

Likewise, each of Hill's major characters is propelled by what is often a seemingly impossible fantasy which he or she lives out to the end. George Haversack, the young husband in *Period of Adjustment*, at the end of the film is still bent on starting up a cattle ranch on which he will raise steers for tv westerns. The young girls in *The World of Henry Orient* live out their romantic crush on grand pianist-imposter Peter Sellers much to the dismay of Sellers and their parents. Reverend Hale in *Hawaii* carries out his Puritan missionary role, which begins as a dream in New England, and he follows it through until it becomes a nightmare in Hawaii. Butch Cassidy and the Sundance Kid go to their deaths at least pretending to believe the illusion that they will continue to be old-time bank robbers in . . . Australia. And Redford makes his fantasy to be a fighter ace come true as he acts in Hollywood at the end of *The Great Waldo Pepper*, while Reggie (Paul Newman) in *Slap Shot* creates a myth about his down-and-out hockey team being sold for a fortune to a Florida club in order to put some life into his dying team. In all cases, without the illusions none of the characters would have gone beyond themselves to reach what they become.

"I'm interested in characters who have illusions," states Hill. "An awful lot of my characters and the characters I am drawn to are people who have ideals that are unreachable because they are glamorized ideals, and they do not really apply to regular life. In fact, when one applies these ideals to regular life, it all falls apart."

Hill's work ranges from the almost pure farce of *Thoroughly Modern Millie* to the serious drama of *Toys in the Attic*, with most of his films combining the comic-ironic and serious elements. While his illusion-creating protagonists come from a variety of backgrounds, all (except for those in *Toys in the Attic*) fall within the mode of ironic comedy.

Hill's films can be discussed in terms of Northrop Frye's theory of comedy. Frye considers the first phase of comedy in terms of the Aristophanic formula, in which "a humorous society triumphs or remains undefeated." The second phase "is a comedy in which the hero does not transform a humorous society but simply escapes or runs away from it, leaving its structure as it was before."[5] Hill's films generally represent this second phase.

These characters tend to be outsiders, children, and/or outlaws with extraordinary "environments" they inhabit themselves. They do not change the society in which they exist. In Aristophanes' plays, characters conceive a zany plan, carry it out with wild success (peace in *Lysistrata, Peace,* and *The Acharnians;* a utopia in *The Birds*). A new order is obtained and maintained in a glorious celebration as Aristophanes' plays close. In Hill's films, in contrast, the tone is bittersweet; the fantasy triumphs of his characters are temporary, and few and far between; or they are maintained only through the power of film as a storytelling medium. The freeze-frame ending of *Butch Cassidy and the Sundance Kid* is a good example: the two heroes live only in the captured moment, the arrested forward movement of film itself, and thus as they are preserved in our memories. Society itself remains unchanged. And yet in *A Little Romance,* Hill suggests, through Daniel's imitation of Redford in *Butch Cassidy,* that stories have the power to affect individuals and likewise their fantasies, as Bettelheim proposes.

Pure comedy ends in celebration. But Hill has often chosen to work with adaptations of novels which end with death, or at best a sense of loss and change. Of the main figures in Michener's *Hawaii,* only Abner survives. Butch and Sundance are murdered as are Billy Pilgrim in Vonnegut's book and Garp in Irving's novel, while Waldo Pepper will die in a crash. Exceptions include *Thoroughly Modern Millie,* which like a Baroque farce exists entirely in a world of its own, and *The Sting,* which was conceived as an entertainment and thus does not adhere to the likely behavior of con men in real life.

Such a form of comedy, bittersweet as it is, falls firmly within much of the American tradition of comic literature and film. In particular I am thinking of *The Adventures of Huckleberry Finn.* Like Hill's films, Mark Twain's novel shows no happy compromise between Huck and "civilized" society. In the end an untamed Huck takes off for the wilderness, refusing to settle down with his Aunt because he has "been there before." For all of the humanity and humor of the novel, there is that sad gap in Twain's work between the individual and society that grew ever more bitter in his later years. Kurt Vonnegut is also within this comedy-as-escape-from-society mode, and it is Vonnegut that Hill likes to refer to in paraphrasing *Slaughterhouse Five:* he sees life as a string of random moments in which you are happy at times if you concentrate on the good ones and ignore the bad.

For Hill's characters, therefore, heroism is an effort of self-preservation and escape from what they perceive to be the hostility and boredom of traditional values and social structures—thus the particular quality of nostalgia in his films. It is not just that these people live out fantasies that conflict with *their* surroundings: the nostalgia is not only for an earlier America, but for a lost childhood as well. In a real sense none of Hill's characters truly grow up. To live one's illusions is to keep alive the child within us all, and to avoid, as much as possible, the adult reality of responsibility and compromises. Director Louis Malle is also fascinated with childhood innocence in films as seemingly different as *Zazie dans le Metro* and *Pretty Baby.* Malle has stated he prefers to focus on children because, "at that age they have a moment of total lucidity. But the moment you become part of this world of adults, you are just one of them: you start cheating and lying."[6] Hill would agree.

Laurence Olivier in *A Little Romance* is no Homeric or Byronic hero. What we respond to so warmly and openly is the nobility of his being able to remain truly young as an old man by inventing and carrying off rich illusions. To watch an aging Olivier in action with his thirteen-year-old friends is to *feel* George Bernard Shaw's remark that it is a pity youth is wasted on the young.

Hill has often been labeled the "master of nostalgia." And certainly many of his films are period movies that evoke a sense of the past: *Hawaii, Thoroughly Modern Millie,* World War II in *Slaughterhouse Five, Butch Cassidy and the Sundance Kid, The Sting,* and *The Great Waldo Pepper.* Yet it is not nostalgia per se that his films are about, for he makes no slavish effort to be historically correct. The use of Scott Joplin's turn-of-the-century ragtime music as a score for the 1930s setting of *The Sting* is a case in point. He is, as he remarks, more concerned with the fantasies and alternative realities his figures inhabit. For better or for worse, and often for both simultaneously, these "environments" tend to be drawn from the past, from a more simple vision of America, or at least from a more innocent conception of life and values.

Consider the Western theme, for instance. George Haversack in *Period of Adjustment* is the young Texan, confused and disturbed by the Korean War and contemporary American society, who wants to set up a cattle ranch. He is clearly unrealistic, but he is admired by his buddy, Ralph, who has compromised his life away with a suburban American lifestyle. *Butch Cassidy and the Sundance Kid* is itself a western, and like many westerns is set in that transitional turn-of-the-century era when the old individualistic values and wide-open spaces were giving way to the increased encroachment of "law and order" and fenced-in land. Butch and Sundance appear romantic, adventurous, and foolish for holding on to a way of life that has passed them by. *The World of Henry Orient,* with its New York City setting, hardly qualifies as a Western, and yet in counterpoint to Henry Orient's supposed "Eastern" sophistication is the zesty enthusiasm of the two girls who are accompanied on the soundtrack by an Elmer Bernstein score that has a Western beat to it: their Western energy is preferable to Orient's comically pathetic pretension. And Daniel, the young French protagonist of *A Little Romance,* grows up as a rabid fan of American films—in particular Robert Redford's roles in *Butch Cassidy and the Sundance Kid* and *The Sting.* Daniel is not American, but his love of American movies makes him the kind of kid he is: an overly bright fellow with the drive and imagination to live out "a little romance" in the face of stodgy schools and narrowminded parents. In all of these examples the idea of the old West becomes the illusion by which these ordinary characters live out extraordinary lives.

*Free-Floating Fantasy.* Creating an environment and inhabiting it is a function of wish fulfillment, and wish fulfillment is a major function of childhood and of cinema. Many, including Bettelheim, have written on the nature and power of cinema to portray and convey fantasies, dreams, states of consciousness that go far beyond the realism of photography and the limitations of time and space. Christian Metz speaks of film as "that other mirror," which reflects our pre-Oedipal egos and represents "desire as a pure effect of lack and endless pursuit."[7]

Much of the popularity of Hill's films, I suggest, comes from his appeal to the child within each audience member, an appeal which Hill makes effectively through his strong sense of story, style, and ironic humor. Nowhere are the dimensions of Hill's portrayal of pre-Oedipal or childlike fantasies more clear than in his lifelong fascination with flying.

In *The Great Waldo Pepper* barnstormer Robert Redford flies down a small country town's main street in his trusty biplane with the "It Girl of the Sky," Susan Sarandon, standing on the wing. It's the best gimmick they can think of to advertise the small-time traveling air circus they belong to.

There is a lot of George Roy Hill in the scene. In fact, it might even be said that his films themselves come down Main Street, America, in much the same way. The "stunt" is entertaining, exciting, dangerous, an exercise of great professional ability teamed with courage, and a living out of a fantasy.

Flying is subject matter and metaphor for many Hill productions. *The Great Waldo Pepper* is devoted to flying in the great old barnstorming tradition and is a nostalgic celebration of a freer, more individualistic period in American history. As a barnstormer, Waldo Pepper can merge his dreams with reality even though he is never able to be exactly what he wanted to be: a World War I fighter Ace. Still, life in the air offers a close second when compared with the "straight" life on the ground represented by Susan Sarandon's family. His flight down Main Street puts the clash in lifestyles between Waldo and mid-America in sharp contrast: his performance is a show, but it's a classy show built on his ability to handle his machine with daring aplomb.

Visually the scene captures the imagination. Hill moved from drama and television, where the spoken word is dominant, to films, where the visual possibilities for expression are greater. His films have reflected a growing awareness of visual imagery and cinematic form. *Waldo Pepper* would be exciting as a visual experience even without a story, simply based on Hill's imaginative use of the camera in the air to put the audience through the thrill of flight, and on ground to capture the compelling action from a spectator's point of view.

The stunt is, of course, part of an advertisement, a preview of the traveling aerial show. Similarly, Hill's films are commercial ventures in the Hollywood tradition. Waldo and Hill are maverick individuals who have their own values and personality and vision, but behind the illusions is economic reality. Entertainment is a sponsored commercial enterprise and, as we shall see, Hill acknowledges his love-hate relationship with the marketplace.

Many of Hill's protagonists remain "up in the air" physically and metaphorically. Jane Fonda does not fly in Hill's first film, *Period of Adjustment*, but in the best visual joke of the film she appears and disappears out of the frame in her newlywed husband's hearse, which is mounted on a hydraulic lift in a garage. As framed, the hearse appears to be floating freely, in defiance of gravity. We laugh. But the joke is a preview of the film: Fonda is herself very much "up in the air" about marriage, and life in general.

In *The World of Henry Orient*, Hill was one of the first American directors to use slow-motion to represent a psychological state. With slow-motion and extreme-low-angle shots, he captures the girls' sense of joyous freedom as they romp through New York, caught up in their own world. Framed against the sky, each girl appears to be floating, happy, free.

The sense of free-floating fantasy and childhood is most strongly indicated in an early version of the *Waldo Pepper* script. As the film is now, we open from a young boy's point of view, but the original William Goldman script went further to show a group of boys in the midwestern countryside in which the film is located. They are jumping from trees and were to have been shot in low angle against the sky to give them the appearance of flying. The sound of a plane engine is called for, while excited young girls look on.[8] Hill cut the scene because he "felt it was too much of a fantasy to incorporate into a realistic film." In a real sense, this scene, which has remained with Hill for years, has finally found its way to the screen in the opening and closing of *The World According to Garp*. Steve Tesich's script, based on the John Irving novel, begins:

A baby appears slowly from the bottom of the screen as if coming out of the womb. . . . the image of the baby rises slowly . . . neck, shoulders, belly and when we get to the feet the nude smiling baby just keeps on going into the air as if captured in extreme slow motion on a trampoline: It goes up, up, up, smiling, laughing, making baby noises, and then starts coming down, down, down, disappearing where it came from only to return again, making more noise, ga-ga-ga, type of noise, laughing and flying high in the air.

The film ends with the same scene. But this time there is also the accompaniment of what has become a theme song, Nat King Cole singing "There Will Never Be Another You." The opening is joyous because we share baby Garp's point of view: the ending, like all of Hill's films, is bittersweet because we know Garp is dying as he is being flown to hospital. The flashback to the opening image coupled with the song that brought Garp and his wife together heightens our awareness of the brevity of youth and happiness, of the need for dreams and romance, and of the violence of life. Even the opening scene is an "illusion." The baby appears to be flying only as long as the camera so *frames* the child against the blue sky of Dog's Head Harbor in 1944.

If cinema is "that other mirror" capable of reflecting our deepest fantasies and wildest flights of imagination, then Hill's films take us through such a looking glass. And through the manipulation of the medium of film, Hill manages to preserve the memory of these worlds of illusion while simultaneously suggesting a sense of the world of reality. In *Butch Cassidy, A Little Romance,* and *Garp,* it is the freeze-frame that permits us to retain these free floating fantasies despite our awareness that the environments these characters have created and inhabited have passed. The gap between the illusion and the reality is the particular ironic double vision that Hill cultivates.

*The Big Con.* Conning and being conned make up much of Hill's films. We have already discussed his characters and their illusions. To focus on the role of the con in their lives is in many ways to over-lap with the need to live out fantasies. To con is to manipulate and to deceive for one's own advantage. It is an outlook that could be purely Machiavellian were it not balanced by a joyful spirit of con-ning-for-conning's sake. And, by extension, what counts for, say, Paul Newman as the seasoned conman in *The Sting* is carrying off the big con as an intricate team effort done with style.

The con takes many forms in Hill's work. In *The Sting,* of course, we see it in its purest form: we watch professional con artists doing what they enjoy doing best. But most of Hill's protagonists are ma-nipulators to one degree or another. Butch and Sundance continually have to dream up ways to get the timid train guard to open the box car, Waldo Pepper lives by trickery and skill as a barnstormer, and Newman as the aging player-coach in *Slap Shot* invents a big con to jolt his losing hockey team into action. Hill's youngsters are capable of ingenious fabrications as they live out their illusions, and Julie An-drews as Millie learns the hard way that being modern means manip-ulating others coldheartedly.

Other characters are possessed by their own illusions and thus have conned themselves. In *The World of Henry Orient,* Peter Sellers al-most believes he is a suave European lover and concert pianist rather than the kid from Brooklyn he really is, while the spinster sisters in *Toys in the Attic* cannot bear to shatter the illusion that they are loved and cared for by Dean Martin, their brother who abandons them to their sterile existence in an old New Orleans home. Similarly, the young honeymooners George and Isabel nearly split up as they see through the illusions they have created about each other in *Period of*

*Adjustment*. And Max von Sydow as Reverend Hale in *Hawaii* never fully sees through the Puritanical vision of life he has conned himself into believing, and has attempted to con a non-Puritan culture into embracing. Hale never understands what Newman knows: revenge is for suckers.

In *The Sting* Newman reflects the ability to be in control of his environment. Modern psychology suggests how important such a sense of play is to an individual's healthy development.[9] William Blake's belief that man must create his own world or be slave to someone else's is also apt. Hill has represented both ends of the scale.

In *Slaughterhouse Five*'s Billy Pilgrim we witness an individual who is as guileless and empty a human as Jerzy Kosinski's humanoid Chance in *Being There*, but who is constantly insulted and abused. And yet ironically as Vonnegut and Hill make clear, Billy "succeeds" in an American society of con men and women because of his total innocence. Newman is able to manipulate the environment in which he lives; Billy Pilgrim, a victim of the horror of life, can only retreat into his midlife fantasies on the planet Tralfamadore.

Garp is the most integrated of Hill's characters. In this recent protagonist, innocence, fantasy, and illusion join together to enrich Garp's double life as a man trying to come to grips with a rapidly changing world and as an author struggling to write as well as he can. In this latter role, Garp, like any artist, is able to express his fears and fantasies in the "sad" tales he spins. That Garp too must die is sad, but at least he has lived and loved and had the satisfaction of seeing two of his three children survive. And as a writer he has left his mark for the future. An artist is a con man to the degree that he manipulates reality for his own ends. Garp goes beyond Gondorff from *The Sting*, however, because a book becomes a means of reaching beyond the self to touch others, whereas the con man's successes are merely in the present.

Garp is also the character closest to illustrating Hill's role as filmmaker. Like Garp's story "The Magic Gloves" (equivalent to "The Pension Grillparzer" in Irving's novel), Hill's films are ironic, comic, but stylish and sad tales that "con" us as good entertainment.

*The Sting* is also an exercise in cinematic conning for the audience on three levels: the opening sketches reveal the set of the film and thus suggest the film we are about to see (Hill appears in the drawing just behind his credit as director). Secondly the use of the preview shots of the actors in their roles frames the film as belonging to the old studio tradition of the 1930s, most specifically the Warner Brothers' gangster films. And the framing of the film with title cards makes us think of the film as both a drama and a story.

To fabricate reality, to tell a story, to work out a con is not necessarily to lie. Aristotle understood that. Poetry, he reminds us in *The Poetics*, is more real than history because history tells us only what did happen while poetry suggests what could and perhaps *should* have happened. "Most of what follows is true," reads the note to the audience in the opening of *Butch Cassidy and the Sundance Kid*.

Hill's cinematic conning thus creates an ironic view of the world as it is and as individuals would like it to be. Irony is precisely the gap between these two worlds. Hill's self-conscious use of style and manipulation of genre forms is a level of "conning" that functions in a double manner. This approach distances us from the material so that we can *think* as well as feel, and it allows Hill to involve himself in his work and yet distance himself from an overly direct and "raw" expression of feeling. At its best, as in *Slaughterhouse Five*, this double vision leads us to a fuller understanding of the double nature of ourselves. At its weakest, as in the closing parade sequence in *Slap Shot*, such control becomes contrived.

"Wit is made, while the comic is found," Freud has said. Conning and filmmaking allow for a blend of both. If there is a danger in Hill's work, it is this thin line between wit and the comic, between the contrived and the spontaneous. Because Hill's vision is, like many American humorists', more ironic than truly comic, he must guard against controlling his films so tightly that the ironic and contrived squeeze out the other elements. Conversely, he must beware of becoming so unreasonably upbeat that even his entertaining fantasies appear ungrounded in reality.

*I Married a Stranger*. If Hill's characters are dreamers and schemers, they are also alone, even when surrounded by others. Again, the tumbling infant in *Garp* makes this clear. Few of Hill's protagonists are lonely, for many find consolation in companionship and friendship; but his films are founded on *individuals* and their stories. Hill has wrongly been credited by some with inventing the "buddy film" with his Newman-Redford efforts. But even *Butch Cassidy and the Sundance Kid* opens after the "silent film" credit sequence with Butch, alone, watching a guard lock up a bank. The duo do not team up until the second scene, again, after we have watched Sundance play out a card game. Of course they are together for the rest of the film, and yet each is given attention alone. In particular Butch is not only the brains and the clown of the two, but also the outsider who sleeps alone when not with a whore and who is framed by himself, lost in his own thoughts, in the montage of old stills used as a transition from the American West to Bolivia.

Early in *Period of Adjustment*, Jane Fonda turns to her husband's best friend and with candid dismay states, "I married a stranger." The friend, who has been married for a number of years, smiles with patient understanding and replies, "We all do that." Her awareness of her situation is the beginning of her realization of the separate illusions each has been holding about the other, illusions that the reality of marriage quickly shatter.

Without a doubt the most isolated of Hill's individuals is Billy Pilgrim in *Slaughterhouse Five*. Kurt Vonnegut sets him up as a loner in the book, but Hill goes further by framing him in the first scene alone at a typewriter and, even more significantly, alone in a snowscape in the second scene. With a quiet, melancholy tune from Bach on the soundtrack, Billy wanders into view as a dot in an all-white, blank, environment in which nothing else exists to serve as coordinates for a "real" world. Billy is unstuck in time, but he is also floating in space.

Alone though they may be, none of these characters feels despair, and many actually feel comfortable in their solitude. Billy handles the horror of the firebombing of Dresden and the sterility of his contemporary American life, by time tripping to the numbly peaceful existence on the planet Tralfamadore. Abner Hale, the single-minded missionary in *Hawaii*, briefly appears aware how much his unswerving Puritan vision has destroyed the love and very existence of those around him at the end, but encouraged by a young Hawaiian convert, he is seen continuing again in the closing shot. And Reggie, the ruthless player-captain in *Slap Shot*, similarly drives away his wife and nearly destroys his bushleague team before he finds the will to keep up the bravado necessary to push and con a team along. Finally, Waldo Pepper is framed alone in his plane during a simulated Hollywood dogfight in the closing shot of the movie. Living out his fantasy of being a fighter pilot at last, he has a happy smile on his face as the music fades out suggesting his own withdrawal from reality.

Jane Fonda (Isabel) did marry a stranger. But the "period of adjustment" that so many Hill protagonists must pass through is the time it takes to understand "we all do that," a knowledge gained by living and with the help of friends.

If the individual is the basis of all Hill stories, the group or crowd is almost always seen in negative terms. John Ford champions the individual as outsider also, but families and groups gather to share births, marriages, deaths, and community events such as the church raising in *My Darling Clementine*. Frank Capra depicts crowds as a multitude of John Does—simple, honest Americans who are the foundation of the country. And Howard Hawks, who could more justifiably be called the father of the "buddy film," celebrates small groups of friends in his movies. For Hill, however, a crowd becomes a dehumanized, asocial mass. "I hate crowds: I think of them as a pack," he says. "They want to see blood or disaster." As Dilhoffer says in *Waldo Pepper* about the crowd at the air circus, "they don't want skill, they want blood." Almost the same line is used again in *Slap Shot* to describe the hockey crowds. Large parties similarly are shown as pretentious and empty in such films as *The World of Henry Orient, Thoroughly Modern Millie, Slaughterhouse Five, Slap Shot,* and *A Little Romance*.

This point can be taken a step further. Hill's individuals are for the most part either children or outsiders—not "responsible" members of mainstream society. *The World of Henry Orient* and *A Little Romance* are surprisingly similar films about rites of passage from childhood innocence to young adulthood, but in each the children live and romp in their own world. Some of the adults are outlaws as well as outsiders in other films. Newman and Redford in their two films, for example, while seemingly "straight" figures are equally outside society: Billy Pilgrim has the American Dream—family, professional respectability, and community recognition—and yet he is as far from being a fulfilled individual as anyone could be. Abner Hale tries to preach his vision of God outside his own culture in another place and culture for which his vision is foreign and destructive.

The family as a social unit fares no better. In both of Hill's "children" films, youths grow up in broken homes or caught between unhappy parents. In *Toys in the Attic*, Lillian Hellman's Southern gothic family is a prison which Dean Martin has left years before and which he must abandon before the film ends. Neither Newman nor Redford has any family ties in the four films they have performed in for Hill, and Julie Andrews is also an isolated "modern" figure entering a city landscape.

Only in *The World According to Garp* do we have a family that tries hard to hold together. Garp derives much of his deepest satisfaction from his wife and children. But in John Irving's novel, the Garp family is struck with violence, lust, hatred, and death as Jenny, Walt, and finally Garp himself are killed. The belief in family survives in *Garp*, and this can be said to be a new direction for Hill.

*The Need for Friendship.* For Hill, friendship lies between isolation and mass conformity. Friendship is important to Hill's characters and transcends even passionate love. Not love, but friendship—man to man, woman to woman, and man to woman—can be seen in each of Hill's works. Hill does not trust the extreme emotion of passionate love, and he would agree with Russell Baker who has said that "Love is responsible for over half the murders on any Saturday night." Hill emphasizes the separateness of couples and families instead of a close sense of sharing or giving. Put another way, friendship emerges from Hill's films as a form of love, and what others might label "love," as in the relationship between Garp and Helen, is perhaps more accurately described as a long-lasting friendship.

The relationship of Butch and Sundance in *Butch Cassidy and the*

*Sundance Kid* captures much of what Hill suggests about friendship. Consider the closing scene of the film as both know they are under fire, trapped in an old building in a Bolivian town. What they don't know, but which the audience does, is that they are surrounded by what seems to be the entire Bolivian army. Out of ammunition, Butch runs out to the horses for more, while Sundance provides cover. Butch makes it back with the ammo, but both are wounded in the effort. Once back, Butch quips, "Is that what you call giving cover?" Sundance retorts, "Is that what you call running?"

The scene is poignant because we know that Butch and Sundance do care about each other. Yet the kind of life they lead does not make for lasting heterosexual relationships even though they both care for Etta, the schoolmarm who follows them to Bolivia, but who exits before their inevitable deaths. As in most Westerns, women are more an interference than a blessing in the film, even though Etta manages to hold her own as an efficient member of the gang. There can be no conventional patterning for this trio on the run. The best they can do is enjoy each other's company in what becomes in spirit if not in fact, a *ménage à trois*.

The two outlaws have each other . . . till death do them part. Their needling of each other even at the point that their end seems clear, is in keeping with the boyish pleasure they derive throughout the film. The attempt is at wit, but the situation is far from humorous. Hill succeeds in creating pathos with his characters' attempts at cheer in the midst of disaster. The script has been criticized as being too glib. But its lines are reflective of Butch and Sundance: they are, like a lot of people, not able to express their deepest feelings for each other in more direct language.

The expression of the friendship is in action, in the subtext rather than the text. When both are wounded, they banter on absurdly about the possibility of moving to Australia while they are helping to bandage each other and to load their pistols. Furthermore, Butch has put his life on the line for Sundance by deciding to go for the ammunition when it was actually Sundance's turn. Finally, we were introduced to each character separately in the beginning; the film ends with a two-shot of both, facing the same fate. Without expressing it verbally, they each know they can count on the other: more than buddies, they act almost as two halves of a single man. Even when earlier in the film they jump off a cliff when pursued by the posse, they do so together (a true act of faith since Sundance can't swim!).

Hill's "buddies" may also be women. *The World of Henry Orient* features the bond between Gil and Val, teenage girls on the Upper East Side of Manhattan. Both are the products of broken homes and stuffy schools, and in Val's case psychoanalysis. They find that friendship and shared fantasy—the pursuit of Henry Orient—become invaluable. Ironically, while many of Hill's adults seem never to have grown up, Butch and Sundance included, his teenagers mature. By the end of the film, Val and Gil are boy-crazy, and although they are together sharing secrets about who-kissed-whom, the pursuit of boys will bring about changes in their intense friendship.

Love-as-friendship is common on several levels in Hill's films. As husband and wife, the missionary couple of Jerusha and Abner Hale in *Hawaii* are kept from a more passionate expression of their love-friendship because of Abner's obsessed Puritanism. Garp and Helen, in contrast, show an appreciation for each other that goes beyond a major theme of the book and film: "lust." Similarly, the young couple in *A Little Romance* are not naïve about the facts of life (they attend but walk out on a porno flick, for instance), but they choose to pitch their relationship on a level beyond passion. The ending of *The World of Henry Orient* suggests yet another form of love crossed by friendship. Val, who has always been caught between her feuding parents, finally discovers her mother's insensitivity and unfaithfulness to both her and her father. Father and daughter are brought closer and decide to live and travel together. "I feel awfully happy in a sorta sad way," Val comments through her happy tears as she hugs her father. At that point they are neither father and daughter nor would-be lovers: they are two lonely individuals reaching out to help each other.

"Nothing ever ends happily," says Hill. It is his double view of the American scene that suggests just how far short of their fulfillment the collective dreams of his characters fall. Hill himself has embraced much of the American experience in his life: he is a Minnesotan who has worked and lived in the Midwest, the East, the West Coast and, briefly, Texas as well. His films are thoroughly American in subject matter (Hill has not made Biblical spectacles or historical epics), and more significantly in temperament. Many observers have pointed out the uneasy conflict in American society between the deep-rooted drive for individualism and personal fulfillment and the equally compelling demands for conformity and teamwork.

Hill is not a reactionary who suggests we should return to an earlier, simpler way of life in which trains could be robbed without the threat of professional posses, in which barnstorming pilots could roam the countryside without the need for federal regulations, in which "old time hockey" was not controlled by coldly calculating business interests, in which con men could pull off ingenious capers, and in which feminism, mad assassins, and fanatical splinter groups did not disrupt the traditional family.

But Hill's films are no blueprints for optimism. In the overall sense, there is quite simply the awareness of mortality: many of his characters die. But in a more particular sense, Hill's films reflect a view similar to that of Arthur Penn, another director concerned with the gap between American myths and their often painful realities: an awareness that both growing up (for individuals) and modernization (for American society) means entering a period in which "there are no solutions." Hill is often the director of nostalgia (lost childhood and of an earlier America). He captures the shared *illusions* of those bygone times. But what makes these American dreams particularly bittersweet is his sense that change is inevitable and that these illusions cannot be sustained indefinitely.

Another Minnesotan concerned himself with the souring of the American Dream. When the first Dutch sailors reached the new world:

for a transitory enchanted moment man must have held his breath in the presence of this continent, compelled into an aesthetic contemplation he neither understood nor desired, face to face for the last time in history with something commensurate to his capacity for wonder.

The narrator is Nick, the author is F. Scott Fitzgerald in *The Great Gatsby*. But while Nick turned his back on the East and the corruption he found there, as appealing as it was in its shimmering decadence, and returned to his home in the Midwest, Hill has continued to explore this territory.

# 2

## Growing Up Amused:
## Early Life, Television, Theater

"A man's maturity consists in having found again the seriousness one had as a child at play."—Nietzsche

Born on December 20, 1922 in Minneapolis to George Roy Hill and Helen Owens Hill, Hill entered a newspaper family. His mother was a Murphy, a strong Irish family that had settled in New Richmond, Wisconsin. Her uncle Will Murphy started the *Minneapolis Tribune* and left the paper with the family when he died. For years young Hill assumed he would go into the business, and in fact, after World War II, he actually did a stint as a cub reporter on a family paper in McAllen, Texas, for a few months before taking off for Ireland.

Hill's father died when his son was nine. Hill remembers his father as a well-respected man who was secretary of the Automobile Club in Minneapolis. Like his mother, his father was of Irish stock from Dublin, where he was related to the Malone and Neary families who then settled in Wisconsin.

Young Hill's first contact with drama came through performances at the Women's Club theater in Minneapolis. He speaks of seeing a show with his brothers, James and Fritz, in which, "It seems there was a horse on stage. Now obviously there wasn't but the *illusion* was so created that I still remember it." The illusion made a strong impression, for he was soon acting in student productions at the Blake Country Day School as well as participating successfully in Debate. The highlight of his acting career at Blake came when he forgot the lines in one play and managed to ad lib his way through. "I couldn't do it today to save my life," he recalls, "but I remember the director turned to me and said, 'You'll go far in this business if you want to pursue it.' I've cherished that remark!"

But the real love of his youth was flying. Weekends were spent listening to pilots and watching them fly at the nearby airports. In those days, of course, flying had nothing to do with Jumbo jets and crowded skies, but rather everything to do with adventure, simple planes, barnstorming stunts, and a way of life that sparked the imagination. His first flight was a treat from his understanding mother who bought him a ticket in a Ford trimotor to Chicago for the World's Fair. Up in the clouds he became as sick as a dog. The plane was forced to land in Madison, Wisconsin, because of bad weather, and the would-be pilot arrived in Chicago by train. Undaunted by such a beginning, Hill started taking lessons and obtained his license by the time he was seventeen. He still owns a plane and stays in close touch with many Hollywood stunt pilots.

When it came time for college, Hill chose to get out of his Midwestern environment and head East to Yale, where he majored in music. Outside the classroom he was a member of the Glee Club and the Whiffenpoofs, for whom he was a bold baritone. In the classroom he delighted in the Classics, particularly Latin, which he considered majoring in through his sophomore year.

But much of his time was taken up with the Yale Dramatic Society of which he eventually became president. In particular, Hill enjoyed doing musicals, and even more specifically he and his friends focused on Gilbert and Sullivan. He speaks of the pure fun of doing *Iolanthe, Patience,* and the *Mikado.*

World War II was on, the year was 1942, and everyone was in a hurry to graduate early and rush into uniform. Hill was no exception. Even though he majored in music, Hill had begun to discover he did not have the talent for it. "I didn't have the ear," he reflects, "I had relative but not perfect pitch." But there was an even more serious obstacle to graduating: the formidable Paul Hindemith. His seminar in music theory was so far over almost everyone's head that Hill felt lost. As a thesis upon which his graduation depended, Hill wrote a sonata for violin and piano. "As I remember it," says Hill, "it was pretty terrible."

Hindemith felt even more strongly about it. Certainly it was considered unpatriotic at the time to fail anyone, but the young would-be naval aviator almost became an exception. When he went to see the professor he saw his score on the table. Hindemith sat there shaking his head. "There's no way I can graduate you on this," he began. "But I'll tell you something. I had the most extraordinary experience last night. I was dragged much against my will to see Gilbert and Sullivan's *Patience*, and I saw you in it and admired you enormously. It's perfectly obvious to me that you are in the wrong field. You shouldn't be composing music; you should be using your talent in a theatrical manner." The composer concluded by saying, "If you promise me you'll give up music as a career and go into theater, I will pass you!"

Hill made the promise and graduated. But though he has obeyed Hindemith's gently withering command, he has remained actively involved with music in his films and in his spare time, during which he enjoys playing the piano, especially Bach.

He was in the navy ten days after graduation in 1942. Soon he was on his way to becoming a naval aviator. In flight school he trained in the Yellow Perils, graduated on December 19 and was on duty as of January 2, 1943. From Minneapolis he was sent to Pensacola, Florida, transferred to the marines and moved to Jacksonville, Mirimar in San Diego, then to Oregon, and finally overseas. He served eighteen months in the Hebrides at Efati and Guadalcanal assigned to SCAT (Southern Combat Air Support) flying R4Ds (a military version of DC-3s). His main job was to take in supplies and pick up wounded. Often no cover was provided, so that the possibility of being hit by ground fire was a constant threat. While stationed in the Solomon Islands he managed to write an autobiographical novel about a flyer in the war, a novel that is buried among his papers and which he feels should so remain.

At Yale, Hill had been strongly influenced by James G. Leyburn, a professor of sociology who also found the time and energy to stage most of the Gilbert and Sullivan productions on campus. "He was a man of immense culture," says Hill and so, taking Leyburn's suggestion, after the war he applied to do graduate work in literature at Trinity College in Dublin. In the meantime he spent a few months in New York and then a few more as a cub reporter on a family paper in Texas. In the fall of 1946 his application was accepted, and he was on his way to Ireland for the first time. His two and a half year stay in Dublin was to be what Hill calls "a turning point of my life."

He speaks of the excitement of stepping off the plane in a country that was simultaneously strange and familiar. He had the new sensation of being in a place in which he knew no one, and yet he had been given the names of an army of relatives to call upon when he chose to. Hill remembers walking "up and down Dublin for days. I had money I had saved up from the war, and to be all alone in a city like that was terribly exciting. I didn't want to meet anybody for weeks."

Ireland was doubly charged for Hill as an ancestral home and as a literary culture of great wealth. At the center of it all was Dublin, a city that always seems tied more closely to the eighteenth century than to the present. "Dublin was marvelous. There were lots of horse carts, bicycles, few cars, and rationing still in effect from the war. We warmed ourselves with burning wet turf that gave off a pleasant smell that permeated the whole city."

Hill made the most of his stay in Dublin in every sense. Academically he plunged into the ambitious project of working on a PhD dissertation on the musical elements in James Joyce's *Finnegans Wake*, attempting an uneasy compromise between his interest in music and literature. Creatively he wrote a second autobiographical novel, this time, of course, about a young American in Dublin after the war. And dramatically he put his acting talents to good use with productions staged by the poet-dramatist Austin Clarke at the Abbey Theater. The plays produced included some of Austin Clarke's material as well as works such as T. S. Eliot's *Sweeney Agonistes*. He has often been said to have been the only American actor to act with the Abbey Theater, but in truth, he is one of the few Americans to act with Irish companies, which for him meant the Lyric Theater which sometimes used the Abbey Theater stage for its productions.

Socially he became good friends with two fellow "literary" expatriate Americans, Gainor Crist and J. P. Donleavy. Donleavy, a Brooklyn boy of Irish descent, was also at Trinity College enjoying the freewheeling life of young single American with many appetites. They were all living the life that became immortalized in Donleavy's glorious first novel, *The Ginger Man* (1955). Hill has frequently been asked if he is the character O'Keefe in the novel; he denies it. What is clear, without a doubt, is that the central character, Sebastian Dangerfield, that "arrogant sensualist who romps through Dublin and London violating middle-class susceptibilities," as one critic notes, was modeled on Gainor Crist, a fellow for whom Hill has much respect and many joyous memories. In fact Hill's Irish novel turned out to "use an awful lot of the same material (by chance) and when I read Donleavy's book, it was so good, I gave up on my own!"

Sebastian Dangerfield appears as a product of comic exaggeration in the novel, but Hill insists that Sebastian is but a tame copy of Crist. Much of Hill's attraction to Crist may have been because of their opposite natures. Hill was shy but ambitious; Crist was boisterous and totally lacking in anything remotely resembling ambition. And while Hill is the first to admit that his memory often serves him poorly, Gainor Crist was the only person he has met who had total recall. He proved this when, soon after Hill arrived in Dublin, Crist came up to Hill at Trinity and asked if he wasn't George Roy Hill, a cadet at flight training school in Pensacola, Florida, whom he had helped to pass his Marine flight test four years ago after meeting Hill only once in a bar the night before the exam. They were close friends from then on.

As friends they could be brutally honest with each other. Crist once told Hill that ambition would kill him. "I told him he was riddled with no ambition and that drink would kill him before ambition got me," said Hill. Unfortunately, Hill's words proved prophetic as the original "ginger man" died in his early thirties of alcoholism.

There were other friends and acquaintances in Dublin including Brendan Behan. And there were many evenings when Hill appreciated the great oral tradition of song, stories, and blarney traded in pubs over a seemingly endless flow of stout.

Unlike John Ford, Hill has never drawn upon his Irish roots for films. He admires Ford's balance of comedy and romance in *The Quiet Man*, but he himself shies away from doing a project that would be so close to him. This helps explain why he has never agreed to Donleavy's proposals over the years that Hill film *The Ginger Man*. "I'm afraid I would lose perspective with anything like that, which is too close to me," he comments. "Mike [Donleavy] has strongly urged me to film it, but I would feel it would be like doing an autobiography of my youth." But when he visits Donleavy in Ireland, they talk of Gainor Crist, and Hill has not ruled out the possibility of doing some kind of story based around him.

Ambition did bring Hill back home. In New York, he continued his acting roles in Cyril Cusack's repertory company and toured the country in Margaret Webster's Shakespearian company where he met and later married actress Louisa Horton in 1951. He was then called back into the Marines as a pilot during the Korean War for two years, reaching the rank of major. That period allowed him to write and to take stock of what he felt about acting. "My main interest in the theater at Yale was that it was just a lot of fun," he observes. "Then I got to where I did not enjoy acting because it was too *painful*. I didn't like to expose myself or summon up emotions I didn't have. Soon after Ireland I did Strindberg's *The Creditors* with Bea Arthur, which got good reviews. But I would break into a sweat and get sick to my stomach before going on stage. And I now get so nervous before crowds at times that I can't function."

Writing became his ticket for off-stage work. By the time he left the Marines he had sold three scripts to television's *Kraft Theater* in 1953. "My Brother's Keeper," the first, concerns the tension surrounding the night landing of a crippled fighter plane being guided in by the control tower. Aired in 1954, this show points to Hill's fruitful career in television for the next five years as writer, assistant director, and finally as director. "My Brother's Keeper" also proved fortuitous because Hill was cast in a minor role in his own show. That alone would not have been significant, but he was chosen by Marion Dougherty who has subsequently done the casting for most of his films.

The genesis of many of Hill's talents as a film director becomes obvious in reviewing his television work. As a writer, for instance, he

*145,918*

wrote alone on original ideas such as "My Brother's Keeper" and "Keep Our Honor Bright" (1953), and he also worked with others on adaptations. Hill's most memorable television show as a director was "A Night to Remember" (*Kraft*, 1956), a tense documentary-drama of the sinking of the *Titanic*, adapted by Hill and John Whedon from the book by Walter Lord.

As a director, however, except for story credit for *The Great Waldo Pepper*, he has not wished to have script recognition even though he works closely with writers and rewrites all of their scripts. When pressed to identify his contributions to specific scripts, he often is unable to recall where his work ends and the scriptwriter's contribution begins. It is fair to say, however, that while he allows his writers a great deal of freedom, he keeps close tabs on the final product, rewriting until he gets the script to the point he feels he is satisfied.

As a television director, Hill had a chance to make use of many of his interests: acting, writing, music, literature, and drama. But editing is what Hill feels he learned best under the pressure of deadlines and short preparation schedules. "When I went out to Hollywood," he states, "I was probably more expert at editing than many who had been in Hollywood for years. My whole thought process of seeing a film before I ever got on the set developed from working for television. Live television was a tremendous training ground for a director."

"Live" should be emphasized. In these productions, theater and cinema met: a director had to have the ability to handle continuous performances by actors, as on the stage, at the same time that he needed to know the language and form of editing in the camera. Editing in one's head before going on the air became extremely crucial for handling the shape, pace, and flow of a drama.

Hill's best work for television and clearly one of the major accomplishments of live television drama was "A Night to Remember," a 1954 production for *Kraft Television Theater* which won Sylvania and Christopher awards as well as two Emmy awards (for writing and for directing) from the National Academy of Television Arts and Sciences. Somehow he managed to simulate a striking disaster, orchestrating 106 actors, six cameras, and a variety of sets. Each set "sank" at a different angle. Hosted by Claude Rains, the show is a model example of how a large-casted story can be told capturing both the sense of overall crisis and of the individual dramas. Furthermore, the highly effective editing from one set to another, often at a frantic staccato pace, was unusual for live television. It is the best example of Hill's later demands for effective editing in his films, most especially in Dede Allen's handling of the complicated cuts in *Slaughterhouse Five*.

Two other television shows are important for understanding Hill's later work: "A Child of Our Time" and "Judgment at Nuremberg," both done for the *Playhouse 90* series. "A Child of Our Time" (1959) shows Hill's knack for handling stories about youth and also demonstrates his ability to work with relatively inexperienced actors. The drama was adapted from the popular autobiographical novel by Michael Del Castillo about his experiences as a young Spaniard who survived the horrors of a World War II concentration camp. Maximilian Schell plays the German prisoner who acts as a father figure and a big brother as he preaches hope in the midst of despair. But the youth, Tanguy, was played by Robert Crawford, then fourteen, who had had very little acting experience. Under Hill's direction, Crawford was nominated for an Emmy award in 1959.

The danger in strong drama is to oversentimentalize or brutalize the action. In "A Child of Our Time," however, Hill continued and refined his ability to create a documentary drama that is tense and moving without being sentimental. It has a direct, purely emotional impact that can be compared to François Truffaut's tale of troubled youth, *The Four Hundred Blows*, which came out the same year. Like "A Night to Remember," this drama used a number of sets, a large cast, and a taut rhythm between group scenes and close-up personal exchanges involving Crawford and Schell. The documentary feel is heightened by some hand-held cinéma vérité point-of-view shots to put the audience through the boy's anxiety, and by an imaginative use of off-camera gun shots to suggest an outside world. Crawford resists the temptation to overplay his part.

Many of his important lines are effective because they are delivered in a muted voice. In one scene, set in the camp during a work detail in the snow, Crawford simply states, "I am going to die." More than the words, the close-up of his shaved head and his expressions of hopelessness convey strong pathos.

"Judgment at Nuremberg" appeared on *Playhouse 90* in April of 1959, just two months after "A Child of Our Times." If "A Night to Remember" was Hill's most ambitious technical accomplishment for television, "Judgment at Nuremberg" was his most topically important work. Here he tackles the explosive subject of the Nazi war crimes trials held in Nuremberg after World War II. Hill's flair for telling individual stories against a backdrop of history again serves him well in this controversial assignment. He interposed documentary footage of Nazi atrocities with a courtroom drama to develop a double vision of crime and punishment. The documentary shots (some taken from Leni Riefenstahl's *The Triumph of the Will* and from Alain Resnais's brilliant *Night and Fog*) are burning reminders of crimes that can never be forgotten. But the courtroom dramas, taken from the actual trial records, suggest the complexity of handling individual cases, the danger of dealing out punishment under the pressure of emotion, and the need for sympathy for individual cases.

Hill's ability to choose and direct a strong cast is evident in this production. Maximilian Schell plays the German defense lawyer who has the thankless task of arguing for compassion and understanding of his clients' situations. Claude Rains is the American judge who must decide all. Other key members of the cast include Martin Milner and Paul Lukas. Schell builds on and goes beyond his role as the "sympathetic German" that Hill had developed in "A Child of Our Time." In a key speech after war documentaries have been shown in court as "evidence," Schell makes an impassioned plea that, "It is inexcusable, it is unfair to show this evidence in this court against these defendants on these charges!" Rains' performance as a patient and reasoning judge is a dramatic contrast to Schell's high-pitched role.

The effective use of film technique makes the theme and drama even sharper. Just before Schell delivers his plea to the court, we have been watching documentary shots of captured Nazi concentration-camp footage. The last scene is of mounds of frail human bodies being bulldozed into large open pits. Hill ends this scene with a superimposition of the documentary footage on Claude Rains' face. The horror of the Nazi crimes seems burned into the judge's brain as he listens to Schell's cry for sympathy.

At the same time that Hill was learning the television trade, he was also becoming a well-respected Broadway director. The first play he directed was *Look Homeward Angel* (1957); it was an immediate critical and popular success. Based on Thomas Wolfe's moving yet sprawling novel taken from his youth in Asheville, North Carolina, the play was shaped by Ketti Frings with, as he has suggested, generous help from Hill. He has an ability to spot and support young actors who then become successful "stars." In *Angel* a young Anthony Perkins illuminated the stage with his special blend of nervous energy and introspective suffering. Jo Van Fleet, Hugh Griffith, and Arthur Hill rounded out the cast to give this American classic a deep resonance. The critics agreed: Wolcott Gibbs of *The New Yorker* felt the adaptation was a "miracle," the performances were "brilliant," and George Roy Hill's direction "flawless" (1957). Other Broadway work included *The Gang's All Here, Greenwillow, Moon on a Rainbow Shawl,* and Tennessee Williams' *Period of Adjustment.*

As in his television dramas and later in his films, the diversity of Hill's work on the stage is the most immediately striking element. He is both eclectic and restless, yet his restlessness is not born from a lack of skill or an inability to find an artistic home. He could easily have stayed with drama or television, made his mark even greater, and retired to comfortable acclaim. But Hill's restlessness is born of curiosity, a certain pleasure of being a loner, and a discomfort with the tried, true, and accepted. He has always "moved on" when it seemed important to do so; from the Midwest to the East, from the East to war, then on to Ireland, and back home again. His Hollywood career has meant a life on both coasts with his four children growing up in New York. Artistically he has moved on as well, from acting to music to literature to fiction to writing for television, and then to directing for the television camera, the stage, and movies. His interests in subject matter have varied from the pure fun of Gilbert and Sullivan to the sober drama of "A Child of Our Time."

After *Period of Adjustment* on Broadway, he turned to film: he has not gone back to the stage except for a semester as a visiting drama professor at his alma mater, Yale, in 1980, when he directed several student productions. Once Hill made the adjustment to Hollywood he felt he could not return to the stage: "I can't cover myself on the stage the way I can in the movies," he comments. "If I have a bad scene in the movies, I can somehow or another get in there and save it with interesting camera angles or some kind of diversion. But when you have a scene that doesn't work on the stage, you can't cut to something else. You have no control. You are completely at the mercy of the actors and their talent. You have *infinitely* more control in a film. You sweat a lot more on the stage."

# 3

## A Period of Adjustment

"The human heart would never pass the drunk test."—Ralph in Tennessee Williams' *Period of Adjustment*

*Period of Adjustment* (1962) based on Tennessee Williams' Broadway play which Hill had directed and *Toys in the Attic* (1963), from Lillian Hellman's play, represent a transitional and ambivalent period in Hill's career—a time when film seemed more an offshoot of his other interests than an all-consuming passion.[1]

These first two films resemble each other in several ways: both are screen adaptations of plays by prominent American playwrights, both are shot in black and white and, for the most part, filmed in the studio, and both reflect basic themes that have become important in Hill's work. Finally, they are transitional works because they are more heavily influenced by drama and television in approach and technique than by cinematic concerns, which Hill had yet to master.

### *Period of Adjustment*

Williams' play is a comic variation of many of his familiar themes about the difficulty of lasting relationships, especially as related to sex, and the clash between ideals and the compromising of those ideals. Two Korean war buddies, George Haverstick and Ralph Bates, meet up several years after the war. Ralph has been practical and has married Dottie, the seemingly unmarriable daughter of a large dairy tycoon in "a Southern city." He is trapped in a marriage of convenience with a frigid wife in a mortgaged house in a condemned subdivision built over an abandoned mine shaft that is caving in. George is a simple country boy from Texas who has just married a Veterans Administration nurse named Isabel who was raised and educated in a strict Baptist tradition. He dreams of starting a cattle ranch to raise cattle for tv westerns, but suffers from "the shakes," a problem that has already affected his relationship with Isabel.

There are comic elements in much of Williams' work. But as an entire play billed as a comedy, *Period of Adjustment* is what even a critic who admired the playwright called "an ambiguous comedy" that is a trite rehash of past material and a play whose concerns with sexuality appear to be homosexual issues dressed in heterosexual garb.[2] It is a talky play that has the structure of a comedy of manners but that in theme and in tone comes closer to a marital melodrama. Behind the humor is a sense of despair about the hollowness of identity, marriage, career, and society. The happy resolution is contrived rather than convincing.[3]

When it came time to do the film, Hill did not enter Hollywood alone. As he has done all of his career, he surrounded himself with a talented cast and crew that helped make his transition to film as smooth as possible. He cast Tony Franciosa, whom he had known from New York, as Ralph, and bouncy Jim Hutton as a thoroughly convincing George.[4] And in the role of Isabel, the virgin Baptist bride, he had the good fortune to cast a very young Jane Fonda, who had been introduced to him by his actress wife. Fonda had already been in three films—*Tall Story* (1960), *Walk on the Wild Side* (1961) and *The Chapman Report* (1962), but this was her first major role and also her first attempt at comedy, a performance that won her critical acclaim as a "great comic actress." Margaret Booth, head of editing at the studio, proved a guiding light in many ways as Hill began directing in films.

Much credit belongs to Isobel Lennart for her adaptation of Williams' play. Certainly Williams was no stranger to Hollywood by 1962; at that time ten of his works had already been turned into films. Williams had worked on many of the films himself, among them *Sweet Bird of Youth*, directed by Richard Brooks, which also appeared that year.[5] But Williams had no connection with the filming of *Period of*

*Adjustment.* The alterations thus belong to Lennart and to Hill, who also helped on the script.

Purists hoping to find Williams' play placed directly on screen are dissappointed with the film. Hill's long apprenticeship in television had taught him the value of adaptation as a creative and flexible art. Lennart's script is such a creative adaptation. The script strengthens and broadens the comic elements, builds the role of Isabel (and so of the female perspective in the story), downplays the motif of the collapsing mine shaft, and explores the nature of "manhood" further than does Williams. Much (perhaps too much) of Williams' dialogue has been kept, and the overall spirit and theme of the play remains.

Thus the reconciliation at the end of the script appears less contrived and more sympathetic than in the original. The period of adjustment is the afterglow of the honeymoon, when romantic illusions give way to the necessity of compromises that two "strangers" must make if a marriage is to work. The script more successfully balances between hope and disillusion, honesty and the need for some forms of self-deception, than does the play.[6]

For all of Lennart's improvements, there remains a static quality to *Period of Adjustment* that suggests the stage rather than the screen. Most of the film is trapped inside the Bates' home. And although the dialogue is witty, the film is more talky than it need be. Furthermore, the long takes in this first film are a far cry from the crisp pacing and editing of Hill's later works.

Despite these limitations there is much that holds up well: Hill captures broadly comic yet sensitive performances from his cast, he has added scenes not in the play to break the one-set feeling of the film, and he began to learn to tell his story in part through camera work as well as through dialogue and staging.

Williams' play is a memory piece set in the present with flashes to the past. The film is immediately more cinematic because it is a chronological work that unfolds directly on the screen in the present. The opening pre-credit sequence is an example. Hill opens with the hospital courtship of Isabel and George and their marriage. Following the credits, we see their honeymoon and subsequent arrival at Ralph's home. In the play all of this action is related later as a flashback by Isabel. On the screen, these scenes involve us with Isabel and George from the start, emphasizing the comedy and romance of their whirlwind relationship so that we sympathize with them when the marriage begins to crumble. More specifically, Hill works the whole hospital sequence into a nonverbal montage during the credits. The pace of this scene exactly matches the brevity of the courtship so that when the sequence ends, they are married. More so than in the play, we *feel* the exhilaration that has brought them together and the blind instability of their new life together once the credits end.

Hill captures the irony of their marriage visually with George's "car." The newlyweds set off in a 1939 Cadillac hearse which George has proudly picked up for five hundred dollars. The car is mentioned in the play, but seeing it on the screen is immensely satisfying. Hill puts the audience in Isabel's position of surprise as the long, black hearse pulls up at the wedding, and he reinforces this surprise by cutting to Fonda's shocked reaction. Every good American couple is really a threesome if we include the omnipresent automobile, thus George's "practical" selection of the hearse is more than just a passing event: It is an ironic comment on the clash of their mismatched fantasies. Isabel has traditional middle-class romantic aspirations while George is in a world of raising cattle in Texas. Hill "frames" this couple and their predicament comically, and ironically from the start of the film long before we get to Williams' dialogue. Added scenes tell us much about the characters. One is the scene mentioned in chapter 1 in which Fonda is seated in the hearse as it is raised and lowered on a lift at a garage. Similarly, there is a scene early in the film that emphasizes George's isolation which does not appear in the play. Shortly after George leaves Isabel at Ralph's, we see him alone at night in a playground. He watches a girl and boy quarrel. The girl finally walks off leaving the boy alone. Hill frames George in such a way that we discover George's sensitivity as we see him begin to make the connection with this younger version of his own marital squabble. Such a sympathetic shot suggests that George is beginning to realize how silly he has been in abandoning his bride to his best friend.

Jane Fonda's comic talent becomes apparent under Hill's direction. In the opening, she appears as a scatterbrained brunette, an early

1960s Goldie Hawn with a Doris Day hairdo and a Marilyn Monroe comic sensuality (especially in the first night of the honeymoon as she stands in the pouring rain). She plays this light role with comic brio. But she has much more to offer as she moves onto a more sympathetic level when she discusses her past with Ralph. She explains her conservative upbringing, her initial attraction to George who as a patient was so "handsome and afflicted," and her disillusionment with the nondevelopment of their marriage. Her phonecall to her father during the height of her problems is a moment of overacting that touches upon both farce and pity as she bawls like a baby while trying to convince her father she is having the time of her life. Even more important, Fonda is convincing at the end of the movie as a woman who is maturing; she quietly reaches out for George as they attempt to bring their period of adjustment to a close.

Juxtaposed to the romantic comedy is a story of the friendship of George and Ralph, a relationship that is also undergoing adjustments. They had become buddies in the Korean War when life seemed much simpler and more attuned to adolescent fantasies of fighting, drinking, and whoring on a grand scale. What we watch unfold, in contrast, is not a "buddy story" similar to *Butch Cassidy* or *The Sting*, but rather a more mature glimpse of two overgrown boys who are trying to grow up in their own ways. They are opposites—George the dreamer and Ralph the practical compromiser—but they join hands in their dissatisfaction with contemporary life as it is. In their drunken exchanges with each other as they toss a football around the living room, they manage to help each other. George becomes less neurotic about sex (Ralph tells him, "When are you going to stop acting like superman? A woman is a human being."). And Ralph is ready to accept his wife for who she is as opposed to how much her father is worth.

The ending is open. George may at least try to live out his fantasy of raising tv cattle. In Williams' play this dream seems rather farfetched. But Hill gives enough character to George through the script and through Jim Hutton's performance that we end the film feeling he just may succeed. At least we want him to do so, especially since he will have Fonda with him at the end of each day.

### *Toys In The Attic*

From adult comedy in *Period of Adjustment*, Hill turned around and did his most serious film with *Toys in the Attic*. By his estimation this is his least successful work, and yet it shows Hill beginning to mature as a filmmaker with a visual awareness.

Lillian Hellman's drama is a tale drawn from the elegant decadence of old New Orleans. Julian (Dean Martin) is a handsome con man with a shady past. He has returned to his New Orleans home from Chicago with Lily (Yvette Mimieux), his beautiful and rich young New Orleanian bride. The drama dovetails Julian's ambitions to become wealthy quickly on a real estate scam, to care for his spinster sisters Carrie (Geraldine Page) and Anna (Wendy Hiller), and to come to grips with his new marriage. Illusion and disillusion, trust and betrayal, are the main themes. By story's end, Hellman suggests a degree of hope by having Anna, the saner sister, escape from their decaying home for her long-dreamed-of tour of Europe, while Julian breaks with the problems of his past by leaving his frustrated sister Carrie and New Orleans behind in favor of reaffirming his life with Lily somewhere else. The toys in the attic are the dusty illusions of misspent lives.

Hill has always managed to use the precredit and credit sequences in his films as opportunities to clearly establish their mood and themes. *Toys in the Attic* is no exception. The film opens with a montage of Lily trailing her husband, unknown to him, through the French Quarter at night. A sense of place, mood, and mystery is immediately established. More important, the film is set up from Lily's point of view so that while Julian is the main protagonist, we are satisfied in the end to know that Lily's suspicions have given way to Julian's new resolve to change his life in order to build their life togehter.

The film demonstrates Hill's ability to find distinctive ways to frame his characters so that the frame comments on the protagonists. The old Victorian home Anna and Carrie inhabit has a long staircase which allows for a number of extreme high- and low-angle shots to suggest the state of the various relationships. From the ground floor to the attic, the staircase enables Hill to show the "distorted" perspectives that have developed between brother and sisters and between sisters and Lily.

A key scene that is well handled dramatically and visually is the confrontation between Carrie and Lily in an upstairs bedroom. Carrie has been smoldering with jealousy ever since she has met the woman who she feels has replaced herself in Julian's affections. Just before this scene, sister Anna had said what Carrie had never been able to admit to herself: "You want to sleep with him [Julian]." We sense Carrie's submerged incestuous desires turn to white hatred for Lily.

In the scene, Lily becomes Carrie's victim. Innocent and insecure, she is too naïve to see the games Carrie plays. "I want you to like me," she tells Carrie sincerely. But Carrie becomes increasingly nasty toward her. As Carrie goes into her closet, the camera suddenly switches to an extreme high angle, looking down on Carrie with Lily seen below her in the distance. This startlingly unexpected shot succeeds in framing Carrie so that while we hear Lily, we watch Carrie and thus share her point of view as she proceeds to devastate her "rival." Even the camera is weighted against Lily and her innocence.

The scene is also effective because of the costumes and set. Lily stands in a white dress against the white curtains of the window: Carrie is framed in the foreground in a dress with almost the same flower print as the wallpaper. Carrie thus appears as an extension of the house where she has wasted so many years. Hill claims that this symbolic visual image was a happy accident that he took advantage of. "When I saw it, I said to myself that she blends right in. She *is* the house: it's perfect!"

Hitchcock always claimed he left nothing to chance in his films. Hill is likewise a careful planner in preproduction. But he feels that luck and accidents are major gifts a filmmaker should grasp and exploit. "You've got to be fast enough to take advantage of things. You have good accidents and bad ones, but the wallpaper dress example in *Toys in the Attic* was a good one."

The confrontation scene between Carrie and Lily is dramatic. Carrie succeeds in breaking Lily by forcing her to realize that Julian was paid to marry Lily by her mother. Carrie then takes advantage of Lily's distress to have her make a fatal phone call revealing the scam Julian has worked out on a real estate deal about to be concluded on a pier along the Mississippi River.

The call leads to the brutal beating of Julian and his former lover, a woman who is honestly trying to help him get ahead. Again the framing is important. This time Hill uses a bird's eye shot in the warehouse to show the complete vulnerability of Julian and Charlotte. They are trapped in a warehouse with a truck closing them off from escape while they are attacked by thugs. Hill films the violence from this distant perspective so that we are not subjected to what has come to be the overemphasis of violence shown in slow motion and in close up for its own sake. The attack is made, and the scene ends with the bodies spread out on the warehouse floor below.

The most significant framing device in the film becomes the wrought iron black fence in front of the old family house, especially in a scene at the end of the film. Carrie has done her best to destroy Lily without success. Julian now understands Carrie's involvement in the phonecall. "Things are going to be fine now," she says in a near-hysterical voice. Julian gives Anna ten thousand dollars for her trip to Europe, kisses her, and leaves the house. Carrie chases after him as he goes out of the gate and along the sidewalk. Carrie is seen through the old fence, hanging onto the bars like a trapped animal in a cage. "You're a failure," she cries in desperation, but visually we are told that it is Carrie who has failed and who must live with her own toys in the attic. The image of Carrie trapped behind the fence of the house in which she has wasted her life with idle fantasies is dramatically and visually striking. Not only does it make clear Carrie's entrapment; it also emphasizes Julian's escape since the camera, like Julian, is no longer a part of Carrie's crumbling world.

Speaking of the scene, Hill mentions that, "It was the visual effect I wanted to make to show that they lived in a compound in which Julian's life was dominated by his sisters." Significantly, the shot is not described in such detail in the script. As has often been the case with Hill's technique, the idea of shooting through the iron fence developed during the making of the film.

What is Dean Martin doing in such a serious drama? The practical answer is that he had been cast for the film by producer Weingarten before Hill came on the project. Martin, who had broken with Jerry Lewis and his old slapstick persona several years before, had already embarked on a career playing dramatic roles in such admirable films as *The Young Lions* (1958) and Hawks' *Rio Bravo* (1959). As Julian, the figure around whom the whole plot revolves in *Toys in the Attic*, he was a definite risk. And yet his performance, despite a somewhat wooden range at times, holds up today much better than one might expect.

Just as Hill works well with children and inexperienced actors, so he is able to effectively break down stereotypes of actors and develop new depths. He enjoys taking an actor or actress and bring out qualities that have always been "there" but which have been neglected or buried or both. According to Hill, Martin "was frightened by the demands the film put on him and so relied on me a great deal." As Julian, Martin succeeds in conveying a sense of perpetual motion and energy that contrasts sharply with the inertia of those around him.

Hill cast the other parts using excellent stage performers with film experience. Geraldine Page had warmed up to Southern decadence with memorable performances in Tennessee Williams' *Summer and Smoke* (1961) and *Sweet Bird of Youth* (1962). As Julian's older sister Carrie, she has what Brendan Gill labeled as all the "sinister sweetness of a chocolate covered Cobra." Wendy Hiller, who had played the role on Broadway, appears as Anna, the other spinster sister who lives with Carrie. Yvette Mimieux as Lily, Julian's lovely but naïve bride, is well cast as the suspicious outsider to Julian's past, his mysterious present, and his peculiar relationship to his sisters. With the inconsequential *Where the Boys Are* (1961) and the dramatic *Four Horsemen of the Apocalypse* (1962) behind her, she handles the delicate balance between a spacey Southern blonde and a loving but insecure young woman who is lost among the machinations of Julian's shady world.

Overall, Hill had two strikes against him before he even started the film. He had wanted to show the script to Lillian Hellman and rewrite it according to her suggestions. He felt that screenwriter James Poe had not done justice to the material, and although Hill rewrote much of the script himself, he wanted Hellman's advice. Time was short, however, and he was not able to meet with the playwright, a fact which did not please either Hellman or Hill. One reviewer remarked about the film that, "Hellman speaks her mind brilliantly but opens her heart rarely,"[7] a comment that reflects, in part, the lack of full development of the script.

The second problem had to do with Hill's lack of strong enthusiasm for the project from the beginning. *Toys in the Attic* is Southern Gothic melodrama in the purest sense, and Hill states he has always been uncomfortable with relentless melodrama:

I think it's just my nature. I'm not interested in doing very heavy dramatic material. My whole view of life is an ironic point of view. Whenever I find something that is serious, as people who work with me point out, I will find some way of defusing the seriousness with irony or comedy or a slightly cynical point of view.

The play had been one of the best dramas on Broadway in 1960, directed by Arthur Penn and starring Jason Robards as Julian. But Hill took on the film because his friend, producer Kermit Bloomgarden, asked him to do so. Hill decided to give it a try.

The most decisive undercutting of the project, however, was a back ailment that put Hill in the hospital. In pain throughout the filming, he directed from a wheelchair. Ironically, while his pain kept him from giving full attention to the script and cast, his affliction helped him cinematically. Forced to see the set from the perspective of the wheelchair, he became fascinated with camera movement and angle. "My camera technique evolved from the wheelchair," he acknowledges, "and so I was more interested in developing a camera style than I was in the basic material." Television had taught Hill to edit in his head. But the limited time and space of TV work meant that he had little chance to experiment with camera technique. Viewed in this light, *Toys in the Attic* is a great leap ahead of A *Period of Adjustment*.

# 4

## New Directions
## *The World of Henry Orient*

"Everything is perfect except for a couple of details."—from Preston Sturges's
*Hail the Conquering Hero*

By the time he made his third film, *The World of Henry Orient* (1964),
Hill was working with confidence and a sense of adventure, both with
his material and with the medium of film. His adjustment had been
made.

 *Henry Orient* concerns two privileged teenage girls caught at that
brief moment of youth just before they become conscious of themselves as women. The location is New York City, and the time is
contemporary with the filming of the story (1964). Soon after Val
(Tippy Walker) and Gil (Merrie Spaeth) meet in the opening of the
film, the stage is set for a tale of adolescent fantasy:

VAL:  Do you want to go adventuring?
GIL:  What do you mean?
VAL:  I mean like jumping right out of your skin and to be absolutely some-
      body else. Not pretending but BEING somebody else.[1]

And, in a receptive state of mind, adventuring is exactly what they
do as they happen upon Peter Sellers, a Brooklyn boy with a fantasy
of his own: Sellers is attempting, none too successfully, to live out
his illusions of being a concert pianist named Henry Orient, complete with a phony French-Hungarian accent. The warm comedy of
the film is generated as these two fantasy worlds clash.

*Henry Orient* was a fortuitous leap forward for Hill as a filmmaker: After the melodrama of *Toys in the Attic*, he turned to a bittersweet comedy of adolescence; after a largely studio-shot New Orleans, he now had the pleasure of shooting on location in his adopted home, New York; after two adaptations of stage dramas, Hill now enjoyed the greater freedom of adapting a novel; after black and white photography in his first two films, he suddenly had the full range of color to work with; and after studio-arranged and -controlled projects, Hill was now his own producer: he had just formed Pan Arts, the company that has handled all of his subsequent work.

Hill drew his story from a novel of the same title by Nora Johnson, who is the daughter of screenwriter Nunnally Johnson (whose credits include *The Grapes of Wrath*, *The Man in the Gray Flannel Suit*, and *The Three Faces of Eve*). The screenplay originally submitted was largely written by Nunnally with the help of Nora. Hill was looking for a script that was different from the kind of material he had previously done. *The World of Henry Orient* struck Hill as exactly what he needed.[2] As is his custom, Hill did much of the rewriting of the script himself, though screen credit remains with Nora and Nunnally Johnson.

Though the film belongs to Gil and Val, the title points to Henry Orient and so to Peter Sellers. Hill's ability to balance seeming opposites is seen clearly in Sellers' role. By 1964 Sellers was near the height of his career as a star and as a widely appreciated mimic. The year before had brought him more glory as a dark satirist for his role as Dr. Strangelove in Stanley Kubrick's disturbing film. How could such a star keep from overshadowing two inexperienced teenagers? There is no simple answer, but as in many of Hill's projects, the right blend was found between the experienced actors and the new ones, and between a kind of pure comedy (Sellers) and a humorous form of pathos (the girls). Sellers achieves perfectly what Hill wanted. He adds his presence and talent to the film, and without upstaging his young admirers.

The story is similar to a screwball comedy of the 1930s, updated and refocused on a much younger set of characters. Hill appreciates many of the old comedies, especially those of Preston Sturges, Gregory LaCava, and Mitchell Leisen. In *The World of Henry Orient*, Val is the "screwball" and Gil an eager partner as they attempt to live out their zany infatuation with Henry Orient. As in the old comedies, these young women-to-be are bright, witty, and a cross between cunning and innocent. And also, as in the screwball films, the basic formula is romantic (girls-meet-boy) with a "happy" ending after a series of misadventures. Finally, Hill's film echoes these earlier comedies by setting the action in an urban location among the well-to-do.

But though there are similarities to the kind of entertaining romantic comedies that Jean Arthur, Katharine Hepburn, and Barbara Stanwyck used to play so well, *The World of Henry Orient* cuts deeper. On the surface the film sparkles as much as a Capra or Hawks comedy. But beyond the breeziness of Val and Gil's adventuring, there is their search for a father figure. Sellers can never fulfill a romantic role for either of the two girls in a conventional romantic-comic sense. Much of the comedy is the distance between their failure to realize this fact, as they magnify Orient's own illusion into absurd proportions, and our awareness of Sellers' engaging yet impotent efforts as an artist and a lover. Both Val and Gil are products of broken homes and affluent absentee fathers. The pathos of the film comes not so much from the friendship of the two girls as it does in Val's final reconciliation with and expression of love to her father. By film's end, her father has in effect merged fantasy and reality as he rejects his hypocritical wife (Angela Lansbury) and swoops Val up as a daughter-partner to live with him "wherever she chooses."

Hill captures a poignant moment in the father-daughter embrace at the end of the film. Val's adventures with Sellers give way to a new life with her father (Tom Bosley). The often madcap comedy that has characterized much of the film suddenly stops as Val hugs her father with tears in her eyes.[3] The moment is moving as a coming together of father and daughter. But it is more than that. Because Val's family is a broken one, like so many in the United States, the father-daughter relationship is also a much broader and more ambiguous one than in a traditional family. The father states in this scene "You're my only sweetheart now," but Hill is not suggesting an erotic and incestuous undercurrent to the line. Even at surface value, the father's words suggest that the "new" family means that in a sense Val will be a wife and daughter figure combined.[4] Furthermore, their need for each other transcends their age and role differences: they are both lonely and alone despite the crowds that have surrounded them and the illusions they have tried so hard to maintain—in particular, the illusion of a marriage for the father, and that of hero-worship and eternal friendship for Val.

*Val and Gil in Wonderland. Period of Adjustment* concerned, in part, the friendship of two war buddies as they attempted to settle down in suburban civilian life. Being buddies is even more at the heart of *The World of Henry Orient*. But whereas *Period* begins with George and Ralph already friends, *Henry Orient* traces the whole life of the relationship between Val and Gil.

Their meeting foreshadows all. An opening pre-credit montage establishes New York at its best as a school bus makes its rounds. Once off the bus, Gil, who has been reviewing her history notes, pauses by an iron fence overlooking the East River and waves to a tugboat captain. She is a healthy but plain-looking girl, who appears simple and sincere. Val virtually bursts into the frame, madly chasing her sheet music, which is blowing in the wind. She is a sharp contrast to Gil because of her huge fur coat (Brendan Gill called Val "the youngest daughter of a woolly mammoth") and her rather aristocratic good looks set off by a mouth full of braces. From the beginning, Tippy Walker's Val is a presence on screen. Her boundless energy, her hyperimagination, her nonstop flights of language make us realize she is in control of the relationship from the start.

If Gil appears a model student and straight personality, Val is the opposite. "I'm unmanageable," she says with saucy pride as she describes how she was booted out of two other schools. Though their conversations often sound like nonintersecting monologues, they are immediately drawn to each other because they are both new to the girls' school they attend, because they hate the same teachers, and, at Val's instigation, they both have a desire for adventuring. They also learn quickly that each belongs to a broken home, though Gil's comfortable brownstone existence with Mom and her Aunt Boothie is depicted as being much more settled and loving than the sleek wealthy apartment in which Val lives with her mother.

After a brief scene in Gil's home, the girls have their first adventure: a romp through Central Park. Hill succeeds in capturing cinematically the feeling of carefree youth while celebrating New York as a city and location. (Brendan Gill says Hill photographed New York in color, "portraying the island as the beautiful impossibility that, on its best days, it manifestly is.")

As we first see them in Central Park on a gloriously sunlit day, they pass by the statue of Alice in Wonderland. It is only a brief shot, but it is a tip that, as in *Alice*, we can expect a looking glass world from this point on. Other books dealing with childhood are also evoked: Sounding a lot like Tom Sawyer, Val claims they are being chased by Chinese bandits because they are "two beautiful white nurses."

Their chase leads them to Peter Sellers, who is in a mad embrace with Paula Prentiss. As he looks up, he catches a glimpse of both girls, staring wide-eyed with curiosity as they pop their bubblegum bubbles and run off. This is their first encounter with Sellers who, as the film progresses, finds those smiling young faces haunt him like Alice's Cheshire Cat. Paula Prentiss is all nerves: she explains she is a married woman about to have her first affair. Sellers tries without luck to lure her up to his apartment in his phony foreign accent. And in one of the best early lines in the film, he voices his frustration as he asks her, "You mean we're never going to be able to get together except on top of rocks in Central Park?"

Hill then cuts to a carefree burst of youth and energy as the girls run through the Park and the streets of their neighborhood, the Upper East Side. The camera follows them from a high angle which continues to pan until the girls run by under the camera; then the camera follows them by so that the image is suddenly upside down. Comedy is often daily life turned upside down, and so is the freedom of youth. Here Hill uses a frolicksome camera to share the experience. The camera then tilts sideways and finally rights itself again.

The scene viewed upside down is only the beginning of the girls' and the camera's romp. Hill next goes to slow motion. From a low angle we look up at the girls as they jump over garbage cans and fire hydrants. The most joyous burst of all is as Val is shot in extreme slow motion, rising slowly into the air, framed with nothing but blue sky behind her as if she were flying or floating as free as a bird, her legs apart for the jump, her school-girl's skirt flying as well. The moment is exhilarating, and it is the camera angle and the use of slow motion that help to make it so. Such techniques are common now, but when Hill shot the scene, slow motion in feature films had only rarely been used.[5] Louis Malle had used it several years before in *Zazie dans le metro* (a film that Hill had not seen) for a similar effect as he captures the carefree anarchistic spirit of Zazie, a young French girl out to enjoy Paris. Hill remembers that he was advised against using such "gimmicks," but he felt strongly that such a use of cinematic technique need not be merely a trick. He got the idea, after all, not from silent comedy but from the diving sequence in Leni Riefenstahl's *Olympische Spiele 1936*.

Slow motion draws attention to itself, but because we have been set up for a fantasy world from the beginning, the use of such distortion not only reinforces the fantasy but also intensifies our identification with Val. We share her intoxication with youth and life. Val's leap is followed by a fast motion sequence of the girls hopping along benches in the Park. Fast motion produces just the opposite effect: when human motion is speeded up, it is reduced to the mechanical. And, as Henri Bergson has pointed out, the mechanical, when applied to the human, is humorous. This is the last part of the romp, and it ends on a light note, keeping the entire scene within the realm of comedy.

Alice was alone in her Wonderland, but Val has Gil. It is the interaction of this twosome that makes up the bulk of the story. Both have dreams and schemes, but it is evident from the start that Val is the more imaginative of the pair, and that Gil plays Sancho Panza to Val's Don Quixote. There is yet another indication that Val is further out on the fringe between experience and reality: she has a psychiatrist. Perhaps this would not be considered unusual today, but in the early sixties teenagers in therapy were still the exception. This fact alone means that Gil (and the other girls) hold Val in awe.

Val has a plan, a role, a scam for every occasion, and so helps Gil, who misses her father. In fact, she misses him most specifically at 6 P.M. when he should be home for supper. Val takes this information and immediately weaves a scenario for Gil's Dad to leave his second wife and return home. "After all," she says, "he's got to go back to his one true love." Gil sits there, crying. Hill subtly suggests that the girls can have it both ways: they can play out fantasies without necessarily believing they will become real. Gil's tears are testimony that she would like to believe Val's scenario would work, and yet she is aware that Dad will not return home at 6 P.M. or at any other time.

Henry Orient becomes the father-substitute for their free-floating need, and so they track him down and trail him with relentless enthusiasm. Their need for a father is best expressed in a scene in which they take an oath to dedicate themselves to Henry Orient. Gil notes that they are no longer children. "We're both practically adolescents," she states, as they make a blood pact and swear an oath:

That whereas love is the most important thing in the whole world, especially true love, hereby be resolved, that Marion Gilbert and Valerie Boyd do solemnly swear that we will live a secret life forever and eternally dedicated to the one Henry Orient.

Elmer Bernstein's score in the background softly plays "Here Comes the Bride," thus emphasizing the marriage-like ritual of their private ceremony in Gil's bedroom.

Part of the freshness of the scene and of the film is that Hill captures these girls before they become aware of their sexuality. It is not that Hill avoids sex in this film and, later, in *A Little Romance*, but that he wants to emphasize what is so often lost in contemporary life: a sense of childhood. "Love is so hard to explain," says Hill, "and love is so often involved with 'lust' which I am not concerned with in these films."

And yet, particularly as viewed today, we are aware of the sexual currents underlying their fantasies, and the way Hill films them. Val, shortly before the oath, falls backward on Gil's bed, legs spread, clutching one of Orient's two records to her stomach, wondering in a wispy voice, "My Oriental Henry. . . . How can I prove to you

that I'm yours?" Later in the film, when they retrieve one of his cig-
arettes and discover that it is an unfiltered brand, they exclaim, "he's
not scared." The lines and their actions are innocent *to them*, but to
us, part of the nostalgia of watching the film is being aware of the
duality of their behavior. Hill does not overemphasize these passing
gestures, remarks, moments; but the subtext is definitely there, point-
ing toward the young women they are soon to become.

*Sellers On Stage*. Peter Sellers had an uncanny talent for totally becoming the character he portrayed. And Henry Orient is one of Sellers' best performances. As in *Dr. Strangelove*, Sellers as Orient had
to play a double role: Strangelove is an "American" scientist who must
continually suppress his Nazi salute and thus his German past; Henry
Orient poses as a world-class pianist and Casanova but often relapses
into his Brooklyn accent when troubled. Sellers handles such comic
schizophrenia with complete mastery.

The comic highlight of the film is the concert scene. Until this
point the girls have only met Orient once (in the Park) and have no
idea who he is. The concert which the girls attend is the third chance
meeting, but more important, it is the "recognition" scene that leads
Val and Gil to swear their oath and live out their fantasy.

Hill carefully prepares us for this fateful evening by paralleling and
contrasting the fantasies and cons of the girls with those of Sellers.
Orient is established from the start as a failure as a seducer and as a
pianist in a conversation with his manager-friend from childhood,
Sydney, who labels Orient a "non-Van Cliburn" as Sellers is being
primped by a hairdresser. Val's problem, on the other hand, is just
the opposite: she is too successful a con for her own good. Just before
Val and Gil bump into Sellers for the second time (on the street as
he is attempting to sneak Paula Prentiss into his apartment building
on the East Side) Val fakes a death scene on the sidewalk. A crowd
of concerned bypassers, including a doctor, comes to her rescue. They
are all convinced by her performance, but Gil, when the scene has
gone too far for comfort, blurts out "It was a joke," and the girls run
off as the crowd exchanges angry words.

Hill pushes this scene just far enough past pure comedy to make us aware that part of growing up is learning to distinguish between real emotion and faked performances.[6] With these forewarnings, the stage is literally set for recognition and confrontation.

The scene begins with Val and Gil in the audience with Gil's mother and Boothie. Cut to Sellers in tails pompously soaking his hands as the orchestra warms up. He is telling his manager about the girls' second intrusion into his life: "Ten more feet and I would have been home," he remarks.

Sellers appears on stage and bows to the applause. As he looks out into the audience he spots Paula Prentiss sitting next to her husband. But as the camera tilts to the row behind her, he spies Val and Gil smiling with wide grins. His face collapses in absolute terror as he heads for the Steinway.

Next is a hilarious satire of pretentious avant-garde music. The piece Sellers plays is a collage of atonal noise accompanied by a full orchestra complete with a conductor who flaps his arms wildly as if he were someone who had stumbled upon a live electric wire. Hill's mastery of the reaction shot is nowhere more apparent than in the comic rhythm of this scene. He cuts continually from the reactions of the conductor to Sellers' bungled performance, to the various states of shock, boredom, and amusement registered on the faces of the audience. Boothie, Gil's aunt, whispers to Gil's mother, "If this is music, what's the stuff Cole Porter writes?" Later a dignified older man with a hearing aid turns it off after sneaking a look at his wife who is completely enthralled by it all. Even the orchestra itself is bored: Hill cuts to two string bass players deeply involved in a game of checkers.

In the midst of such orchestrated noise, it's hard to imagine how any musician could mess up. But Sellers manages royally. Completely self-possessed, Sellers hits a steady trill on the piano and then looks up to see the conductor shaking his head "no." Sellers then slides back down the keyboard and then proceeds to slide back up, his hair flapping, his eyes closed, his head thrown back. When he opens his eyes, the conductor is shaking his head again. This time the conductor mouths "B FLAT" slowly, and Sellers suddenly, insecurity in his eyes this time, switches notes on his trill, and the orchestra, which has been holding the note waiting for the honorable Henry Orient, pounces back into the score once more. The brief wrapup of the concert now becomes pure farce as we have a tilted shot of the horns and clarinets, as a man hits the bass drum with a beanbag, and as another man plays a steam whistle, but at the wrong time.

John Simon calls this "Steam-whistle Concerto" an example of the screenwriters' and of Hill's "militantly anti-intellectual" approach to the material.[7] But Simon seems to have missed the whole thrust of the film. The scene is a comic-satiric sendoff of Henry Orient and the kind of music *he* is associated with. Hill and his screenwriters are not thumbing their noses at Carnegie Hall and high culture in general. Given the framework of the film, the orchestra is entirely consistent with Orient's pretentiousness, a form of pomposity that needs to be deflated.

But the scene continues. Once the orchestra has reached a farcical crescendo, we cut to a close up of Val who is totally carried away by the moment. The scene is hardly "militantly anti-intellectual," but rather a comically exaggerated moment to show how intoxicated Val has become with Henry Orient. The irony and the comedy spring from the con that Orient has effortlessly pulled off on the willing young girl who is so deeply involved in the illusion of the moment that she cannot see that Orient's behavior is laughable. With this final reaction shot, Hill shows us the trickster tricked, the con artist conned. Val is still in Wonderland, a land where she can convince others she is "dying" but in which she cannot recognize the ludicrous nature of others.

The scene is worth viewing repeatedly to see how skillfully Hill has built the movement of the concert with humor while advancing the story and establishing the growing relationship between Val and her father-substitute. The scene is also instructive as to how much Hill elaborates and adds to a script to obtain the effect he wants. As written, the scene is relatively brief. Hill added much of his own. The reaction shot of the old man with the hearing aid would be one example. Hill claims the inspiration for this touch came from an old Peter Arno *New Yorker* cartoon in which an old man with a hearing aid sits with his bosomy wife at an opera. The woman turns to her husband and says, "You have *so* got it turned off!"

Much of the scene, in fact, was improvised. Hill had the concerto specially written for the film and then worked on the kinds of reaction shots he thought would work best. A crisp editing style maintains the rhythm of the scene. Hill also encouraged Sellers to fill out his satiric portrayal of Henry Orient. Sellers' accent, his self-possessed sweep of the keyboard, his pleading look at the conductor are all the results of the late character actor's inspired comic talent.

If Hill followed his script perhaps too literally in *Toys in the Attic*, he showed with *The World of Henry Orient* that he could expand and improvise effectively off the script, using it as a blueprint for the final scene.[8]

*Beyond Innocence. The World of Henry Orient* shows two girls who use their fantasy life and sense of play as a way to help them grow up. The games they have played have been innocent fun, but they have also been a rite of passage. The film ends a year after their Henry Orient kick when they meet again to discuss their latest discovery: boys.

Val's dream of Orient crumbles as she learns of his affair with her mother. Here slapstick and farce blend into pathos as Val is drawn closer to her father, who finally decides to take control of his life by leaving his wife ("Sometimes people get married for the wrong reasons," he explains to Val). They join together and live in Rome for a year. But even this bond is not enough, for Val needs to go beyond her father and her childhood fantasies to discover the reality of "boys."

The closing scene, a year later, rounds out the film while leaving the future of the girls open-ended. We watch the girls meeting again, dressed as young women now, less spontaneous, more self-conscious. But as soon as they are in Gil's bedroom, complete with a YALE banner on the wall, they are the friends they used to be, at least for the moment. The topic of conversation is boys and necking, and rock music on the soundtrack clues us into their altered states.

Hill takes us to the brink of the loss of innocence and then leaves us there. The girls are on their way to womanhood: they are adolescents and no longer *idol*escents—followers of Henry Orient.

François Truffaut has remarked that anybody who says he has had a happy childhood has a bad memory. Hill disagrees. "I can sit and remember marvelous times from my childhood," he says, "and I can also remember miserable times: sometimes I feel I had the happiest childhood one can imagine, and yet there was also the fact that I was shy and often on the periphery of the social and academic groups." *The World of Henry Orient* is carefully poised between innocence and experience, suggesting both.

Besides being a critical success, Hill's third film became the official United States film at the Cannes film festival in 1964 and was well received. This was the encouragement he needed for himself and his young company to continue to go beyond typical Hollywood patterns.

# 5

## Who's in Control?

"Strip away the phony tinsel and you can find the real tinsel underneath."—
Oscar Levant on Hollywood

The next two films, *Hawaii* (1966) and *Thoroughly Modern Millie*
(1967), took Hill in the quite opposite directions of historical epic and
musical comedy. Such diversity of genres has baffled the critics who
constantly accuse Hill of restlessly hopping from genre to genre without settling down. Hill sees it differently: his interest has always been
in telling a story and finding a story that pleases him, and so he has
attempted various kinds of film. Screenwriter William Goldman appreciates this characteristic in Hill: "I think he is one of the most gifted
directors in the world," Goldman states. "He is one of the few directors who can do anything: he can do big or little, funny, hard . . .
anything at all!"

With these two films, Hill was able to move further away from his
earlier stage and television background and explore the possibilities of
telling a story in a large-scale production. Each film is important in
its own way, and yet neither came off as Hill had wished them to be
because of clashes with studio heads. The question of who was in
control of each project became distracting, and finally resulted in
damaging battles over the finished films.

### Hawaii

There is much that seems unlikely about the beginnings of many of
Hill's projects. *Hawaii* was no exception. It is hard to imagine a more

disparate trio than the epic-historical novelist James A. Michener, George Roy Hill, and the blacklisted scriptwriter Dalton Trumbo.

*Hawaii* seemed ready made to fit the tried and true Hollywood formula of adapting a blockbuster novel into a popular film. What's more, it contains in its chronicle of the rise and fall of Hawaii, enough war, love, passion, conflict, and storms at sea to rival earlier Hollywood successes, *Gone with the Wind* in particular. And while there had been large budgeted films before, most notoriously, *Cleopatra* (1962), *Hawaii*, which was done for $10 million, was clearly extravagant for its time.

Yet from the beginning Hill saw more than mere entertainment in the project. Made at the time that Vietnam was just becoming a major issue, *Hawaii* as Hill presents it becomes not merely a tale of missionaries in a pagan land, but by extension a metaphor for Vietnam and the "rape" of any culture by another. According to Hill: "What I wanted to do was to present the dangers of exporting a culture and way of life into a totally alien society on the assumption that our way of life was better than theirs."

Handed the possibility of several screenwriters, Hill found himself most sympathetic to Dalton Trumbo, whose strong sense of social and political awareness was well-known.

"I'm not a political creature, really," Hill reflects, "especially compared to Dalton; but we agreed on Vietnam." Thus though Trumbo was at first leery of Hill, they soon found they had similar thoughts about *Hawaii*. Michener, meanwhile, was supportive of their efforts, but chose not to be involved in the project.

The script as it emerged focused entirely on early Hawaiian history as reflected in the life of missionary Abner Hale. Trumbo highlighted Michener's material showing Hale as a simple, earnest man who sincerely believed in his calling to spread God's word to the natives. What becomes clear from the beginning is the complete cultural clash of Hale's values with those of the Hawaiians.

The cultural conflict is handled well in two ways. First, the opening is set in New England so that we feel a sense of the Puritan background from which Hale emerged. A good half hour of the film is devoted to capturing the flavor of the Yale Seminary and in showing

Hale's courtship of Jerusha Bramely, a young New England lady brought up in a much more refined atmosphere than Hale, who is a Yankee farmer. The white houses set against snowscapes serve to stress a sense of place as well as to suggest the moral frigidity of the characters.

When the scene switches to Hawaii, the contrast could not be greater. Hill went to a lot of trouble not only to film on location, but to choose those islands that were still unspoiled and thus representative of an innocent Hawaii. After the frozen simplicity of the New England landscape, the verdant richness of Hawaii assaults the eye in lavish hues that would be taken as merely postcard photography had it not been for the American sequence. Thus even before the drama unfolds, Trumbo and Hill visually establish how different the environments are for these two cultures.

The narrative also contrasts the culture by framing the story from a native Hawaiian's point of view. As the film opens at Yale in 1819, we hear a voice-over narrator who turns out to be a young Hawaiian prince, Keoki, who is studying for the ministry. He becomes a key figure in the story as he at first attempts to reconcile the white man's Christian values with his own native traditions. He is moderate, temperate, and patient. But in the end, Hale is so obstinate in denying the young prince his rightful ministry that the Hawaiian returns to his people, forsaking the church.

Beginning the film through the prince's eyes properly reminds us that, as the title suggests, the story ultimately belongs to Hawaii and not to Hale. The movement from innocence to corruption and destruction that Hale's mission inadvertently brings in is constantly viewed as it affected the natives. It is as if *Moby Dick* were to be rewritten from Queequeg's point of view. This fact alone lifts the film beyond the usual Hollywood historical epic in which the story is simply told from the heroes' point of view rather than that of the victims.

*Hawaii* is also the tale of the downfall of a good man destroyed by his own obsession. As scripted and finely acted by Max von Sydow, Ingmar Bergman's memorable knight in *The Seventh Seal*, Abner Hale has a flinty righteousness and obdurate self-possession that reminds us of Captain Ahab and Hawthorne's Reverend Dimmesdale combined.

He sincerely believes in the minister who sends him off to sea stating he is, "To bring the heathen to the Lord and civilize him. . . . They came to a nation in darkness; they left it in light."

But Abner is more than a stonyfaced New England preacher: he is a simple man at war with his natural desires to love and be loved. It is this human side of him that Jerusha Bramely (Julie Andrews) brings out. Hill handles the courtship with warm humor and delicate observation. "I have no graces," says an awkward Abner as he tries to express himself to a sympathetic Jerusha who finally accepts him despite her passionate love for a whaler (Richard Harris). Hale's real growth is his discovery of his love for Jerusha. At the birth of their first child, he cries as he holds his wife and says, "I love you more than I love God." His love makes it possible for us to feel sympathy and pity for Hale at the end when he has lost everything and everyone except himself and his love of God. Standing alone by the sea he states simply, "In this place I have known God, Jerusha Bramely, and Malama [the native queen]. . . . Beyond that, a man needs no friends."

Pauline Kael saw the value of *Hawaii* as more than just another spectacle off the Hollywood treadmill. "Even the things done badly are interesting because we can see what those who made the film were trying to get at, and why, and how hard it was to get as much as they did. It would be a loss if people couldn't respond to a movie like *Hawaii* for its characters and subject matter."[1] As a film about the corruption of Hawaii, Hill's project is devastating. But also as a parable applicable to other situations such as Vietnam, the message is contemporary and pertinent. "We didn't go into Vietnam viciously," remarks Hill, "but it's like the old saying that the missionaries went over to do good and they wound up doing very well!" *Hawaii* shows missionaries who went to save souls and became landowners and businessmen instead.

Kael's remarks are apt because in many ways the film was ahead of its time. A few years later, when Arthur Penn made *Little Big Man*, a story about Custer's Last Stand told from the Indians' point of view, no one missed the relevance of the film to the United States' Southeast Asia involvement. To view *Hawaii* today is to be clearly conscious of the parallels. But in 1966 the film was often dismissed as another *Mutiny on the Bounty* extravaganza with bare-breasted natives and palm-treed sunsets. But Kael's words have been vindicated, and *Hawaii* remains a film that continues to grow in importance as it is revived and reviewed.

The large degree of authenticity that Hill strove to capture in the film is remarkable. The opening sequence during the credits establishes a virgin paradise of sky, sea, and land. But, as usual in Hill's films, casting was equally significant. Casting director Marion Dougherty said *Hawaii* was the toughest job she ever had. Hill wanted an authentic 400-pound Polynesian queen who was regal and over six feet tall. Most casting directors would have given up and used someone from Los Angeles or the Bronx. But after six months of traveling the Pacific Islands, Dougherty discovered Jocelyne LaGarde, a descendant of the last king of Tahiti.[2]

Jocelyne LaGarde may easily be the most sympathetic and "complete" woman in Hill's films. She had no acting experience, but from the moment she enters the film, lowered on board the missionary's ship in a sling, she commands attention as a robust yet sweet woman with royal blood. Like the young missionary preacher-to-be, Keoki (well acted by Manu Tupou), Malama tries her best to make sense of the white man's morality, more to keep peace on the island than out of any personal belief. But as Hale becomes more demanding in his morality, the Queen becomes upset. "Too much law make people sick," she says. When asked to divorce her husband because he is her brother, she asks Hale if this means the previously happy natives should ban all twenty-three kinds of incest. She is an Earthmother, a presence—and her death of a broken heart toward the end affects us even more than the death of Hale's wife, Jerusha.[3]

Julie Andrews is well cast as Jerusha. In *Hawaii* Andrews is given a dramatic range well beyond the "sweet" performances she had given in *Mary Poppins* (1964) and *The Sound of Music* (1965). She conveys a sense of New England upbringing, yet there is enough spark and sensuality to her characterization to make us feel how much she has given up (including her sailor boyfriend who reappears on Hawaii) to follow Hale. Jerusha's life is that of quiet acceptance of Hale and a warm friendship with the Queen and her native Hawaiian traditions. The women, therefore, come off much better than the men as mediators able and willing to live in a multicultural environment in friendship.

Technically there is little of distinction in *Hawaii*. Its strength is in its scope, characterization, and authenticity. There is, however, one short moment—when Jerusha nearly dies giving birth to her first child—that is so remarkable it seems out of place in the film. Until this point we have seen the story from the men's perspective, but suddenly we experience childbirth from Julie Andrews' view. Jerusha's face is seen in close-up, surrounded by black as we hear off camera, "It's a boy!" Softly the black fades to pale grey and gradually lightens even further. It is an unexpected and memorable moment that exactly captures the feeling of life returning to the mother after a close brush with the void.

If Julie Andrews represents a force of love, Max von Sydow carries the weight of unbending faith and damnation. When the natives finally turn on him and return to their native religion, von Sydow stands like King Lear on the blasted heath, alone and raging. "DESTROY THEM UTTERLY," he commands in a super close-up of his battered, unforgiving face. The irony is tragic indeed: he has ended up damning the people he has come to save. And yet as conceived in the script, portrayed by von Sydow, and directed by Hill, Abner Hale is tragic rather than foolish. While Hale is narrow-visioned, he is also a man who has tried to live by his dreams, his ideals, his faith, only to see them crumble. Hill may be known for his comic touch, but this dramatic moment is carried off with a sensitive effectiveness.

Not all went well on the *Hawaii* project, however. The disputes were involved and bitter. Hill felt the production was mismanaged and quit before shooting began. He felt he wanted more control over the film than the Mirisch brothers had given him, and, as he comments, "I had, in effect, written a letter that got me fired," once the film was in production. Hill would have been replaced by the producers except for a large problem: the Polynesian cast refused to work for anyone else. Hill claims he even tried to convince some of them to go back to work, but they held firm. "I had acquired their loyalty without realizing it," he reflects.

The time and energy consumed bickering with studio heads obviously distracted Hill from giving full attention to the film. Hill feels the final film was not the work he had wanted to make since he was caught between trying to please the studio and doing justice to his script. The weaknesses show up in the fragmented feeling the film creates as the last years of the Hales' lives are rushed through while some of the earlier scenes are allowed to run on too long.

## Thoroughly Modern Millie

*Thoroughly Modern Millie* is all style and surface, but that is exactly the fun of it. Wrapped up in one film is a collage blending silent comedy (with a special nod to the window-ledge-hanging talents of Harold Lloyd), romantic comedy (or clichéd romantic formulas parodied), the myth of the poor country girl and the Big City, fairy tales (especially Goldilocks, Cinderella, with strong doses of *The Wizard of Oz* in the character of Dorothy, played by a miscast but competent Mary Tyler Moore),[4] a murder-mystery complete with an evil old woman (appropriately cast with Beatrice Lillie, a reminder of similar light-hearted farces of the past) and a couple of silent-but-deadly Chinamen, all involved in kidnapping young waifs and selling them off on the white slave market, as well as a screwball comedy with Carol Channing with her raspy laughter throwing Gatsby-like parties at her estate and commanding everyone to "be happy." Star-crossed lovers, mysterious dirty deeds, practical and impractical jokes, and a zany final chase, all wrapped up with music and an ever-quickening pace that leads to a surrealistic farcical ending that reminds us of the Marx Brothers inspired mad finale in *Duck Soup*.

Hill emphasizes that *Millie* was not meant to be a comedy, a musical, or a satire: pure and simple it was a farce. The challenge, therefore, was to manipulate these stereotyped characters, these clichéd situations, and the overly familiar plots and subplots with enough speed and wit to keep the audience amused enough so that the bubble of sheer delight would not be popped. "I wanted it to be a soufflé," Hill remarks, "I knew it had to stay afloat by its own mindless nonsense."[5]

Stylistically, *Millie* is a tour de force. If little originality appeared in the filming of *Hawaii*, the camera and film technique become a major element here. We have seen how Hill began to experiment with a sense of comic surrealism in *Henry Orient's* Central Park romp scene. But from the beginning to the end, *Millie* celebrates film itself. In fact, Hill conceived of the film as "more of a cartoon than a real movie." Hill often employs title cards to let us in on the characters' thoughts ("I wish my bust wasn't so full" says Millie's first card) newspaper headlines, overhead framing of characters (especially in the elevator scene), iris-in and iris-out, fast motion, a scene "flip" as the whole image turns over, split screen, and even subtitles for some Chinese crates at the end of the film ("Big Marty's Tart Shop"). And as usual for a Hill production, the editing and pacing are well controlled so that the action builds to a dazzling, dizzy montage conclusion with an explosion in a Chinese fireworks factory that doubles as a front for many illicit businesses.

The film is well color-controlled to suggest, if not the twenties as they were, certainly the twenties as they were pictured and remembered. "I wanted to reproduce the three-color scheme of the thirties, when they had the first color plates in the national magazines," Hill explains. They had black and white and two other colors. The result was a very specific look for the period.

The opening sequence, for instance, is done in a controlled grey. We feel the film is almost a black and white film at this point, but as Millie (Julie Andrews) is transformed from a country lass to a true "modern," color is introduced. Color stylizes each scene, as each sequence takes on a different dominant hue. The elaborate dance number called the "Tapicoa" is shot in yellow, while a chase episode becomes bright red. Romance is made even more obvious as Millie's friend Dorothy (Mary Tyler Moore) in a white dress falls in love with Millie's boss, Mr. Graydon (a cardboard John Gavin who, as Hill remarks, is a "perfect James Montgomery Flagg hero"). Graydon is clothed in black while Millie (the loser), caught in the middle, wears black and white.

Millie, of course, wants to be what she conceives of as "modern." The dialogue contains clipped lingo with words such as "terrif" and "swell" and "stenog" (for stenographer). Predictably she deals with "modern" only in material and external ways, hiding her true feelings until she at last states "moderns don't cry." This is her illusion that she proceeds to live out with disastrous yet comic results. Because *Millie* is cast in the realm of farce, it differs from Hill's other works in remaining upbeat throughout. Millie's illusions must fall. However, she learns from experience and from Carol Channing, who turns out to be the wise fool of the lot, who counsels Millie to "Follow your heart— no raspberries."

The fun and energy that shine through in this film, despite the heavy hand of producer Ross Hunter, suggest the original gaiety Hill enjoyed through Gilbert and Sullivan at Yale. Far from being a side step away from a developing career, *Millie* should be viewed as an experiment that combined Hill's growing command of cinematic technique with his earlier involvement in musical farce.

Take as an example the romantic office scene between an eager Millie and a distant Mr. Graydon who is all business and zip. It is Julie Andrews' first day on the job as a stenographer, and as she opens the door and sees John Gavin for the first time, we hear part of "Hallelujah" chorus from Handel's *Messiah*. She is enthralled. She begins to sing "Baby Face" out loud while the "Hallelujahs" serve as comic-ironic contrast. Hill caps this moment by ending up with "You've got the cutest little . . . Hallelujah!" Where else but in Gilbert and Sullivan's imaginative musical word play can we find such delight in breaking up the familiar to make us laugh?

"I think *Thoroughly Modern Millie* would have been one of the best things I've ever done in terms of technique if they had just left it alone," Hill states. To discuss this popular musical farce cleverly scripted by Richard Morris is to examine what Hill wanted it to be, and what producer Ross Hunter finally turned it into.

Hill had never done a film musical before, but his experience with Gilbert and Sullivan and his direction of *Greenwillow* on Broadway whetted his appetite to have a try at one. Perhaps he was also attracted to the script because it could be shot primarily in the studio and not on an island thousands of miles away with a cast of thousands of natives. *Hawaii* is not without its charm and humorous moments, but surely after the high seriousness of the story, *Millie* must have seemed even more attractive. The story does not try to be anything more than a breezy good time. It was entertainment in the purest sense. As Hollis Alpert wrote, "No one is going to be made any wiser by this exercise in calculated camp. The film will not help in the slightest degree in alleviating poverty or ending the war in Vietnam, but audiences are to know what they paid for and get value in return."[6]

In this spirit, Hill undertook to direct this spinoff of the popular British review *The Boy Friend* (itself beefed up for the screen by eccentric director Ken Russell). Although the connection between *Hawaii* and *Millie* is slight, it nonetheless exists in the figure of Julie Andrews. According to Hill, Andrews was given the script since she had starred in *The Boy Friend* on stage. She in turn passed it on to Hill. Originally there was no music in the script. Thus Hill transformed a well-written farce into a musical farce, choosing the music himself. For the most part he preferred period songs which included standards such as "Baby Face," "Poor Butterfly," "Stumbling," "Japanese Sandman," "Jazz Baby," and "Rose of Washington Square."

Hill's run-in with producer Ross Hunter came over control of the film. Both men are strong-willed, and each had his own view of what the film should be. If Hill wanted a light but delightful soufflé, Hunter wanted a hundred pound wedding cake with all the trimmings. Hunter has specialized in slick commercial entertainment ranging from *All That Heaven Allows*, *My Man Godfrey* (the remake), and *Pillow Talk*, down to *Flower Drum Song*, and since *Millie*, *Airport* and *Lost Horizon* (the lifeless remake). He is, as Brendan Gill stated, "the misguided champion of cinematic overkill."[7] Gill clarifies his remark by saying that for Hunter, "twice as large is twice as good, twice as loud is twice as convincing, twice as long is twice as funny." Hill could not have disagreed with Ross' philosophy more.

After much bitterness in post-production, Hill was removed from the film and given no say about the final form of the film. At two hours and eighteen minutes, Hunter left in much that Hill would have edited out (the Jewish wedding scene, for instance). Furthermore, Hunter decided to add an unnecessary intermission and thus draw special attention to the film. He changed the musical sound of the film by bringing in André Previn and recording a louder, fuller soundtrack. Thus an important element in Hill's version was done away with. According to Hill, "I had a wonderful kind of Paul Whiteman sound with no highs and no lows, like the old radio sound. It was a very tinny sound of the period that I worked hard to get, and Ross Hunter rescored it with André Previn and a thousand strings!" Hill was also most disenchanted with the addition of an intermission: "It was like taking a soufflé out of the oven half way through and asking 'how's it doing?'"

Though Hill felt the film was badly mangled, it turned out to be the most successful movie that Universal had done until that date. And, it is worth noting, it was brought in for under $5 million, a price that seems almost insignificant when compared to contemporary musicals such as Francis Ford Coppola's $26 million plus *One From the Heart*.

# 6

## "Just So We Come Out Ahead"
### *Butch Cassidy and the Sundance Kid*

"It's easy. Like Butch Cassidy and the Sundance Kid jumping off the cliff. It's only a couple of marriages and a child."—Annie in Tom Stoppard's *The Real Thing*

*Butch Cassidy* is a parody and a reaffirmation of Westerns and the spirit of the West. In one sense, the film belongs to a long Hollywood tradition of Western spoofs that would include Will Rogers' silent farces, Chaplin's *Gold Rush*, Keaton's *Go West*, on up through satires such as *Cat Ballou* (1965). The script is composed of memorable one-liners ("I don't know where I've been and I've just been there") usually delivered by Newman who plays the wit to Redford's straight man. And there are many farcical moments such as the scene in which they blow up not only a railroad car but also the money contained within it, which point to the unexpected ineptitude of the robber-protagonists.[1]

But whereas most Western spoofs are simply that and no more, *Butch Cassidy* creates a dialectical tension between, on the one hand, the comic and the conventional codes of a Western, and on the other the combination of the historical Butch and Sundance with the contemporary late 1960s sensibilities. The result is a film that manages to draw upon our memory of Western movies in order to playfully satirize them while simultaneously involving us emotionally in the lives of Butch and Sundance, "two-bit outlaws on the dodge," as a sheriff friend calls them. Thus the film goes beyond satire to reaffirm the power of the Western as a genre capable of reaching us.

The film appears as unusually stylish because of this self-aware double vision it projects: it is not only a version of the Butch and Sundance story, but also a film about film and about the images and myths that can be generated by the media. For this reason, the opening sequences are a key to the whole work. The film begins with an empty dark screen upon which flashes "The Hole In The Wall Gang" and another title card, "The Hole In The Wall Gang led by Butch Cassidy and the Sundance Kid are all dead now,"/"But once they ruled the West," and in the jerky black and white of an old silent film we see figures on horseback robbing a train while Burt Bacharach's haunting theme song plays softly in the background. The credits flash by as the old film continues. Several points are established immediately: the "newsreel" format presents the story as history; we know the outcome—their deaths—before we begin; even as a newsreel, their lives have already taken on the aura of myth ("once they ruled the West") and it is by means of a film-within-a-film that this information is served to us. The film is silent. Thus the music, a simple yet melancholy piano tune, functions much like Kurt Weill's haunting songs for Brecht's productions to set a general mood while also making us aware of the artifice of the work ("old" newsreel combined with an updated imitation of period music).

The second part of the opening sequence introduces us to Butch and Sundance. Beginning with a close-up of Butch Cassidy (Paul Newman), this sequence is shot in sepia by cinematographer Conrad Hall to create a feeling of faded photographs of the period. A series of close-ups informs us that a bank is closing for the day and that it has an elaborate set of locks and bolts to protect itself. When the guard completes his ritual task, the first exchange of the film occurs:

NEWMAN: What happened to the old bank? It was beautiful.
GUARD:    People kept robbing it.
NEWMAN: Small price to pay for beauty.

Besides establishing Butch Cassidy as the wit of the duo, this introduction also foreshadows the difficulties both will face as they attempt to use their nineteenth-century frontier robber ethics and techniques against twentieth-century technology and efficiency. Butch would prefer to rob banks because, unlike trains, "they don't move." But tighter bank security forces them to take up hitting trains until that option is closed by a professional security force hired by the railroad owner, who hires Lord Baltimore, the best Indian scout in the business, to help out. The opening newsreel tells us of their deaths. The opening dialogue points ultimately to Bolivia and their "freeze-frame" death at the hands of the Bolivian army.

Sundance's opening establishes the close friendship between Butch and himself and also suggests how much of a living legend they have become. Once again in close-up, we are presented with a poker game in progress, shot in sepia-rose. Sundance (Redford) comes off as playfully ironic as he utters his first word of the film in answer to the question from his card opponent, who asks how is it possible that he never loses: "Prayer." Butch arrives to mediate the gunfight that would surely have followed had he not appeared. Once the name "Sundance" is mentioned, the opponent becomes terrified, as he learns who he is facing. The legend is more effective than reality. It is a short-lived victory, however, for despite the myths that have spread about them, they will spend the rest of their lives trying to outrun the reality of the new West.

The progression of the opening is from empty screen to old newsreel to sepia photography of Butch and Sundance. The rest of the film, except for the New York sequence, which is handled by means of still photographs, is presented in full color. The ending concludes as we began: We are made aware of the ability of cinematography to both capture and mythologize reality: Butch and Sundance are caught in a freeze-frame which turns sepia colored and becomes a photograph within a larger background.

Media, role-playing, and the generation of legends are represented in a variety of ways throughout the film. Newspapers, for instance, act as a silent "chorus": A gang member quips to Cassidy early on that, "I just love to read my name in the paper, Butch." Etta (Katharine Ross), the third member of their intimate group, informs the two friends that the papers have reported them as dead after the long chase sequence. Like the opening newsreel, therefore, the papers have the power to report the news and to fan mythology through "slanted" or downright misinformed journalism.

Furthermore, all three are aware that they are playing roles, and Butch in particular perceives himself as a performer. As mentioned this self-awareness is evident from the opening poker sequence. Later, when they are robbing a train, the engineer stands aside without resistance so that he can watch the famous Hole in the Wall Gang in action. When they visit a friend who is a sheriff, they tie him up before they leave so that it will appear he has been mistreated. And in the Bolivian segment they are aware that they have created a new set of legends about themselves as the "Banditos Yanquis." Most important of all is Etta's speech to them before they depart the American West: she offers to do anything for them except watch them die. "I'll miss that scene if you don't mind," she states suggesting that even their deaths will be performances. Finally, the bicycle sequence done to the sound of Burt Bacharach's joyful tune "Raindrops Keep Fallin' On My Head" features Butch and Etta as playful performers and would-be lovers. The scene appears to be a moment out of time, a romantic-slapstick diversion from their downhill slide toward death. But even this performance foreshadows the conclusion. Both Newman and Ross clown on the bicycle—the symbol of the new life that has made their existence obsolete. But then Ross quits the "scene" to become a spectator as Butch's act becomes ever more foolish and daring. "I'm free, nothin's worryin' me" says the song, yet Newman, riding *backward,* crashes through a fence, falls off, and is chased by a bull. Butch's performance is a comic vision of their own downfall, an ending due in large part to their "backward" outlook and their failure to adapt to a forward, advancing society.

A scene that would have further clarified the relationship between media and myth was, unfortunately, cut from the film. William Goldman had scripted a scene just before the end when in a Bolivian cinema they see a fictional film that turns out to be a fabricated version of their own deaths. Legend and life come into sharp contrast and focus as this somber foreshadowing flickers across the screen. The conclusion of this important scene is as follows:[2]

SHOT #

709    THE SCREEN
and a title reading: "Ruthless evil men, they stopped at nothing"
followed by a CLOSE UP of the gang. (NOTE: in this "movie," all
the actors should be dressed as the real people were dressed, and
they should look like the real people as much and possible.)

CUT TO:

710    THE AUDIENCE
hissing louder now.

CUT TO:

711    BUTCH AND SUNDANCE
BUTCH (to Sundance)
Did it say we're dead? We're not dead.

CUT TO:

712    THE SCREEN:
and a title reading "Their leaders were Butch Cassidy and The
Sundance Kid." This is followed by a SHOT of "Butch and Sundance" grappling with a small child.

CUT TO:

713    THE AUDIENCE:
as suddenly the hissing doubles in volume and—

CUT TO:

714    THE SCREEN
as "Butch and Sundance" are tying the child to the railroad tracks
in order to stop the oncoming train and—

CUT TO:

715    BUTCH AND SUNDANCE
            SUNDANCE
        —we didn't do that—never—
            BUTCH
        —damn right we didn't—Etta,
        you tell 'em—
And as he glances around for her—

CUT TO:

716    CLOSEUP—ETTA—NIGHT
She is just leaving the theatre now and this is the first of a series
of shots of her—all of them walking shots as she moves away and
into the night—all of them closer and getting closer.

CUT TO:

717    INT. TENT THEATRE—BUTCH AND SUNDANCE—NIGHT
Butch whirls back to the screen as suddenly the audience is cheering like crazy and—

CUT TO:

718 THE SCREEN

as the Superposse appears. The cheering SOUND grows louder as the "Superposse" take out guns and begin FIRING.

CUT TO:

719 THE SCREEN AND BUTCH AND SUNDANCE WATCHING IT

                    BUTCH
          (as "Harvey Logan"
           is gunned down)
          Hey that's Harvey—
          (grabbing Sundance now)
          They didn't get Harvey then—
          you think they got him later?
                    SUNDANCE
          —I don't know, I don't know—
          (as News Carver is shot)
          —they just got "News"—
He turns quickly, glancing back to where Etta exited.

CUT TO:

720 CLOSEUP—ETTA

Walking. The SOUND of the crowd inside the theatre is terribly loud in the night. She continues to move away.

CUT TO:

721 INT. TENT THEATRE—BUTCH AND SUNDANCE WATCHING SCREEN

                    BUTCH
          (as "Flat Nose"
          Curry dies)
          —there goes "Flat Nose"—My
          God, they're getting everybody.—
The audience is SCREAMING now and Butch turns on them—
                    BUTCH
          Shut up, you people—

CUT TO:

722 CLOSEUP—SUNDANCE

                    SUNDANCE
          (riveted on the screen)
          Butch—

CUT TO:

723 BUTCH AND SUNDANCE

                    SUNDANCE
          (grabbing Butch now)
          Look—they're coming after us!

CUT TO:

724   THE SCREEN
as the "Superposse" takes off after "Butch and Sundance"

CUT TO:

725   BUTCH
turning again to the screaming audience—
>BUTCH
>This isn't how it was—it
>wasn't like that—shut up—

CUT TO:

726   THE SCREEN
the "Superposse" is closing the gap on "Butch and Sundance."

CUT TO:

727   BUTCH AND SUNDANCE
staring at the screen and—

CUT TO:

728   THE SCREEN
as "The Superposse" draws nearer, nearer and

CUT TO:

729   BUTCH AND SUNDANCE
on their feet now, caught up in the action on screen, talking softly,
almost in spite of themselves—
>BUTCH
>—They'll never get you—
>SUNDANCE
>—move—you can do it—move
>BUTCH
>—come on you guys—
>SUNDANCE
>—all the way—
>BUTCH AND SUNDANCE
>(together)
>—come-on-you-guys—

But on the screen, the Superposse continues to close in.

CUT TO:

730   A SERIES OF SHOTS
And this next sequence consists of quick cuts to:
A. BUTCH AND SUNDANCE
watching the screen
B. THE ACTION ON THE SCREEN
C. THE AUDIENCE
cheering wildly, the SOUND always building.

D. ETTA

walking away her face always growing as the CAMERA COMES CLOSER AND CLOSER to her.

On the screen, the Superposse forces Butch and Sundance into a corner where they can't ride any more and Butch and Sundance get off their horses and try to climb to safety up the rocks that have cornered them, but the Superposse is too quick for them, too smart, and before Butch and Sundance are halfway up the rocks, the Superposse is already firing and the audience is SCREAMING itself crazy as Butch gets winged and the explosive nature of the SOUND carries through the night to Etta, who continues her walk away from it all, and on screen now, Butch is hit again, Sundance too, as the Superposse continues to fire on them. Butch is dead as he slides to earth. As Sundance dies, Etta's stunning face fills the screen. HOLD ON Etta . . . HOLD . . .

FADE OUT

Hill says he "felt that the implications of the audience seeing Butch and Sundance watching their deaths on the screen were a little heavy-handed and unnecessary." Yet although Hill and Newman felt the scene was arbitrary, others wanted to include the scene. Hill at times regrets that he didn't leave it in (it appears in Bob Crawford's documentary, *The Making of Butch Cassidy and the Sundance Kid*). Ironically, what looks like newsreel footage at the beginning of the film is actually the film Hill shot for the Bolivian cinema scene, so in that sense, a foreshadowing effect is obtained. But Goldman's script goes even further, for it also includes Etta's parting scene. She leaves them fully aware that the film is prophetic and that these men are too blind for all of Butch's talk of vision and bifocals to see this simple truth. As written, it becomes Etta's scene, a scene that would have added a stronger sense of character to her role.

*Behind The Scenes.* "I felt guilty getting paid," says Robert Redford about working on *Butch Cassidy and the Sundance Kid*. He was not alone. Hill had spent much of his energy on his previous two films butting heads with studio chiefs, but suddenly everything clicked for those concerned with *Butch Cassidy*.

Screenwriter William Goldman explains, "It was a rare experience in which the people working on it had a pleasant time, and it came out well."

Paul Newman enjoyed making the film more than the attention he received afterwards. "The experience of making that film was more important than the legacy somehow: those three months of work were what was important."

The film was a breakthrough for all associated with it. For William Goldman it was an even larger hit than his previous film, *Harper*, and it was his first original screenplay. For composer Burt Bacharach, "Raindrops Keep Fallin' on My Head" became almost as familiar a tune as "Yankee Doodle." Robert Redford had his first major success, and Paul Newman strengthened his already impressive career.

For George Roy Hill, the film was an unexpected hit that not only put him at the top of the Hollywood pecking order, but also became the film that guaranteed him the artistic control and freedom he had been striving for.

And for the Western genre itself Hill's film became a classic that will probably run forever on the revival circuit and television. It has what Ezra Pound used to identify as the mark of a true classic: an irrepressible freshness over long periods of time.

The film began with writer William Goldman. He had never written a Western before, but he was fascinated by the various accounts of the lives and legends of the two leaders of the famous Hole-in-the-Wall Gang.[3] "Cassidy was the most popular gang leader of his time along with Jesse James," states Goldman. The Hole-in-the-Wall Gang was in fact the biggest and most successful gang in the West. "And yet," smiles Goldman, "Cassidy was no good with a gun, nor was he a fighter: he *must* have been affable!" The more he thought about this outlaw duo and their misadventures in America and later in South America, where they supposedly met their deaths, the more he was attracted to them and simultaneously amazed that a million movies had not already been made about them.

During the Christmas vacation of 1965–66, while teaching at Princeton, he finished what became the first draft after eight years of thinking about the project. Besides simply telling the story of these two friends and Etta, Sundance's girlfriend, Goldman wished to treat the pathos of characters who attempt to repeat their past. When the American West closed in on them, they tried to transplant themselves to South America, into a culture they did not understand and with a language they could not speak. "I was terribly moved by these three people who died (except for Etta) in a foreign place not speaking the language," Goldman says.

Although the facts of their lives are very hazy, Goldman attempted to remain more faithful to what is assumed to be true than the typical western that exists in a mythical universe of its own. More than one critic has taken Goldman to task, for instance, about what seemed to be contemporary dialogue (Newman's constant refrain, "Who are those guys?" referring to the superposse) of Butch and Sundance. But Goldman states he doesn't believe that real Western folk spoke the way people talk in a John Wayne film. "After all," he concludes, "we're talking about 1901, not 1801, and that wasn't all that long ago." More important, he worked in details that were finally dropped from the film. Sundance, for instance, was originally from New Jersey, and Goldman had scripted about twenty pages of his return there before going to Bolivia (subsequently replaced by the New York trip montage). And in the Bolivian segment, he had shown them aging, as they lived in South America for a number of years. "My movie script was darker than the film," Goldman states, "because of these elements."

When the script was offered to Hill, it had already been considered by other directors, and had been sold to 20th Century-Fox for $400,000, which was, at the time, the record sum for an original script.[4] According to Hill, Paul Newman had read it but was not keen on it. It was then passed on to Steve McQueen, who came back to Newman and asked him to play Sundance. He would do Butch. At that point Hill was approached, but he would only agree to do it if they switched roles. "Paul didn't want to play Butch because he didn't think he would be able to do comedy," remembers Hill. "But I explained he should play comedy like anything else." Newman became convinced.

McQueen at this point departed, upset with the changes. It was at that point Hill found Redford and pushed for him. Richard Zanuck, who was the producer at Twentieth Century-Fox refused; he favored Marlon Brando for the role. Brando, however, was at the time involved with supporting the Black Panthers, and so Zanuck thought of Warren Beatty, who agreed to play the role. Hill persisted with little luck in suggesting Redford even though he did not have a large reputation at the time. The stalemate was finally broken when Newman went to Zanuck and threatened to resign if Beatty were cast. Zanuck reluctantly signed up Redford and the production was under way.

From the start Hill was clear that he was making a western with humor rather than a comic western. "I just don't think that genre works," he says. And though Goldman had made an effort to be as true to the facts of the duo as he could, an important element in the script and thus in Hill's direction was the emphasis on legend and myth. "What I wanted to do was to open up a myth to see what was inside it and then close it back up again," Hill remarks about the overall effect he sought out. His growing sense of cinematic style, therefore, served to emphasize the mythical elements of their lives, especially as applied to the freeze-frame ending.

Style for Hill once again becomes an integral part of the work. It is this point that Hollis Alpert admired in the film in a review that favored *Butch Cassidy* over Sam Peckinpah's *The Wild Bunch*, which was also based on the Butch Cassidy material and released in 1969. According to Alpert, "Our best American directors have been attracted to the Western because it affords them opportunities for the cultivation of style."[5]

*Butch and Sundance As Trickster Figures.* The double nature of Hill's approach to narrative is also reflected in the double nature or ambiguity of his main characters. Butch and Sundance are in fact trickster figures. According to Claude Lévi-Strauss, the trickster as seen in the coyote of American Indian cultures, "must retain something of the duality—namely an ambiguous and equivocal character."[6] The trickster is a mediator between opposites: between, in *Butch Cassidy*, women and men, law and non-law, comedy and emotion, performance and reality, words and actions, youth and aging.

As a pair, a male couple, this duo becomes even more ambiguous if considered beyond the surface value of male friendship. Clearly they are men-as-boys, two adolescents much like Western versions of Huck Finn and Tom Sawyer, who are bound together by their profession, who are the best of friends, but who never seem to face a problem that will divide or separate them or give them reason to question their relationship. They are, like trickster figures, half way between myth and reality, caricature and character. Paul Newman admires Butch for these reasons. According to Newman, "There is such bravery in Butch when his ambition and his sense of himself always exceed his talent. It's always touching when Butch is struggling against his own inadequacies!"

Such figures are inherently attractive to us because of their choice to live outside of respectability and the responsibilities most of us face in daily life. And that their illusions of themselves do not finally triumph, that indeed the trickster is often tricked (by himself and others), adds sympathy and pathos to our interest in these half-mythic, half realistic men.

Furthermore, we must acknowledge the importance of Redford and Newman in creating the charm and resonance of the film. This duo was a breath of fresh air in 1969 for an American society worn out with the daily horrors of Vietnam, racial strife, drugs, and rising crime. These good buddy outlaw vagabonds were also a satire of contemporary American society: they chose not to lead the straight life, yet in many other ways they appeared to represent a nostalgic past that seems to have existed only in Hollywood studios and in our own active imaginations. Going against the ultra-realistic grain of the day in filmmaking, Hill cast Redford and Newman as "stars": clearly they are meant to be both Butch and Sundance *and* movie people who are more witty, more charming, and more handsome than the actual characters ever could have been.

When we see the film in this light, we can better appreciate its subtlety. The film clearly goes beyond what some critics have found to be the one-dimensional quality of Hill's work.[7] The ambiguity of the Butch-Sundance relationship, in which they find more genuine comfort and companionship together than they ever find in Etta, is part of the playful charm of the entertainment. That the film suggests but does not explore or resolve dualities and tensions, much like the Indian coyote trickster, may be seen as a more accurate social barometer than at first expected.[8] That an audience is always ready for good "entertainment" (Hollywood's basic reason for existence) is obvious. But the popularity of these two outlaws who escape to Bolivia instead of facing up to the hopelessness of their past career in a changing America suggests that many in the audience consciously or subconsciously wish to escape—if only vicariously—the unattractive realities of contemporary life. Finally, beneath the witty banter and seemingly carefree attitudes is a sobering reality: they cannot win on their own terms. For all of the good humor and cameraderie, we cannot help but be affected by their destruction, a destruction that is both puzzling and intensified by the ambiguity of their relationship and their seeming lack of self-awareness.[9]

*The Hill Touch.* We have previously examined the skill with which Hill handles the poignancy of the closing moments of the film. The lines belong to William Goldman, their engaging delivery to Newman and Redford; but the overall effect owes much to Hill's direction. Hill was bothered during rehearsals before production began with what Butch and Sundance would be *doing* while they talked. Of course much of the impending tension and doom is created by the crosscuts to the growing artillery outside on the rooftops. But they needed something to do to make their last moments more than throwaway lines. The credit goes to Hill for thinking of the idea of their bandaging each other's hands. This simple gesture shows their friendship, and it also shows us that they do have an unspoken awareness of how greatly the odds are stacked against them.

The scene is beautifully controlled in yet other ways. There is a movement throughout the film from dark to light and back to dark. The film begins with a black background as the "old" film comes on, and Newman appears in sepia color out of the shadows. In numerous other scenes as well Butch and Sundance burst from the dark into the light. Such shadowing is literally a foreshadowing and a motif that helps establish the melancholy background to their witty banter. Not

*Period of Adjustment:* a frustrated Isabel (Jane Fonda) rings up her father while her husband George (Jim Hutton, on right) and Ralph (Tony Franciosa) look on.

*Toys in the Attic:* Julian (Dean Martin) is caught between his love for his wife Lily (Yvette Mimieux) and his family ties to his sister Carrie (Geraldine Page, on right). Note Carrie's patterned dress which appears almost as an extension of the wallpaper and thus of the house itself.

*The World of Henry Orient:* Henry Orient (Peter Sellers) pretensiously poised for his concert performance.

*The World of Henry Orient:* Valerie Boyd (Tippy Walker) and Marian Gilbert (Marrie Spaeth) as two adventurers loose in New York.

*Hawaii:* Abner Hale (Max von Sydow) and his wife Jerusha (Julie Andrews) together with the Holy Word.

*Thoroughly Modern Millie:* Millie Dillmount (Julie Andrews) strikes a pose reminiscent of Harold Lloyd in *Safety Last*.

*Butch Cassidy and the Sundance Kid:* Butch (Paul Newman) and Sundance (Robert Redford) in the freeze frame pose that signals their death.

*Butch Cassidy and the Sundance Kid*: Group portrait of the original
Butch and Sundance and other "friends."

*Slaughterhouse Five:* Billy Pilgrim (Michael Sacks, center) marching through the streets of Dresden as a prisoner of war.

*The Sting*: Johnny Hooker (Robert Redford) and Henry Gondorff (Paul Newman) pose by the poker table that launched the con against Doyle Lonnegan (Robert Shaw).

*The Great Waldo Pepper*: Waldo Pepper (Robert Redford) and director George Roy Hill examine Pepper's plane.

*The Great Waldo Pepper:* A wing-walking stunt representative not only of the aerial acrobatics within the story but of the fancy stunt flying done by ace flyers for the film.

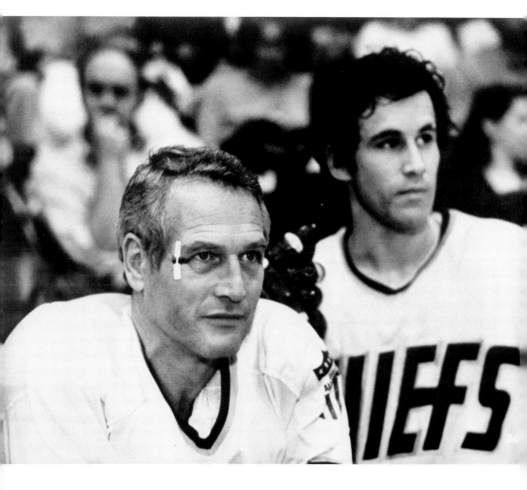

*Slap Shot:* Battered player-coach Reggie (Paul Newman) watches on while his gadfly team member Ned Braden (Michael Ontkean) sits beside him on the bench.

*Slap Shot:* Director George Roy Hill dons skates as he waits for Paul
Newman to be sound-wired for an action shot.

A *Little Romance:* Julius (Laurence Olivier) is flanked by his young friends Lauren (Diane Lane) and Daniel (Thelonious Bernard).

*The World According to Garp:* Transsexual ex-football star Roberta Muldoon (John Lithgow) receives a warm greeting from three generations of Garps, including Robin Williams as T. S. Garp and Glenn Close as Jenny Fields. (Courtesy of Warner Brothers)

*The World According to Garp*: T. S. Garp (Robin Williams) confesses his love for his wrestling coach's daughter, Helen Holm (Mary Beth Hurt), who becomes his wife. (Courtesy of Warner Brothers)

only is the frontier closing in on them, but the darkness is swallowing them up. In the closing scene they are once again in the shadows. But as the film ends, they burst out one last time into the bright light of day and of memory as the freeze-frame captures them and transfers them into a still photograph.

The effect is to capture them at their best as they are in motion on the run and still alive, although the soundtrack of the Bolivian bullets undercuts the image. Still they are spared the indignity of dying before us. The freeze-frame ending was Hill's idea: it is not in the script. It became the perfect way to follow through on Hill and Goldman's desire to take these characters out of the past, bring them into the present, and return them again both to the past and thus to myth and legend. Made two years after the success of Arthur Penn's *Bonnie and Clyde*, which destroyed the "romance" of the outlaw couple by showing in slow-motion their massacre by unseen lawmen, Hill's film chooses the opposite effect. We *hear* wave after wave of bullets on the soundtrack and thus know that they must die, but the freeze-frame which becomes a faded photo in a book preserves the duo as a myth, a story, a page from history.

The concluding scene is also well directed in terms of camera angle and distance. The motif of vision is continually brought up by Butch who says, "I got vision and the rest of the world wears bifocals." Yet everything in the story points to the fact that neither he nor Sundance can see what is clearly changing around them. If Butch has vision, it is hindsight. Sheriff Bledsoe makes this explicit:

You just want to hide out 'til it's old times again, but it's over. It's over, don't you get that? It's over and you're both gonna die bloody, and all you can do is choose where.

We have seen how this is visually represented by Newman riding backward on the bicycle during the "Raindrops" interlude. In addition, unlike John Ford, who shoots almost entirely in medium and long shot, Hill emphasizes close distance. If we watch the film closely, we notice that a very large percentage of it is shot in a medium to tight close-up. At such a short distance it is impossible to see what is going on outside the borders of their own lives. Of course, the close-up also serves to intensify our identification and sympathy for these affable outlaws.

In the last dialogue we are no longer in close-up. The camera is at a medium-long distance and mounted at a high angle looking down on the duo. After being involved with them throughout the film, Hill is now beginning to draw back, and let us see both characters together at a distance. The high-angle serves to further foreshadow their vulnerability.

All of these elements are expertly orchestrated to produce an ending that is both bitter and sweet. The humor in *Butch Cassidy* is not the locker-room material of Mel Brooks' popular *Blazing Saddles*. The humor and kidding become for the most part an expression of concern and a way of covering up darker truths. We should not doubt that Butch and Sundance know they will die. If they had not picked up all of the clues that had been mentioned, there are several more worth reviewing. Etta, of course, has left them because she did not want to watch them die. And if that alone were not a strong enough foreboding, Hill and Goldman convincingly use violence near the end to show Butch's psychological reaction to killing for the first time in his life. As we see Butch shoot some Bolivians, we watch them scream and fall in slow motion. Newman is clearly horrified by the experience. "What I wanted," states Hill, "was to show the duo falling out of themselves." He feels the scene is not as effective as it could have been, but I suggest it does give us the *sensation* of what they feel. It is all the more powerful because of their inability to articulate how they feel. Much of the poignancy is thus our realization that they know they will die and yet they try to remain as cheerful as possible.[10]

Hill's contribution to the film is further felt in the transitions used to get from the American West to Bolivia.

The bicycle scene existed in the script but not as it appeared in the film. According to Hill, Goldman could never get a scene that pleased both of them. Then Hill suggested what became the version used, which worked both as the first of three musical interludes and, as we have seen, as a further expression of Butch's character and his attraction to Etta. The song was written for the film, but not until the rough cut was finished. That too was suggested to Burt Bacharach in a general form by Hill who always takes a personal interest in controlling the music used in his films.

The second musical interlude was the New York City sequence. Goldman had scripted a live-action scene with dialogue, and Hill wanted to shoot it on the set of *Hello, Dolly*, which was in production at the time. Zanuck refused, however, because *Dolly* would not have been released by the time *Butch Cassidy* came out. "So I asked him if I could shoot it still-camera and incorporate our actors into those sets in that fashion." He agreed, and the results were not only intriguing as a stylish montage that evoked an atmosphere of turn-of-the-century New York, but the switch from dialogue to still image and music helped evoke another dimension to the characters of the "family of three." We have been watching a Western: now swiftly we see the trio as Eastern dandies, posing in a variety of roles. Historically the montage is correct, because they did sail from New York, and it is also accurate because both men were East Coast boys (Sundance from New Jersey and Butch from Pennsylvania).

But the effect of watching this montage is also one of having our preconceptions of the Western destroyed. The genre in its classical form conforms so rigorously to a landscape of the wide open spaces that we almost feel it is representative of a continent apart from the East. The typical Hollywood western does not encourage us to realize that many of the cowboys did come from elsewhere and that they went home from time to time. In Hill's New York montage we realize a sense of the West as connected to the "real" world. Furthermore, the montage telescopes the group friendship of the three outlaws into a short sequence.

Yet another Hill innovation was the transition from the New York montage to Bolivia, accomplished by fading in color from black and white. Much like the beginning of the film which slowly bleeds into color as Butch and Sundance ride the range, this transition brings us once again out of nostalgia and the past and into the narrative present. Far from being merely "artsy," Hill's techniques further the thematic structure of his film.

Hill's protagonists are ordinary people with illusions that cannot be sustained. They are not heroes. And yet *Butch Cassidy* shows with ironic humor how a couple of ordinary characters who happened to be robbers became legends. There is first of all the transformation of their names from Robert Parker to Butch Cassidy and Harry Longabaugh to the Sundance Kid. They too must have come West caught by the lure of adventure. Early on Butch says, "Y'know, when I was a kid, I always figured on being a hero when I grew up." "Too late now," replies Sundance. Butch is upset: "You didn't have to say that—what'd you have to say that for?"

Hill's favorite exchange takes place during the first train robbery. After all of the trouble the Gang goes to robbing the train, a gang member announces, "There ain't what I'd call a fortune in here, Butch." Butch doesn't break stride as he replies, "Just so we come out ahead, News; that's the main thing." Hill laughs when he thinks of this line: "They were not heroes, just small time businessmen!"

If they were heroes, they would come out ahead in every sense. But because Butch and Sundance are really Robert and Harry, they do not. Therein lies the nostalgia and the pathos of this beautifully balanced film.

# 7

## Unstuck in Time
### *Slaughterhouse Five*

"Why is war man's greatest pleasure?"—Walker Percy, *The Message In The Bottle*

Shot in 1971 while the Vietnam War was still raging, *Slaughterhouse Five* served, as did Kurt Vonnegut's 1969 novel from which it is taken, as a story concerned specifically with World War II, but echoing all war and by association reflecting the futility of Vietnam. But, going even farther than Vonnegut's book, the film becomes a satire of the suburban American dream of the 1950s and 1960s that Hill had concerned himself with in *Period of Adjustment*.

*Slaughterhouse Five* was George Roy Hill's most completely realized film until *The World According to Garp*. Building from Vonnegut's bitterly ironic novel about the firebombing of Dresden by American forces toward the end of World War II, Hill fashioned a movie in which his sense of style and form, his growing mastery of cinematic technique, and his ability to suggest the significance and magnitude of a historical moment through the lives of a few characters found a harmonious fusion.

Finally, *Slaughterhouse Five* is an outstanding example of professional teamwork. The script (Stephen Geller), the casting (Marion Dougherty), cinematography (Mirislov Ondricek), editing (Dede Allen), production design (Henry Bumstead) and music (Bach) are orchestrated by Hill with complete self-assurance.

*Vonnegut Transcended*. In an unreleased documentary on the making of *Slaughterhouse Five* shot by assistant producer Robert Crawford, Vonnegut when asked how he feels about the film, replies, "You've probably never heard any author say this before, but the film is better than my book!"[1]

Both Vonnegut and Hill were surprised with the outcome of the film. Hill at first rejected the project as too difficult even though he had enjoyed the book. It was only when screenwriter Stephen Geller came in with the first draft of a screenplay that Hill began to see the possibilities.

There were two major difficulties to overcome in adapting Vonnegut's extremely popular novel: what to do with the opening chapter in which Vonnegut appears as himself giving the personal and historical background to Dresden and thus his story; and how to capture a cinematic equivalent of Vonnegut's catch phrase, "And so it goes."

The opening chapter is critical to the success of the novel. In it Vonnegut appears as the novelist, the fabricator of fiction, explaining his craft. He also establishes the authenticity of the story. Vonnegut was at Dresden as a prisoner of war (an irony itself since Vonnegut comes from German-American stock), and experienced the horror of the firebombing—an event that could be compared only with the dropping of the atomic bombs in Japan. (135,000 people died, mostly civilian.)

Obviously Vonnegut could have conveyed something of this in a prefatory note. But the opening chapter accomplishes at least four important tasks: (1) it fuses Vonnegut's roles as witness and writer; (2) it provides background on Dresden; (3) it explains the subtitle of the book, "The Children's Crusade," as his effort to write not just another "war book" but rather a book that reflects the stupidity of all wars; (4) it sets the tone for the rest of the book.

What Vonnegut shares with the reader is the dilemma of how to write about an event so painful and which, until recently, has been so carefully hushed up by official sources that it would appear to others as the product of an overactive imagination. Billy Pilgrim's story becomes Vonnegut's way of exorcising his experience, and ironic humor ("And so it goes") becomes Vonnegut's tone and means of protecting himself from the horror of what he has experienced.

The opening chapter is pessimistic: wars have, are, and will be fought. And like Dresden, which was not a military target but a cultural center, the innocent will always suffer and die. Vonnegut reports that when he tells others he is writing an anti-war book, a character says, "Why don't you write an anti-*glacier* book instead?"

The chapter ends as Vonnegut sets up his story:

It begins like this:
Listen:
"Billy Pilgrim has come unstuck in time."
It ends like this:
Poo-tee-weet.[2]

As we turn the page to chapter 2, we read, "Listen: Billy Pilgrim has come unstuck in time," and the story begins.

Before Stephen Geller showed up with his script, Hill had turned down the project because he could not figure out how to do it without actually using Vonnegut himself in the opening of the film, having him describe the territory covered in the first chapter. Geller simplified the novel and eliminated this problem by beginning directly with Billy's story. As the film opens, Billy is typing in the dark shadows of his study in his suburban home in the "present." In superclose-up we see the IBM ball punch out "I have come unstuck in time."

This switch from the novel has several effects for the film. It immediately removes Vonnegut and the background perspective from the story and makes the film a first person point of view. The time travel that we shall experience is clearly established as representing what is happening in Billy's head, a point of view that we have no way of escaping from, no means of gaining a distance from. The film's opening also removes Vonnegut's didactic tone. Vonnegut has said that, "As I get older, I get more didactic. I say what I really think. I don't hide ideas like Easter eggs for people to find."[3] George Roy Hill, on the other hand, has always emphasized *story* over ideas, preferring to allow whatever relevance the story may have to develop from the characters and plot rather than being imposed on them from above. Hill has not hidden Easter eggs in *Slaughterhouse Five*, rather he begins *in medias res* without telling us what is going on. From the beginning we are as puzzled as Billy is with no help from Vonnegut or Hill to guide us through his time tripping. Hill trades the didactic for the dramatic.

Finding a cinematic equivalent for Vonnegut's ironic tone—"And so it goes"—was more difficult. "And so it goes" in the novel becomes almost a form of punctuation. And it is definitely a constant intrusion by Vonnegut upon his material. Whatever happens to Billy, Vonnegut is there to undercut it with his seemingly casual irony which masks his personal hurt. How does the film manage this? Certainly lost in the film is the accumulated effect of the repetition of Vonnegut's phrase. But Hill uses his *editing* to juxtapose scenes ironically, much more so, as we shall see, than in the book. And he carefully contrasts foreground and background action so that they comment on each other.

"One example of finding a cinematic equivalent," comments Hill, "is in my presentation of death. I tried to make it seem casual." The climax of the novel and the film is the execution of Edgar Derby, the high school teacher who befriends Billy and becomes something of a father figure for him. The bitterest irony of the book is that Derby is shot for stealing a teapot from the rubble of Dresden after the horror of the Allied destruction (in the opening chapter Vonnegut informs us he really knew of such an absurd execution).

Hill sets up the scene as prisoners work to clear rubble from the smoldering city in search of survivors. Edgar discovers a small china dancer (instead of the teapot in the novel), that is a reminder of the high culture of the old city and a symbol of the miracle that *anything* so fragile could survive. While Billy remains in the foreground, German soldiers drag Edgar off, place him against the rubble, and execute him. The speed of the action, the confusion of languages, the smoke of the debris, all mean that Derby's death is over before we or Billy fully realize what has happened. Billy goes berserk; when he catches on, it is too late. Hill cuts to a shot of a German soldier look-ing at the china doll and then tossing it away: Derby died for an ob-ject considered worthless by those who killed him. Hill's irony grows naturally out of the action. There is no intrusion by, for example, a voice-over narrator. In a way, the irony of Derby's death strikes us even more strongly than in the novel; we don't know it is coming (though we do hear several times that Derby is dead), and his death is not reduced to one ironic level by the repetition of a single phrase.

There is yet another change in the film: the absence of Kilgore Trout, Vonnegut's eccentric science fiction writer who wends his way through Vonnegut's novels. Vonnegut has him become a strong influence on Billy Pilgrim who is an admirer of Trout's strange novels. Besides simply livening up the book, Trout serves the function of suggesting that Billy's tripping is partially induced by Trout's notion that writing is a kind of letting go of one's fantasies and wildest imagination. With Trout gone from the film, the narrative is even more concentrated on Billy. The effect is to make Pilgrim more alone and alienated from others and thus more within his own fantasies than in the novel.

Furthermore, Geller and Hill have simplified the whole concept of the planet Tralfamadore. "I wanted to make it a fantasy that would incorporate Billy's experience," says Hill. "I wanted the Tralfamador-ians as *ambiance*, not as creatures." And so for the Tralfamadorian sequences, we see Billy, and later Billy and Montana Wildhack, alone in a large transparent dome. We do not see any Tralfamadorians. Rather than go for little green men and special effects, Hill keeps the focus on Billy. (The voice of the Tralfamadorian is that of George Roy Hill himself.) Similarly, the spaceship that comes for Billy is not a flying saucer or a space shuttle run by aliens; it is simply a growing point of light that whisks him off softly, peacefully, again suggesting how easily it could be a dream, an hallucination.

As Hill cuts back the details of Tralfamadore, he also eliminates any mention of Tralfamadorian novels. In the novel Vonnegut pro-vides us one more possible seed for Billy's "unstuck" condition. Billy in the novel learns that Tralfamadorian novels are written in such a way that, "All moments, past, present, and future, always have ex-

isted, always will exist." Billy's story is thus in actuality a Tralfamadorian fiction. Put another way, he has become so caught up in his
own fantasies that they have doubled back on him. Without this information, the film locks us even more tightly inside the seemingly
disjointed maze of Billy's memory and imagination.

*Cutting Up Billy's Mind.* More so than any of his other films, the
effect of *Slaughterhouse Five* depends for its success on its editing.
We've seen how Hill himself learned from his television days how to
edit in his head, a talent few directors can claim. To capture the sense
of Billy coming unstuck in time, Hill worked closely with Geller on
the script to detail and build the intricate number and juxtapositioning of shots and scenes that appear in the film.

But even with such a carefully mapped out script, the editing of
Dede Allen stands out as strongly distinctive. Allen came onto the
film as one of the most respected editors in the business. Her name,
in fact, has been intimately linked with American cinema since the
1960s, for it is her brand of "nervous montage" that added so much
to the originality of *Bonnie and Clyde* (1967), especially the remarkably edited death scene at the end. She worked in the industry for
fifteen years before cutting her first film *The Hustler* (1961), continued with Kazan's *America, America* (1963), and after the runaway
success of *Bonnie and Clyde,* she cut *Alice's Restaurant* (1969) and
*Little Big Man* (1970), all three for Arthur Penn.

*Slaughterhouse Five,* however, has been her most challenging project to date. While most of the cuts were set up in the script, Allen's
great talent, according to Hill, "is the timing of a scene to make it
work. She has an exquisite sense of where to cut *within* a scene."
Dede Allen feels that she is intuitive about editing, "It's really a matter of taste and making the scene play. . . . Obviously I have a very
definite reason for doing things; I'm very disciplined."[3]

The intended confusion of *Slaughterhouse Five* is that it covers an
ever-switching series of scenes between three time periods in three
different locations: The War sequence follows Billy through the events
surrounding the bombing of Dresden; the "present" is 1965 in Ilium,
New York, where Billy is a well-thought-of family man and success-

ful optometrist; and the briefest segments are devoted to Billy's outer space planet, Tralfamadore, and his fantasy of living with a movie sex symbol, Montana Wildhack.

By tracing the cuts through the first part of the film we can better understand the complexity of the editing and the contribution it has made to the film.

SCENE #1. We open in the deep shadows inside a house as a young woman cries out "Daddy" from outside. A shot of the house establishes a wealthy suburban estate [filmed in Minneapolis, Hill's birthplace]. Cut to the interior shadows again which now reveal a middle-aged man with glasses at a typewriter. He is typing a letter to the editor of the Ilium paper. "I have come unstuck in time," appears letter by letter in extreme close-up with the harsh metallic stabbing of each letter amplified on the sound track as well. Another loud sound intrudes and we are suddenly watching a Nazi tank moving through a snowscape.

#2. The credit sequence features the snowscape which completely whites-out the screen. A quietly haunting musical piece plays on the sound track [compare to the similar use of quietly nostalgic music at the beginning of *Butch Cassidy*]. Beginning as a dot on the horizon, Billy slowly comes through the snow, wrapped in a blanket, which as the film goes on, becomes an enveloping security object for him. If he is isolated in the shadows of his house in the "present," he is seen as totally isolated in a snowscape in the "past." His isolation is so complete that he appears to be free-floating in space, and thus *visually* unstuck not only in time but in space as well. As he comes along a snow bank, he is suddenly yanked down.

#3. Cut on Billy falling, back to the typewriter to establish the present.

#4. Cut to the planet Tralfamadore where Montana Wildhack sits in their glass and steel dome reading Life magazine.

#5. "Who the fuck are you?" is the jarring question we hear as we cut back to the snow as Billy is assaulted by some American soldiers. One of them is Paul Lazzaro, Billy's assassin in the future, a hyped-up New Yorker who is an angry paranoid ready to kill at any moment. Much more clearly than in the book, the Lazzaro-Pilgrim antagonism is established from the beginning.

#6. Cut to Tralfamadore as Montana calls out, "Billy, are you time tripping again?" We see Billy, middle-aged, in wire-framed glasses.

#7. Cut back to the snow where the small group of Americans is captured by the Germans.

#8. Cut to Billy's bedroom in Ilium. Billy is in bed with his hefty wife, Valencia, who states, "I never thought anyone would ever marry me."

#9. From the silence of Billy's bedroom we cut to the noise of the prisoners captured by the Germans. Billy is yanked from the line and pushed down.

#10. Cut to his wedding in Ilium to his boss' daughter, the one we have seen in the bedroom in a scene that, chronologically, follows this scene.

#11. Germans herd Americans into box cars. Billy is wrapped in his blanket.

#12. The blanket becomes the linkage for this cut as we hear Billy's mother talking to someone else in the "present." Billy peers outside his blanket with the camera taking his point of view so that we see Billy's mother staring at us, stating, "Billy, the war is over." The man she has been talking to will turn out to be Mr. Rosewater who is writing a book on Dresden, though he was not there.

#13. The war is not over for Billy. Cut to the cattle car as one man, Roland Weary, dies and Paul Lazzaro blames Billy and swears revenge. Lazzaro makes his threat emphatic by telling the story of a dog that bled to death after being fed a broken clock spring.

#14. From an extreme high angle in the present, we see an operating room in a hospital with Billy on the table. His head is wired. "You're going to sleep," the doctor says and Billy is hit with electroshock as we hear a loud sound.

#15. Again sound is used to bridge time shifts. A train whistle sounds and we see the prisoners' train arrive at the concentration camp at night. In this scene Billy is given a ridiculous red and black coat and silver boots to wear so that he is made to look like a fool. Edgar Derby is introduced as a friend to Billy and antagonist to Paul Lazzaro. As they enter a prison building, the camera moves in for a close-up of a showerhead, a shot that suggests the gas chambers.

#16. But in a surprise cut, as the camera pulls back from the same showerhead, we see Billy as a young boy taking a shower with his father before entering a swimming pool. Billy's father subsequently picks up his son explaining he will learn to swim, and tosses him into the pool. Billy sinks like a bucket of cement. [How carefully many of the shots were planned in pre-production is exemplified here. Hill himself carried the shower head into Prague, Czechoslovakia, where the Dresden scenes were shot, to make sure of the visual continuity between the two scenes described.]

From these opening scenes the themes and rhythm of the film are established. We begin in the present, move to the past, and then to what can either be called the future or simply Billy's suburban white, middle-aged, male fantasy life on Tralfamadore. The importance in length and subject matter is weighted toward the War and Dresden (the past). In terms of numbers of scenes in these first sixteen cuts, there are seven war scenes, seven in Ilium, and two Tralfamadorian sequences. From the start Hill's alteration of Vonnegut's work is clear. Vonnegut begins with the present, goes to Tralfamadore for a number of flashes and then finally moves on to the War.

The editing suggests the various ways in which Billy can come unstuck. These include sound overlap (the Nazi tank, the train whistle), sudden or violent action (being yanked down a snowbank, electroshocked, or sinking in the pool), or the linkage of an object, such as his blanket, used between cuts. Allen also establishes a rhythm between moments in which Billy is being threatened or made the center of attention and those times when he is cut off, isolated, alone, floating in snow as a soldier, sinking in water as a child, hidden in shadows at the typewriter. Confrontation and isolation, violence and detachment are played against each other constantly.

That film editing can heighten the sense of surrealistic confusion more completely than the printed page of the novel should be clear. Vonnegut needs to tell us what is going on. Hill can manipulate us as he chooses, throwing us into a scene directly. Because he has excluded the author, the effect of his cuts resembles exactly what Billy is experiencing. We too become pulled, yanked, badgered, threatened, and caressed.

The editing of *Slaughterhouse Five* helps convey Billy's confusion and passivity. Hill admires Dede Allen for knowing exactly where to cut in a scene, and it is characteristic of her sense of "nervous montage" that scenes are interrupted, broken off, uncompleted. Billy is not making connections with himself or others.

One scene is particularly exemplary. In the German prison, the Americans are asked to elect their own leader. Paul Lazzaro nominates himself. Billy follows by nominating Edgar. A voice overlap then leads into a Lions' Club election in Ilium at which we see Billy being chosen president. There is a quick cut back to the prison and then back to the Lions' Club. At the Club, Billy begins to speak, saying, "I want you to know I'll do my best . . ." but the line is completed by Edgar Derby in the prison having just been chosen leader of the group. His speech is an impassioned partiotic speech characteristic of his idealistic vision of the world.

The scene does not occur in the novel. But as Stephen Dimeo has pointed out, it effectively captures Vonnegut's spirit in cinematic terms.[4] Cutting within a scene and even within a single sentence shows how far Billy has come unstuck. Yet it also establishes the strong father-son relationship between Billy and Edgar Derby. The editing presents the two elections in two locations as happening simultaneously, yet we know Billy's election is modeled on the kind of speech Derby gave.

*The Three Faces of Billy.* Some critics complained about the editing and about the intentional jumbling of three rather unrelated stories. Penelope Gilliatt, for instance, was impressed with the war sections but found the other two segments more like a comic book spoof. "All of the scenes in real time," she notes, "are done with feeling for human attentiveness, with a comic sense of the behavior of different nationalities locked up together, and with piercing truth in the sound of Bach and the shots of lost baroque pieces as the Allied prisoners of war march through Dresden."[5] Why add Ilium and Tralfamadore?

The most realistic and moving scenes are in the Dresden part of the film, as we shall see. But there is a need for the other two sections as well. Billy's name alone clues us to his double role as an Everyman and a nonentity. As Billy he is an eternal child who will never become "William" or "Bill," and he is also an echo of that other significant innocent in American literature, Billy Budd. But while Melville's allegorical figure was able to strike out in anger, Billy Pilgrim is utterly incapable of such violence. As "Pilgrim" he is a comic parody of *Pilgrim's Progress* and of our Puritan forefathers. Instead of progress there is regression into fantasy, instead of a religious search and journey, there is the passive existence of an individual cut off from himself as well as from others. We need all three sections to the story in order to see Billy's three faces: as child-soldier, as good citizen and family man, and as a time traveler in his own universe.

One critic calls the book and film "a savage attack on the spiritual poverty of the American culture."[6] I would soften "savage" to "cynical." Vonnegut makes it clear in his opening that Dresden is not an isolated event; it is part of the fabric of human history. Similarly, the film does not "savagely" attack American culture, but rather, it shows how the bombing unhinged Billy enough so that his life forever after became a purposeless mental wandering. The basis of the film (and the book) is in the reality of the war: the integration of the other two segments is necessary to show, how *as perceived by Billy*, his American life became an empty shell. Without the Ilium and Tralfamadore sections, we would have, as Vonnegut notes, only another typical war story.

In many ways, Billy Pilgrim can be compared with Chance in Jerzy Kosinski's novel and Hal Ashby's film, *Being There*. Kosinski's book about the effects of television on our culture is also an allegorical work that draws no conclusions. Billy like Chance is a non-person produced by a white, middle-class American society. And like Kosinski, Vonnegut is cynical about that society's ability to "innocently" wage a war in which the innocent suffer and then attempt to return to "normal" in the regulated life of the suburbs. Billy and Chance are uninteresting as humans because they lack the depth, emotion, and consciousness we expect and need in a rounded character. But this is the point: both Vonnegut and Kosinski take a non-person and hold our attention by forcing us to think about these emblematic exaggerations. And to hold our attention when the characters themselves are incapable of doing so, the authors have made the style of their books as important as the content.[7]

Who is Billy?

We know very little about his youth except that he has a father who drops him in the pool and a large mother who still treats him as a child after the war is over. In the army, however, it is important that he is not just a soldier, but a chaplain's assistant. The film captures this well as Billy hurriedly and mechanically recites the Lord's Prayer to himself when attacked by Lazzaro and Weary at the beginning of the story. The Lord's Prayer is the extent of his religion. If he is indeed a pilgrim, the only holy land he finds is in his mind and its name is Tralfamadore. Instead of being a seeker, he is a receiver: things are done *to* him. He, in fact, *falls* into one moment after another. From the moment he is yanked down the snowbank at the beginning of the film, he continues to fall, pushed into the snow by the Nazis, falling face forward into his soup in the prison, sinking to the bottom of the pool as a child, and falling out of the sky when his convention-bound plane crashes in America. His death, shot down while giving a speech on time, is his final fall. Careerwise, his movement is from chaplain's assistant to an optometrist with faulty vision of his own as demonstrated by his wire-rimmed glasses. As a husband and a father (the role of the son is beefed up in the film to add yet another irony as the problem teenager becomes a proud soldier), he simply goes through the motions, more attentive to his dog than to the people around him. These scenes appear as caricature because of Billy's total alienation. But part of the reason they are caricature is because those around Billy are unable to notice him for what he is.

Vonnegut is cynical. But in his focus on war and its effects, he is less so than in some of his other works such as *Breakfast of Champions*. The film maintains Vonnegut's spirit, but softens and sharpens it simultaneously.

First there is the presence (or should we say absence?) of Michael Sacks on screen as Billy. In the book Billy remains a name, but Sacks' presence on film conveys a certain quiet sweetness along with his seemingly indestructible innocence and passivity. Hill took a chance in casting Sacks, an unknown, in the lead.[8] Sacks' boyish looks, even as he ages, and awkward, shy behavior help us accept him as more than the human blank he appears to be in the novel.

Secondly, Eugene Roche brings a warmth and personability to the role of Edgar Derby. Like many Hill characters, Billy needs a father figure. And in Derby the pilgrim hooks up with the patriot. But in the film the scenes between them build nicely the parent–child relationship as Derby misses his son and Billy needs someone to look up to. The hospital scene in which they look at each other's wallet photos exchanging "nice! nice," is particularly well done. Hill can balance differing moods, and in that scene the delicate line between absurdity and sympathy, caricature and character development is maintained.

The realism of the Dresden scenes also adds an emotional level missing in the novel. Hill, who had admired Milos Forman's early films, insisted on hiring his impressive cinematographer, Mirislov Ondricek, even though he did not speak more than a few words of English at the time (the only other English-speaking director he had worked with was Lindsay Anderson on *If*). Ondricek, shooting in his native Czechoslovakia, succeeded in giving the film rich, dark hues for the Dresden scenes that contrast sharply with the brightly lit American sequences and the artificial light of Tralfamadore.

The entry of the prisoners into Prague is one of the most memorable scenes in the film. Hill and Ondricek work together to use Prague to best advantage in capturing something of the spirit of Dresden, one of the cultural centers of Europe, before it was destroyed. The music of Bach beautifully sets the mood as the soldiers are marched through the streets. Hill cross-cuts effectively between the marching soldiers and tracking close-ups of the "Dresden" population along the streets and of the grand baroque architecture and statuary of the city.

The authenticity of the place and the people is strong indeed. The faces of the young and the old citizens are not those of a crowd rounded up by central casting in Los Angeles. Hill's on-location shooting was important to grounding the film in a reality that contrasts with the American suburban world and the studio-made Tralfamadore. There is also the role of the German prison officer played with Eric von Stroheim-like staunch nobility by the Czechoslovakian Friedrich Ledebur, who is best remembered for his performance as Queequeg in John Huston's *Moby Dick*. He adds a solidity and dignity to his role that is not unlike von Stroheim's in Renoir's *Grand Illusion*, a film that appears to have influenced Vonnegut in his writing of the book (particularly the use of the spirited British prisoners) but which Hill claims he was not consciously alluding to in his film.

The scene serves a double function: it introduces us to Dresden and its culture, and it further develops Billy: In his strange coat and silver boots, Billy, oblivious to his image, appears as a harmless blend of the Pied Piper and the Scarecrow from *The Wizard of Oz*. He is led out of line by the children to play until an enraged citizen stops the fun. The scene is one of Hill's best both for its visual richness and its economy of style in conveying, more clearly than the novel could possible do, the glory of Dresden.

Henry Bumstead, the production designer who won an Academy Award of his work on *Slaughterhouse Five*, did a fine job of capturing the three different phases of Billy's life in the sets he designed. But "Dresden" is his best work according to Bumstead himself.[9]

If Billy is a victim during the war, he is a success during the American scenes. Yet his success is shown to be a farce: Billy remains detached from wife (robustly played by Sharon Gans), family, and community. Billy's crisis during the war was not just his witnessing of the firebombing itself, but the grief caused by the loss of Derby. Billy's problems are compounded in civilian life by the crash of the convention-bound plane, which heightens his hallucinations and brings on the need for electroshock (as seen in the early scene).

Unhinged, Billy goes through suburban life in a haze. Yet at his center is a peaceful, distant void. Psychologically the loss of his father-friend brings on a regression to childhood, which is represented in the film by Billy's boyish attachment to his fire engine and his dog. Likewise he sees those around him through such two dimensional eyes. Stanley Kauffmann, while admiring the film, found the suburban sections a "trite cartoon,"[10] but this is meant to be the point. Billy is incapable of growing up, of living in the same American landscape that Garp inhabits in *The World According to Garp* with such joy, pain, and a full sense of life in between.

Hill goes further than Vonnegut in creating a cartoonish suburban life for Billy. And yet he does so with humor and compassion. Sharon

Gans is a balloon of a woman as Billy's wife, but she is a warm balloon who enjoys life and loves her husband. Her mad race to the hospital that ends in her own death is both a farcical chase scene straight out of silent comedy and an expression of her concern for Billy (which is certainly more emotion than Billy shows for her). The daughter is cast much in the same mold as her mother but with less hysteria. She too is concerned for her father and appears as a sympathetic figure when she explains the death of her mother from carbon monoxide poisoning. Again, we should keep in mind that what we see on the screen is basically given to us from Billy's perspective. The double vision of his family and community as ridiculous and yet at times sympathetic is appropriate because it is how *Billy* sees things. This contrasts with the novel in which Vonnegut's narrative voice comments upon, satirizes, and frames the events.

The third of Billy's personas is his Tralfamadorian identity. From the reality of war through the regression to a "childhood" suburban existence, Billy finally begins to trip through time, fulfilling his middle-class, middle-aged fantasies. The tawdryness of Tralfamadore is once more indicative of Billy's own imaginative impoverishment. The set is classic Sears catalogue, the atmosphere that of a Holiday Inn. Valerie Perrine plays lusty Montana Wildhack, without a brain in her head but with a busty body that aches for Billy. And true to male fantasies and Hollywood as it has represented them over the years, we see Perrine exploited as she stands bare-breasted (there are no shots of Billy in the raw to balance the picture). The loss of a father-friend in the war, and the lack of meaning in suburbia are transcended on Tralfamadore, where an uninhibited Billy finally shows *some* spark, a twinkle behind his gold-rimmed glases before the lights go out and they begin to mate.

*Destruction and Renewal: "I Was There"*. By chance, Billy's roommate in a hospital back home after the War is Professor Bertram Copeland Rumfoord, Official Historian of the United States Air Force. As Billy listens to him under the security of his blanket, he learns that Rumfoord is writing a book on Dresden. "I was there," states Billy, but the historian and history in general pass Billy by (Vonnegut played the role of Rumfoord, looking very much like Mark Twain in the first take of the scene. But when the scene had to be shot over again because of Billy's poor makeup job, Vonnegut was unavailable and another actor had to take his place).

The scene takes on more irony in the film than in the book because of its simplicity and directness: It is precisely the scene needed for the audience to be reminded that "objective" historians will actually write their "own" versions of what happened (and Rumfoord is clearly a revisionist historian), while the personal experience of war is another reality altogether. *Slaughterhouse Five* has suggested that reality through the scrambled time sense of its participant-protagonist.

Hill brings the film to a violent climax and then to a peaceful ending with effective dramatic brevity.

Much like his earlier television dramas, the actual day of the bombing is handled in semi-documentary style. FEBRUARY 13TH, 1945: 3 P.M. flashes on the screen as we watch the citizens and children going about their business, playing games. Hill builds tension as he flashes other times on the screen followed by brief scenes. If Billy is unstuck in time, he (and the film) present the actual day in clear chronological order. Just before the bombing there is an effective scene with the sudden entry of Campbell, the American Nazi leader of the "Free American Corps." In his powder blue uniform decorated with American flags and the swastika, he is a strong visual representation of the ludicrous-gone-dangerous. Hill builds the drama well as both Lazzaro and Derby take verbal potshots at him.

The actual bombing scene is brief. What Hill wanted to emphasize was the aftermath, not the attack. Here again Hill has a sharp eye for the dramatic as the prisoners parade out of the slaughterhouse that has ironically saved their lives, carrying candles as they silently march through the dark wreckage of a city. The pathos of the moment, as usual, is not caught in Billy, but in those around him. The teenage boy who has been guarding them and flirting with a young Dresden girl earlier in the film is now seen running away, charging into a flaming building searching for his father. Later he finds the body of his love which he burns.

Vietnam is directly brought into the film while it is only hinted at in the novel. Billy trips back to the present as his son, who has earlier appeared as a mangy hippie, enters his bedroom with a cropped head and in a Marine uniform. He is on his way to Vietnam, full of patriotic verve. He is not as passive as Billy, but like his father he is off to war to fight the "good cause." Billy says nothing.

Hill begins to intercut Tralfamadorian scenes with the aftermath of Dresden. The cuts are no longer confusing because we feel by now Billy's need to transcend the horror of Dresden. The cuts from the reality of the destruction to Tralfamadore make Billy's fantasy seem all the more pathetic and yet natural too. It is Billy's only defense against the past pain.

After Montana Wildhack comes into Billy's life and dreams, Billy trips back to Derby's death. Hill cuts from the execution to Montana spinning around, much like the spinning china doll Edgar died for. "Billy, do you like it?" she asks trying out a new outfit for him. Billy's ability to sublimate has almost become perfect: the doll itself has now been transformed into a live doll full of pleasure for him alone.

But Billy is not content with sexual pleasure by itself. His Tralfamadorian fantasies turn Montana into a domesticated woman as she asks to have his child. And, after a cut to his daughter and her husband talking of finding a psychiatrist for Billy, we cut back to Montana already pregnant.

Having viewed Derby's death, we are ready for Billy's. Paul Lazzaro finally has his revenge as an ancient Billy addresses a large crowd in a large, blandly modern hall. As Billy speaks in a raspy broken voice, the camera circles him as if it were his fate closing in on him. "Hello, farewell" he says and dies, his old face dissolving into his young face as a soldier. At this point Hill has added a highly original image of Billy that visually captures his whole situation. We are back in Dresden after the bombing, and Billy is trying to carry a large grandfather clock across a street when he falls with the clock on top weighing him down and obscuring him from view at the same time. Helplessly he lies on the ground pinned down by "time," one hand feebly waving above the clock which is set for the time Dresden was bombed.

While still in Dresden time, a voice overlap from Montana brings us to the final scene: "Billy, we had a baby." Back on Tralfamadore there are fireworks in the dark sky outside their dome. The firebombing of Dresden has become the fireworks of renewal and hope as Billy and Montana seem destined for familial bliss on a planet more than 400 billion miles from earth.

Hill's characters create an environment and inhabit it. Yet for all of his other protagonists, that environment is on earth. How starkly Billy Pilgrim stands out in Hill's films: his fantasy can only be fulfilled outside of time and outside the earth. Vonnegut's book is more realistic as it ends on this planet with birds chirping in springtime: "Poo-tee-weet." Hill's film leaves Billy floating through his own imagination, unstuck in time and place, far beyond everyday reality.

It is a disquieting ending. Compare it, for instance, to the close of *Butch Cassidy*. There the freeze frame preserved the duo as vibrant rogues. *Slaughterhouse Five* closes with the opposite effect. As Hill says, "Billy never drove a single scene: he is always reacting or acted upon." The seeming joy and sense of celebration at the end is one further indication of how far Billy has retreated and withdrawn from any real human warmth and fulfillment.

Not even the gentle closing strains of Bach can erase the hollowness of Billy's triumph.

# 8

## The Big Con
## *The Sting*

"I am no more guilty of imitating 'real life' than 'real life' is responsible for plagiarizing me."—Vladimir Nabakov from *Nabokov's Dozen*

*The Sting* (1973) reunited Redford, Newman, and Hill in an immensely successful box office hit. Not by accident is the theme song Scott Joplin's quietly melodic tune "The Entertainer." With *The Sting*, Hill presents entertainment in its purest sense: we not only have a yarn about a Big Con, but also the audience is playfully shown that entertainment is itself a con, an illusion, the capturing of imagination. Once again Hill's narrative approach is double-layered. We enjoy not only the tale but also the way it is told, so that the ability of film to manipulate narrative and film conventions for the purposes of entertainment becomes the final con.

*The Set Up.* For a while, it looked as if *The Sting* would not get off the ground as a George Roy Hill production. Hill was at the time becoming involved in helping Steven Spielberg set up his second film, *Sugarland Express*. As soon as he read David S. Ward's script for *The Sting*, however, he wanted to do it, and since it was clear even in those pre-*Close Encounters of the Third Kind* days that Spielberg knew what he was doing in Hollywood, Hill turned his attention to the project.

Originally, David S. Ward, who had just written *Steelyard Blues* (1972) was to direct his own script with Peter Boyle in the role of

Gondorff. As conceived in that early version of the script, Hill notes, Gondorff was a "slob of a man." Also included in the original draft, Hill adds, was "a motif of bodies being sent down cement mixer chutes!" When Hill was approached to do the project by producers Tony Bill and Julia and Michael Phillips *(Steelyard Blues)*, he agreed if he could have total charge of the film. They accepted.

Hill claims he did not set out to do a Redford-Newman film. He did approach Redford, who at first turned it down. When Redford later agreed to play the part of Hooker, Hill asked Newman if he would play a secondary role. Newman read the script and felt he didn't fit the part. At that point there was some talk of turning the film into a "buddy" story similar to *Butch Cassidy and the Sundance Kid*. Redford was strongly opposed to any such attempt. Then one afternoon at Newman's apartment in Manhattan all three discussed the story once more. Hill mapped out how the relationship could be put in juxtaposition as one of the "transfer of the crown from the King to the Prince," but Newman was still uncomfortable. Stalemate. Later, in the hallway, there was a long silence as the three of them waited for a delayed elevator. Hill broke the silence saying, "What are we worried about? *The Sting* is a pop piece, we enjoy working together, we'll have fun, so let's do it." They all agreed, and appreciative of a stalled elevator, they began work.

The mobster was the other major role, and Hill wanted Richard Boone. But Boone, very much an independent personality, refused to play third fiddle to Newman and Redford. Hill then chose Robert Shaw and changed the name of the gangster chief from Lorrimer to Lonnegan, thereby converting him into an Irish underworld figure, a twist that Shaw plays to perfection with his thick brogue. (The limp that Shaw exhibits throughout the film adds to his character but was a necessary addition. Shaw injured his knee in a handball game the day they began rehearsals. Once again, Hill capitalized on adversity to improve a film.)

Hill revised the script for *The Sting* less than any other film project he has worked on. The basics of the film are in David S. Ward's early versions. There is the tale of the Big Con as two small-time con men set out to trick one of the biggest mobsters of all with a little help from their friends and a lot of guts and cunning. Set in the Depression in Chicago, the script is an upbeat story about a big caper that succeeds and which the audience is made to feel sympathetic to, since the victim is a ganster-businessman (with no sense of humor) and since the con is motivated by revenge for the death of Luther, a "family-man" small-time grifter. The clipped dialogue, the intricate plotting and subplotting of the con, and the division of the film into segments or "chapters" complete with headings are all to be found in the November 21, 1972, version of the script.

But Hill's contribution to the script can easily be seen in his personal notes on the first draft and in their final form as represented in the "final draft" of December 15, 1972. In general, Hill strengthened the sense of motivation and narrative drive of the tale. In the original, Luther has no family. By giving him one and by slicing out an early bar and whorehouse scene, Hill increases Hooker's motivation for revenge and our identification with the "fairness" of that revenge. Hill's reputation for cutting away anything that hinders the drive of the main plot is well supported here as well. A well-written early scene has Hooker pulling a con in the men's room of the Chicago train station. Its value is that it is the only scene in which we see Hooker alone pulling a con (small time as it may be). Redford liked the scene and argued in favor of keeping it in. But Hill cut it on grounds that it slowed the film from reaching its main plot: the teaming up of Hooker and Gondorff to plan and execute the Big Con.

Hill's notes to the first draft show his concern for details. He suggests that music be used with the title cards to set the mood and connect the scenes. The Scott Joplin music was added much later, as we have discussed. Similarly, the use of a *Saturday Evening Post* style to the title cards in drawing and format was Hill's idea, as was the imitation of old Warner Brothers gangster films in the use of cameo introductions at the beginning of the film and in the framing of scenes throughout. "I purposely copied the stylistic elements of the *Saturday Evening Post* and the early Warner Brothers films. For instance remember how no extras would be used in street scenes in those films: Jimmy Cagney would be shot down and die in an empty street. So I deliberately avoided using extras." Hill also notes on the first draft that many shots should have the look of Walker Evans' Depression era photographs in which people stare into the camera "flat on." Hill also wrote in set colors and clothing suggestions for the characters in this first draft.

*The Sting* won George Roy Hill an Oscar for Best Director of 1973. The decade since the release of the film has not diminished its appeal, a fact that adds even more prestige to Hill's accomplishment. Clearly the film stands as a landmark in Hollywood entertainment of the 1970s. Robert Redford goes even further in his respect for Hill's direction. "I suspect that when people have forgotten about the critics, they will remember George's films. I think George's work will be seen as outstanding in years to come, and *The Sting* is one of the best."

*The Tale. The Sting* is a tale told as if it were a series of Chinese boxes, one inside the other. Unlike *Slaughterhouse Five*, this film appears to have a simple, straightforward drive. Yet, the film quickly establishes the idea that appearances are deceptive with Redford's first street con (tricking Mottola, the mob courier, out of thousands of dollars).

Like *Thoroughly Modern Millie* and *Butch Cassidy*, *The Sting* is both a period piece and a variation on a film genre, in this case the gangster-caper film. That the film is an "entertainment" is clear from the four levels of framing Hill employs. First, there is the opening shot of the old Universal Pictures spinning globe, which immediately casts the film as an "old" movie (Hill's first "con"). Hill continues this motif as he borrows from the thirties films the cameo star introduction of characters before the story begins. The cameos not only serve as a playful reminder of past films and of the characters in the present tale, but they also enable Hill to pull off a con that we accept and do not discover until the end of the film. We are introduced to "FBI AGENT POLK," and we have no reason to doubt that he will appear. But, at film's end, the extra "kick" to the Con is the discovery that even the FBI agent had been a fabrication by Gondorff to trick police lieutenant Snyder.

The second framing device is the *Saturday Evening Post* magazine format drawings. These include Hill himself standing, as drawn, behind his credit. We recognize that beginning with a story book or the printed page is itself another long-standing Hollywood convention. This format suggests other old films as well as a world of "printed" tales.

Third, there is the chapter division of the tale into six titled segments plus the opening sequence in Joliet, Illinois. The opening of the tale itself could be a documentary: "SEPTEMBER 15, 1936" flashes on the screen over a freeze-frame of a run down small town street showing a photograph in the style of Walker Evans. It then comes to life. But once Hooker has met Gondorff, the Con is on, and the film too assumes a sense of style and control which parallels that of the protagonists. As in a magazine (the *Post* drawings again) or a novel or silent film, the chapter-title cards break the flow and help structure what we watch and read. Thus we have THE SET UP, THE HOOK, THE TALE, THE WIRE, THE SHUT OUT, and what we are led up to, THE STING.

Finally, the music of Scott Joplin also helps frame the story. David S. Ward had written in cues for some brassy Chicago blues of the period to help locate the story as a Depression piece. But Hill opted for Scott Joplin's sweet yet melancholy piano tunes, representing the turn of the century and a less specific sense of place.[1] Says Hill, "The film is meant simply as an entertainment, and I wasn't worried about the anachronistic elements." Furthermore, the music not only helps create a mood, but it serves to connect the divisions of the film, as we hear Joplin's tunes (arranged by Marvin Hamlisch) playing along with the title cards and drawings. The feeling is as if we were being entertained by a piano player between acts at the theater or during a silent film. The delicate quality of the lone piano and the arrangement, like the piano scores in *Butch Cassidy* and *Slaughterhouse Five*, also help soften the brutality of the action on screen (especially the murder of Luther).

*Hooker's Initiation. The Sting* shows less than exists. The film is a series of cons from start to finish. Beginning with the framing devices in the opening, Hill builds our trust, plays on our willingness to become gullible, and then exposes how we, like Lonnegan, can be taken.

The first con within the film is the street scam pulled off by Hooker

(Redford) and Luther (Robert Earl Jones). The scene is set in Joliet, Illinois, during 1936. The opening image is one of a rundown street caught in a freeze frame.[2]

A lone figure named Joe Mottola comes down the street as the camera zeroes in on his fancy white winged alligator shoes. We track with the shoes into what looks to be an abandoned tenement building only to discover a numbers office bustling with activity. It is quickly established that this is no small-time operation (the character on the phone says, "they did 14 grand in Evanston, 16.5 in Gary, and 20 in Cicero"). Mottola is handed a thick envelope with the day's take and told to catch the 4:15 train to Chicago. Mottola takes the money and heads out into a narrow alley on his way to the station. Hill and Ward have thus introduced us to a big-time operation and kept our attention through close-ups on Mottola.

We identify with him, and so we are as surprised as he is when he is swindled. What happens? In the alley Mottola hears shouting and sees a "thief" race toward him chased by an older black man. A young stranger (Redford) is coming along from the other direction. Redford yells to an uninterested Mottola to cover his end of the alley as he manages to trip up the thief, sending the wallet he carries flying. Redford kicks the wallet to Mottola as the thief flees. The black man arrives to claim his wallet which Mottola hands to him. When the black man (Luther) exposes a thick wad of bills, both Redford and Mottola are surprised. Luther then proceeds to explain that he runs some "slots down in West Ben for a mob here" and that he has to get the cash to the right people by 4 P.M. Because his leg is hurt, he offers either of the others a hundred dollars to deliver the money. Hooker bows out, afraid of walking "into a bunch of knives." Mottola volunteers. He takes the money and puts it inside his pocket with the other money.

Hooker then worries about the safety of carrying the money in so vulnerable a spot. Taking a handkerchief and calling for Luther's money, he places it in the handkerchief and asks for his other wallet too. Mottola hesitates but places it on top. Redford wraps them up and slips them inside down his pants into the crotch: "Ain't no hard guy in the world gonna frisk ya there." Redford hands him the handkerchief and Mottola slips it into his crotch and leaves. Inside the taxi, Mottola breaks into laughter at the thought of his easy steal. But as he unties the handkerchief, he discovers nothing but toilet paper.

Hill and Ward have duped the audience as much as Redford and Luther have made a fool of Mottola. At first, of course, we suppose that this minor gangster has conned two innocents (though Luther does say he works for the mob) out of a handsome sum. We recognize the stranger as Hooker, but we have no idea of his role. In fact, because he is usually cast in romantic and heroic roles, we are doubly surprised to find out Redford is in on the con (again although he was a robber in *Butch Cassidy* he and the camera are open about his profession). Our surprise is as great as Mottola's at the con, and we enjoy it all the more because we realize that it is a mobster who has been tricked. Like Mottola, we instantly understand that what we didn't "see" was the switch, a switch that Hill has purposely withheld from us.

Hill and Ward have hooked the audience and caught it in a double bind. On the one hand the street con sets us on our guard against being tricked again: we are ready to watch every move extremely carefully both to protect ourselves from being conned but also to experience the sheer pleasure of watching the "how" of each trick. On the other hand, Hill has shifted our sympathies to Hooker. We are thus doubly vulnerable, as we begin to trust Hooker and as we are now limited to what he sees just as, in the opening, we were limited to Mottola's point of view.

As the film finally turns out, we are taken in on a large scale. In one case it is because Hooker does not know what is happening though Gondorff (Paul Newman) does: we do not know that Loretta is "Salino," a female hit man, and we do not know that the mysterious black-gloved hand we see in an unknown location handling a gun belongs to someone Gondorff has sent over to protect Hooker from Salino. Finally, as we shall see, we are taken in by both Gondorff and Hooker in the faked "killing" sequence at the end of "the sting." We have spent nearly two hours delighting, as "insiders" in watching the set-up of the sting. We enjoy this privileged information that the victim, Lonnegan, does not know despite his suspicions. But the fun of the ending is that we discover that Hill and Ward have not told all. Beyond what we think we know, no matter how "in" we are made to feel, there is still that extra sleight of hand that is the mark of a thoroughly professional con man and entertainer.

Gondorff is the master from whom Hooker must learn if he is to revenge Luther's death (Luther was murdered by Lonnegan once he discovered that Mottola had been taken) and improve his skills. Yet once again appearances deceive. Our first shot of ·Gondorff shows him pressed against the wall of his bedroom in a drunken stupor. Could this be the "Great Henry Gondorff" Hooker had heard so much about? Why should we trust an aging drunk who repairs amusement park rides in a faded part of Chicago? (The amusement park is itself deceptive: it is a front for Billie's cathouse located upstairs.) The relationship Hill establishes between Gondorff and Hooker is archetypal. The story of initiation of a younger man by an older father-figure who is wiser than he appears to be, a relationship that is both serious and humorous, is a contemporary rendition of a story at least as old as Homer's *Odyssey*. There, Odysseus is disguised as a weary vagabond who carefully (with the aid of a goodly amount of necessary deception) guides his son Telemachus into manhood through a series of increasingly difficult tasks and tests.

That Gondorff is the guru of guile is clear from the beginning of "The Set Up." Once he has heard Hooker's story and signed himself up to go after Lonnegan, Gondorff quickly rounds up a motley crew of con men not seen since the pages of Dickens, Gay's *The Beggar's Opera*, or Brecht's *Three Penny Opera* (though without their sense of social commentary). Gondorff orchestrates the plan with the efficiency of a corporation chief executive. Hooker has learned his first lesson about The Big Con. It is to be both far more complex than the street scams he has lived on in Joliet, and it depends on specialization, discipline, and teamwork.

Gondorff comes fully to the forefront with his glorious poker game aboard the twentieth Century Limited Train in part two, "The Hook." The idea is for Gondorff to hook Lonnegan by beating him at his habitual New York-to-Chicago poker game (Lonnegan's only vice according to "intelligence" reports) and thus to make him angry enough that Hooker can play on Lonnegan's thirst for revenge in order to capture the big-time gangster. As carried off in terms of writing, acting and direction, it is one of Hill's most memorable scenes.

Billie begins the sequence by skillfully stealing Lonnegan's wallet. Gondorff is happy to find $25,000 in cash which he switches to his own wallet as Hooker watches. The stage is set. But Hill builds tension by cross-cutting to Chicago and Gondorff's organizer, Twist, who is preparing the "Club" in which the con will later occur. The poker game is, in fact, framed by the Chicago segments which open and close "The Hook" like a trap snapping shut. This cross-editing is particularly effective, for while Lonnegan is being tricked at cards on the train, we are aware the larger scam is ready to be pulled on him as soon as he reaches Chicago.

Gondorff is both a card shark and a ham actor. Hooker's street scam that opened the film was clever, but it was child's play in comparison to the sustained talent operating at close quarters at the card game (and we feel a sense of claustrophobia in the dark tightness of the card room aboard the train). Gondorff plays a loud-mouthed drunk who riles Lonnegan all the more because he never gets his name right ("Mr. Lonneman" at first and then "Lonnihan" without the "Mr."). The drunken newcomer quickly takes the first round when he calls Lonnegan, who produces a solid two pair. Gondorff puts down three tens.

The Big Play comes in the third round after a cut to Twist in Chicago. We know that during a break in the game, Lonnegan had a deck of cards fixed. When, back in the game room, Gondorff hands him the deck to cut, Lonnegan swiftly substitutes his deck for Gondorff's. Of course we half expect Lonnegan to overturn the upstart Gondorff as the stakes rise and the other players drop out. Finally he calls, and Lonnegan lays down four nines. We now see that Gordorff is holding four threes. He then sighs as he stares at Lonnegan's hand in disbelief and proceeds to throw down four jacks. "You owe me 15 grand, pal," Newman says with one of his winning smiles.[3] Lonnegan has a "stare that could kill," David S. Ward writes in the script. But the game is not over: Lonnegan must now fumble for his wallet and discover it missing. And, finally, he must hear an unexpected honest answer from Hooker when he comes to collect:

LONNEGAN
Your boss is quite a card player,
Foley. How does he do it?
HOOKER
(matter-of-factly)
He cheats.

Lonnegan is hooked by Hooker who comes on strong as Gondorff's defecting partner. It is now Hooker's turn to prove he is proceeding with his initiation: he is face to face with Lonnegan, the man who ordered Luther's murder, and he must not only control his feelings but also try to live up to Gondorff's high standards of acting.

Throughout the scene, and the film as a whole, Hill's cinematic style is shaped by the tale he is telling. Because our focus is on Gondorff and Hooker and their abilities to con, the photography and camera movements are extremely simple. In *The Sting* there is nothing of the cinematic razzle-dazzle of *Thoroughly Modern Millie*, the tricky time-tripping editing of Dede Allen in *Slaughterhouse Five* or the sense of spaciousness created by the camera work in *Hawaii*. *The Sting* depends largely on close-ups and middle-distance shots caught with a stationary camera. Such simplicity allows us to watch the action. But, as noted, it is a deceptive simplicity since Hill's camera also conceals as much as it reveals: how did Hooker switch handkerchiefs in Joliet, and when did Newman come up with four jacks when we, like Lonnegan, were watching him the whole time?

*Nerves and Brains.* Gondorff clearly sees the Big Con as a form of initiation for Hooker. While gangsters and con men in other films have family and women to worry about, for these two hoods, women are, for the moment, a distant second, and family is never mentioned except in connection with Luther.[4] In this light, Gondorff, though he never expresses it, obviously takes a fatherly pleasure in breaking in Hooker. Yet Gondorff is more than a father figure. The Big Con is shown as a man's world that puts a premium on a boyish spirit of play.

The relationship between Gondorff and Hooker is made most clear at the end of the fourth section, "The Wire."[5] Hooker has been in trouble with Lonnegan and has been beaten up. He tries to hide this and the fact that he has switched rooms in order to try and work things out on his own. Gondorff comes down firmly on him for this breach of communication:

GONDORFF
You can't play your friends like marks, Hooker.

Hooker doesn't reply. He knows Gondorff's on to him.

GONDORFF
You know how easy it'd be for one of Lonnegan's guys to nail you?
HOOKER
All we need is a couple days, Henry. A couple days and we'll get Lonnegan down and stomp on 'em.
GONDORFF
You just won't learn, will ya. Hell, you come in here, I teach you stuff maybe five guys in this world know, stuff most grifters couldn't do even if they knew it, and all you wanna do is run down a bullet (pause).
You're just like all them new jerks. Lotsa nerve and no brains. And ten years from now when me and the others are through and you dumb guys are all dead there won't be one gee left who knows the Big Con was anything more than a way to make a livin'.
HOOKER
A couple days; that's all I'm askin'. I can stay clear that long.
GONDORFF
(trying to be angry and failing) Christ, they'll probably miss you and hit me.

Hooker must learn what to hide and what to reveal to his friends and partners. Conning is the art of fooling others, but, Gondorff makes apparent, among the "team" all cards must be known. The last direction for Gondorff ("trying to be angry and failing") is important because it is not his style or character to blow up at Hooker in a traditionally patriarchal way (contrast his behavior with that of John Wayne in *Red River* as Montgomery Clift's initiation leads to open conflict). Gondorff has made his warning but can't resist ending on a wisecrack. The speech has been a serious one, however, and we learn just how serious in the next segment, "The Shut Out," when we discover Gondorff has assigned a man to the job of saving Hooker's life. As a true professional, Gondorff does this cooly, quietly, and without our knowledge (or Hooker's). Gondorff likes Hooker, but he is not willing to take chances.

Nerves and brains are what Gondorff has to offer the apprentice con man, and Hooker proves, in the end, that he has learned well from his mentor. But the night before The Sting, the rapid pace of the film slows down for a moment as the two men talk about conning and the past. They are both aware that after The Sting they will have to split and go into hiding. This is their last opportunity to talk openly. Hooker asks about Gondorff's past record as a grifter, and Gondorff obliges him by reflecting on Chicago in the old days. He makes it clear that times changed when the "Wall Street boys" tried to start investing money for the con men. For Gondorff, the wedding of Big Business and the Big Con was the beginning of the end. "It really stunk," he says, "No sense in bein' a grifter if it's the same as bein' a citizen."

Gondorff, the master con, finally lets us in on why he is in on the job. In part it is in memory of Luther, but revenge by and of itself is for suckers, as he exclaims. And in large part he is doing it, as he tells Hooker, because it "seems worthwhile, doesn't it?" His revelation about the Wall Street boys, however, provides a third deeper and more personal motive for his behavior: getting back at Lonnegan is a way of showing his disgust for mobsters who try to put up a respectable and legitimate façade to the public.

The Big Con is not just a "how-to" course. It is also an initiation into an attitude toward the "art": it is a philosophy of life. That Hooker learns the lesson well is seen in the last scene. After The Sting has been pulled off, and the two rise from the floor after being shot "dead," Gondorff asks if Hooker wants to wait around for his cut of the money. "Naw," he replies, "I'd just blow it." Gondorff nods, and then they walk off together down the alley and turn the corner. Hill and Ward keep their characters' motives pure. They are not in the con for the money at all, but rather they have lived out a caper for reasons that have nothing to do with greed and capitalism. We leave them going off, romantically individualistic in the American tradition of Huck Finn heading out for the wilderness, their backs to the camera. Such purity is an impossible ideal, but that is its attraction as an entertainment, for through Gondorff and Hooker's victory, the audience vicariously triumphs over both Big Business and the Mob.

Hill's tale fulfills the romantic American myth that with brains and nerves an individual can succeed at what he sets out to do—no matter the obstacles of real life, the chances against such a "Sting" being pulled off, the likelihood of the two being caught later, the implausibility of plot twists.[6] What counts is that the story is rooted in the American spirit of individualism and that it satisfies our need for wish fulfillment. At a time when "realism" is carried to crushing and depressing extremes in art, literature, and film, Hill, like Gondorff, stands nearly alone in reminding us what stylish and intelligent entertainment can be like. *Rocky* is also about winning, but Sylvester Stallone's battered face in the closing shot reminds us his success comes from a harshly real environment in which muscle and animal strength predominate. *The Sting* celebrates brains over brawn and nerves over power.

Contrast the closing of *Rocky* with that of *The Sting*. Both films make the audiences leave the theater feeling like winners. But while Rocky will be nursing a bruised body for weeks to come, Newman and Redford, flashing their engaging boyish smiles at each other, rise from the floor, their stylish tuxedos barely ruffled.

*The Sting* and Its Critics. There is no doubt that a large public has delighted in *The Sting*. Many critics, however, have been less than kind. Jay Cocks is typical of those who are unwilling to accept the film on its own terms. In his *Time* review, Cocks wrote, "This isn't a movie, it's a recipe. The people who put *The Sting* together followed the instructions on the *Butch Cassidy and the Sundance Kid* package: one Paul Newman, one Robert Redford, a dash of caper. Stir in the same director, if available."[7]

Redford, who has certainly made his share of socially "significant" films (*All The President's Men*, *The Candidate*, and even his directoral debut in *Ordinary People*) is upset by such a simplistic view of the function of entertainment. "I think *The Sting* is a totally relevant film," Redford remarks. "What is the purpose of entertaining people? You want them to feel a little better than when they came in, and if

you can do it by making them cry, think, be provoked, or simply enjoy a story, that is relevant." Hill more modestly claims the film was
made to be enjoyed for the fun of it. "As the credits suggest," he says,
"we are here to tell you a yarn, not to involve you in an emotional
way." For Hill, film is exciting because it has such a great capacity
for entertaining large numbers of people. That he wants the film to
be viewed on this level is also clear at the end of the credit sequence
when we hear a voice (Marvin Hamlisch's) start up the music with
"A one, a two." And the film is on.

Even if we accept the film in the spirit it was made, there is still
another criticism that has often been leveled at *The Sting*. Pauline
Kael sees one of the few differences between *Butch Cassidy* and *The
Sting* as the swapping of mustaches between Redford and Newman
("Newman now has the dashing ornament").[8] The differences do,
however, run much deeper.

Overall, there is the sharp contrast between the open spaces and
the sense of continual motion in *Butch Cassidy* and the confined,
city landscape composed of interiors in *The Sting* (even in the long
train sequence, we have no real sense of motion). More important,
as Newman noted, *The Sting* is a tale of initiation, of the passing
along of a craft from an older man to a younger one. It is not really
a "buddy" film in the sense of *Butch Cassidy*, in which part of the
charm of Butch and Sundance is that they never seem to learn anything at all (or they are unable or unwilling to express it). Redford
points out that *The Sting* is not a sequel to *Butch Cassidy* moved to
the city. Commenting on why *The Sting* is not a buddy film, Redford
says, "if you think about it, Hooker and Gondorff are not in the same
scene very often. Newman and I hardly ever come into contact with
each other in the movie, but everyone says what a great relationship
you have in the film."

The separateness of Redford and Newman in *The Sting* is worth
noting. Despite Cocks' cry that "this isn't a movie, it's a recipe" the
fact is that *The Sting* carefully avoids merely repeating the success of
*Butch Cassidy*. The opening segment belongs to Redford as we watch
the small-town grifter become involved in big-time trouble. Redford
and Newman appear together in the few scenes necessary to show the

set up of the Con, the updating of the progress of their stunt, and at the end as they carry it off. But in between these meetings, we focus on how first one and then the other is able to handle himself *alone*. In the case of Hooker, we watch his growing skill at adapting his streetwise skills to indoor charades. In contrast, the most memorable scene in the film, the poker game on board the train, belongs entirely to Gondorff and thus to Newman's performance as the aging confidence man.[9]

Finally we note that Butch and Sundance were robbers while Hooker and Gondorff are con men. The difference between these pairs is not only the difference between their occupations and relationships, but also the contrast in how Hill presents their stories. Part of the pleasure and pathos of *Butch Cassidy* is that we know more than the characters do. In *The Sting* we know less, often a *lot* less, than the protagonists.

# 9

## The Corruption of Sport

"Amerikans love caustick things; they would prefer turpentine tew colone-water, if they had tew drink either. So with their relish of humor; they must have it on the halfshell with cayenne."—Henry W. Shaw, *Josh Billings' Meditations*

With his next two films, Hill continued his career as a maverick director with the courage to break new ground. *The Great Waldo Pepper* (1975) gave him the chance to explore a lifelong obsession, flying, whereas *Slap Shot* (1977) allowed him to follow through on a subject he knew very little about: ice hockey.

As different as these projects are, they appear in retrospect as companion pieces in Hill's career because each is concerned with the corruption of a sport and the way of life that went along with it. They are also united by their main characters who are depicted by the Redford-Newman combination going solo. Furthermore, both are cast against their more light-hearted roles in *Butch Cassidy and the Sundance Kid* and *The Sting*. In these more recent films, both are portrayed as con men who can be blatantly deceptive and nasty when they choose to be.

Finally, the nostalgia both films evoke is one for a simpler America where competition and capitalism did not so crushingly spoil the sheer fun of sport.

### The Great Waldo Pepper

*The Great Waldo Pepper* goes further than *Butch Cassidy*, the previous Hill–William Goldman collaboration, in focusing on the delicate balance between myth and reality, conning and sincerity, and the need for, yet the danger of, hero worship. The very titles of these two Hill–Goldman films suggest the emphasis on the male individual as hero and myth. Likewise, *Pepper* is set historically at a moment of change in American society. In *Butch Cassidy* it was the close of the frontier; in *Waldo Pepper* it is the late 1920s and the post-World War I switch from rural values to an urban orientation. And like *Butch Cassidy*, *Waldo Pepper* "starts light and ends dark." In fact, as we shall see, *Waldo Pepper* darkens so much that it lost many of the critics and a fair share of its audience.

There is a clear double vision in all of Hill's films. But the contrast between fantasy and reality is especially sharp in *Waldo Pepper* in which the regulated and traditional sense of life-on-the-ground is played off against Waldo Pepper's freedom in the sky where, as a barnstorming pilot wandering around the Midwest, he is his own man. He is his own best companion (in a narcissistic sense his real partner is his plane: he is much closer to it than to any of the people in the story), and even as Andrew Britton has perceptively pointed out, a kind of "trickster-god who comes down 'from the heavens, all for you.' "[1]

*Behind the Scenes.* Although Hill had considered a flying film for a long time, he hesitated following through on the idea because it was such a personal subject. "Waldo Pepper was my early life," Hill states simply. Nothing really happened until Robert Redford made a move. According to Redford, who laughs when he recalls the genesis of the movie, "Hill's obsessive interest in flying got so boring sometimes that I thought I would have to leave the room or break it with some obsession of my own." Redford pushed for a film because the idea of building a story around the age of barnstormers after World War I was "romantic and colorful and rich, and I thought it would be a good film." William Goldman was called in and asked to write up the script, but personal differences between Goldman and Hill led to a shelving of the project.

Meanwhile Hill made *The Sting.*

About a year after their initial conversations, Goldman and Hill did get back together and brainstormed about barnstormers for ten days in New York. The result was the beginning of a script, which was completed in 1973. From the start, it was clear that this work would be Hill's most personal film. *Butch Cassidy* was entirely Goldman's script. "*The Great Waldo Pepper* was George's baby almost entirely," says Goldman, who had the responsibility for fleshing it out and "making it work."

Hill looks back on the filming of *Waldo Pepper* as perhaps the most challenging and enjoyable production he has been involved with. Films about flying were certainly not a novelty in Hollywood, where Hawks' *Only Angels Have Wings* and *Dawn Patrol* and William Wellman's *Wings* became classics of their kind. But in few other films about the early days of aviation has the sheer joy of flying been so well captured as in *Waldo Pepper*. "There is not a process shot in the film," says Hill with pride. Every stunt was intricately worked out and executed with precision. Hill himself took to the sky and piloted the camera plane at times to get exactly what he wanted. Hill's obsession even rubbed off on the cast. Redford did his wing walk with no double in one shot (though he was not far off the ground). "The dumbest thing I ever did," he reflects with a gleam in his eye. And Hill gives actor Edward Herrmann special honors for not using a double in the spectacular shot of the plane piloted by Art Scholl flying upside down and practically brushing the ground. "The gutsiest bit of flying I've ever seen," Hill remarks.[2]

"*It Shoulda Been Me.*" *Waldo Pepper* unfolds with a classic American simplicity, almost as if the stark beauty of the Midwestern landscape were filmed by Andrew Wyeth rather than by the talented Robert Surtees (*The Graduate, The Last Picture Show,* and *The Sting* among others). Yet there are three principal dimensions to the myth of the hero in the film that give it a particularly rich resonance. First, like *Butch Cassidy* the film is framed within a world of artifice and cinematic reality. *Waldo Pepper* opens with a clever spoof of the old Universal trademark: a small plane is seen circling the globe. The film is immediately set as both a period film and a movie about flying.

Second, Hill personalizes his film and adds yet another level to the framing of the story by cutting to a model, as near as he could make it, of his own childhood scrapbook of famous barnstormers. With a light but haunting piano tune in the background (much in the spirit of the music used to set an opening mood in *Butch Cassidy* and in *Slaughterhouse Five*) the scrapbook introduces us to our subject and also reminds us that most of these men are *dead* (their birth and death dates are given under their photos).

William Goldman is quick to mention that death is strongly fore-shadowed in *Waldo Pepper*, as it was in *Butch Cassidy*. In fact, he states that the title of the film originally was to have included Waldo Pepper's dates: 1895–1931.

The framing of the story by the old Universal logo and by the scrapbook is the first dimension of the myth of the hero. The second has to do with Waldo Pepper as he projects himself to others and as others perceive him. In *Butch Cassidy* it was primarily the media that turned Robert Parker and Harry Longabaugh into Butch and Sundance. But in *Waldo Pepper* Hill and Goldman show us as the film unfolds that Waldo Pepper is, like the name itself, a carefully constructed persona who appeals to different people for various reasons. To children he is an adventurer, to hard-working, straight-living farming folk, he is a breath of fresh air in their otherwise humdrum routine, and for the young ladies, he is a romantic hero-god, who might sweep them away.

The opening scenes prepare us for this side of Pepper. Our first view of him is in fact seen through the eyes of childhood. We open with a young boy, Scooter, fishing. This could be the introduction to *Huck Finn* except for the rumble of a distant airplane on the soundtrack. The boy drops his pole and begins to race across a field after the colorful biplane that is zooming overhead. The time is 1926; the place is Nebraska. The boy reaches a large field as the plane touches down. THE GREAT WALDO PEPPER is painted on the side of the plane as Robert Redford (who was thirty-six at the time, but who never looked more dashing and certainly looks as if he were younger—as the script describes him), springs out of the cockpit and with a large smile that flashes his perfect teeth, waves and exclaims, "Hello, good people!"

Goldman in the script writes, "He wears beautifully shined boots and a white scarf and an airman's jacket and he looks believe it or not, dashing. People don't look dashing anymore, but they did then, some of them anyway, and Waldo does." He is too good to be true, too handsome, too adventuresome, too much a hero, or so he seems. And yet, Pepper is soon given human dimensions as we watch him tease Scooter into running into town for gas on the promise of a free ride. Scooter fulfills his end of the bargain only to watch Pepper take a string of folk up and then offer to pay him off without a ride. Scooter prevails, however, and Pepper finally gives in, taking the young Nebraskan and his dog on the flight of their lives.

Paul Zimmerman meant to be ironic in his description of the film as having the, "lively, outdoor appeal of a teenage adventure film," [3] but in many ways this is exactly the spirit and value that Hill has so successfully captured. Flying is and has been, especially in the early days, a romantic idea, the stuff of childhood dreams, as it was for Hill himself. A scene that would have underscored the adolescent appeal of flying even more strongly and which Goldman was personally fond of, was finally dropped from the script.

The February 15, 1973, version of the script marked "First Final Rewrite"[4] contains a prologue. It is as follows:

FADE IN ON
THIS KID. Maybe he's ten, freckled and bright eyed. Very American looking. And we're in CLOSE UP. And there are a lot of boys who are going to lose a lot of sleep over this one when she gets a little older. SHE's looking up at something just now, we don't know what yet, and she's so excited you can almost feel the pounding of her heart. Now—
CUT TO
THE BOY. Not quite so close up this time. He takes half a step forward, then hesitates, stops, and moves nervously back and forth, as we
CUT TO
THE TEN YEAR OLD GIRL, AND NOW ANOTHER GIRL THE SAME AGE JOINS HER. This one is pretty too, and she too stares up at the same gentle angle, and she's just as excited as her friend, and they stand there side by pretty side, watching and waiting, watching and waiting.
CUT TO
THE BOY. He takes a deep breath, slowly starts running forward and as he does
CUT TO

THE TWO PRETTY GIRLS, and whatever's going on, it's just too exciting, they simply can't stand it and, keeping their eyes on the BOY, they reach out for each other's hands, find them, clutch each other tightly as we
CUT TO
THE BOY, running faster now, picking up speed as he tears across this enormous green hill, coming closer and closer to the edge of it and beyond that edge there's one hell of a sheer drop off but that doesn't seem to matter, because now THE BOY is really racing, and the edge is just ahead and
CUT TO
THE GIRLS, watching, clinging to each other, their eyes wide, going wider and now
CUT TO
THE BOY, suddenly extending his arms out wide, launching himself off the edge of the cliff, and
CUT TO
THE GIRLS, waving joyously as THE BOY soars over them, changes his arm position, banks, flies back over them a second time, waves back, then starts to climb as the GIRLS stare after him, their eyes filled with wonder.
CUT TO
THE COUNTRYSIDE AS THE BOY SOARS ALONG, and Jesus it's beautiful, green and sunlit and pure and now
CUT TO
A DIFFERENT BOY SOARING THROUGH SPACE.
CUT
A DIFFERENT GIRL WATCHING THIS DIFFERENT BOY, but that same look of dreamlike wonder is in her eyes too.
CUT TO
STILL ANOTHER BOY, running along the roof of a barn, and when he reaches the edge he too starts to fly and
CUT TO
ANOTHER BOY poised in a treetop, but only for a second, and as he glides into space
CUT TO
THE SKIES, and it's full of flying children.
CUT TO
THE GROUND and the GIRLS are there, beautiful and awed and waiting and
CUT TO
THE SKIES, and now the BOYS are starting to come in from unexpected angles, soaring up from the bottom, zooming in from the corners, and the GIRLS begin clapping and waving and crying and everything's going faster, getting more and more wild, and it's all reaching a peak now, and the GIRLS

just love it, they really do, you can see it in their eyes as they watch their heroes, and the flying dream is perfect, and no one ever crashes, never, not once, not yet, not here . . .
(New from somewhere distant there is the sound of a motor.)
END PROLOGUE

Hill cut the scene, because, as he says, "I felt it was too much of a fantasy to be incorporated into a realistic film." The movie plays well without the scene, as it follows Scooter's point of view. But the scene is illuminating for it shows how strong a sense of the lure of flying Hill and Goldman wished to convey. As written the scene is filled with the action and rhythm of childhood adventure (with a definite sexual undercurrent that comes to a climax as the prologue ends and the sound of a real motor is heard).

Finally, the opening also serves to suggest Pepper's origins. He too must have been an excited youth attracted to the open skies.

But Pepper is more than an image and a barnstorming pilot: he is also a master storyteller and con man himself. The next scene shows Pepper as a dinner guest with Scooter's family. The group, which includes Mary Beth (Susan Sarandon) is seated around the table eating as Pepper is asked if he is the best pilot in the world. "I'm the second best,"[5] Redford replies, and he is off explaining his battle record as a fighter pilot in World War I dueling with the best pilot in the world, the German ace Ernst Kessler. There is a clash of values between Pepper and the farming family as the father says, after Redford explains Kessler shot down over seventy Americans, "That don't make a man a hero." To the father only an honest day's work is worthwhile. The whole family is taken in, however, by his battle account, including Mary Beth who stares at Pepper with the wide open excitement described in the excluded scene about the girls watching the boys "fly."

It's not till a little later when Waldo is on a movie date with Mary Beth that the truth of his deception surfaces. At a soda shop after a Valentino show, Waldo and Mary Beth run into Waldo's rival on the barnstorming circuit, Axel Olsson (Bo Svenson in a rather one-dimensional performance).[6] When Mary Beth speaks of the great aerial battle with Kessler, Olsson exposes Waldo as a liar. Waldo pauses and comes back with "It shoulda been me!"

The line tells us who Waldo is. And this is the third level of the myth of the hero: the fantasy Waldo nourishes of what he wanted to be and was not. If he is a con artist, a daring pilot, and an entertainer, he is also a believer in his own myths: it *should* have been his fight, but it wasn't. Again a comparison with Butch and Sundance is instructive. Butch is upset that the film they see of their lives is not true (in the excluded scene we've discussed). Butch has a clear sense of reality and cannot understand the need for legend. He is, as we noted, a businessman of sorts trying to come out ahead. Waldo, on the other hand, is attempting to live out a fabricated legend. In this sense, he does not see himself as a liar or even as a typical con man: he would like to believe it is immaterial that he was not present at the dogfight. He feels he is good enough to have been there and to have shared the glory of fighting and flying.

The film concerns Waldo's attempt to live in the glorious past when the present is fast becoming the future around him. As Andrew Britton points out in his article, Waldo is indeed similar to the archetype of the trickster, the semi-mythical figure who is caught between contradictory abilities and limitations, a figure who is both hero and fool, victor and victim.[7] As a trickster figure Waldo is similar to the protagonists in *Butch Cassidy* and *The Sting*: their occupations and situations make them outsiders involved in their own myths and thus unable to break through and establish other romantic or lasting relationships outside themselves. In the so-called buddy films, Newman and Redford had each other to fall back on, but Waldo (and, as we shall see, Reggie in *Slap Shot*) are alone.

*The Great Waldo Pepper* is Hill's most neglected work, although it was a modest box office success, especially in Europe. Pauline Kael notes that it is "bright and clear," with "the coolness of a schoolboy reverie." But it is more than this. Nebraska in the early 1920s is a well chosen location to show how swiftly the United States was moving from an unsophisticated agrarian society that would turn to barnstormers as one form of live entertainment, to a much more regulated culture represented in the film by Dillhoefer's commercial traveling Air Circus, and, finally, to the banning of all such stunts by the regional air director. "I'm a flyer," protests Waldo.

"That kind of flying is finished," rejoins Newton Potts, the Federal official. Waldo Pepper attempts to live out his fantasies caught between these opposing forces.

Waldo is so deeply involved in his own myth of himself as a hero that he cannot give up the past. He wants desperately to duplicate the most dangerous stunt of all, the outside loop, which his self-chosen rival, Kessler, threatens to perform, and eventually does (in reality it was General Jimmy Dolittle who first did this stunt). "You're not a bad sort," says Dillhoefer to Waldo, "but you're dangerous." He is so dashing and glib that his dangerous side is not apparent at first. But before the film ends, Mary Beth dies, his engineer friend Ezra also dies attempting the outside loop in his newly designed single wing plane, Waldo is badly banged up, and, as the ending suggests, he too will die in a crash in 1931.

Hill and Goldman agree that Mary Beth's sudden death grounded the film for many audiences. Hill now regrets that he ever dropped Susan Sarandon off the wing. William Goldman suggests the scene and the effect of the film could have been saved: "It would have been the easiest thing in the world to have changed it by adding an insert shot of Susan (or her double) falling into a pond and then waving." Neither Hill nor Goldman set out simply to tell a romping story. But the flavor of the first part of the film is so bright that Mary Beth's death proved too sharp a switch to the darker second half. Hill feels part of the problem was that Susan Sarandon turned out to be such a lively character in her role that she won the hearts of the audience. The script calls for a simple farmer's daughter, and Sarandon is in contrast a feisty woman in search of adventure. Goldman goes further and points out that another difficulty was the audience's unwillingness to accept Redford as anything but an affable good guy. "If we had Jack Nicholson in the part," he observes, "they would have expected the darkness, but because Bob was a happy-go-lucky Errol Flynn type, the audience met Susan's death with glacial hatred."

Mary Beth has to drop out of the script, however, either cast away, injured, or killed. She has to go since Waldo cannot be tied down to anyone else because of his pursuit of himself as a flyer-hero. It is, in fact, appropriate that she at least be badly injured in a flying stunt, because what we watch in her performance is how totally she becomes a part of show business herself as she transforms herself into the "It Girl of the Sky." Once she has cast off her traditional family ties, her narcissism knows no bounds:

I get to pick the clothes, And I get to pick what words you use about me in the sign. And I want my name the very highest on the sign and I want my name bigger than anybody's.

What she has fallen in love with is not so much Waldo Pepper but with herself as a star. But she lacks Waldo's double vision of himself as a con man and a believer in the myth at the same time. She is literally carried away by the excitement of it all. Goldman makes this clear in the cinema sequence in which Waldo explains to Mary Beth what will happen in the film they are watching a split second before it happens on the screen. She believes it's because he knows so much about human nature, while we know it's because he has seen the film before. She believes the illusion; Pepper knows that the movie Sahara is the back lot of a Hollywood studio. Waldo tells her, "[Valentino] may be a great actor and all but he's no hero."

"He isn't?" Mary Beth asks naïvely.

"Not a REAL hero," replies Waldo.

Much of the attractiveness of *Waldo Pepper* is in such a direct archetypal presentation of the con man and the myth of the hero. The film gains in resonance all the more because it echoes similar treatments of the pattern of the con man in American literature and film, most notably in Herman Melville's *The Confidence Man* (1857). Melville weaves a clever narrative of a Mississippi riverboat journey during which the Protestant ethic is called into question and tested by the "confidence man." Like Twain's *Huckleberry Finn* and Hill and Goldman's *The Great Waldo Pepper*, the Melville tale is set in the Midwest, beginning in St. Louis on April Fool's day. The opening description of the central character closely resembles that of Waldo Pepper:

His cheek was fair, his chin downy, his hair flaxen, his hat a white fur one, with a long fleecy nap. He had neither trunk, valise, carpetbag, nor parcel. No porter followed him. He was unaccompanied by friends. From the shrugged shoulders, titters, whispers, wonderings of the crowd, it was plain that he was, in the extremest sense of the word, a stranger.

Furthermore, Melville notes that the confidence man was "quite an original genius in his vocation."

Waldo Pepper, who arrives out of the heavens and flies back into them at the end is every bit as much an engaging yet enigmatic loner in tune with his own dreams and uncomfortable within society.

Like Melville's confidence man, Waldo is all the more alone because of his ambivalent relationship to the general public. "Hello, good people," is his opening line, but before the film is over he is dive-bombing the crowd at the Flying Circus which begins to gather around the wreckage of Ezra's plane. As trickster, con man, and would-be hero, Waldo is in a double bind: part of being a hero is being recognized as such by others. Barnstorming is show biz, and as such needs the general public. And yet Waldo literally sees himself "above" the others, unwilling to settle for the white Protestant working and middle class mentality.

Waldo gets along with individuals but cannot relate to the crowds. As Dillhoefer says of the audience, "they don't want skill, they want blood." As a barnstormer it was different: when Waldo dropped out of the sky into a field, he was surrounded by farmers and children who came running to greet him. The Flying Circus, however, turned flying into mere entertainment in which showmanship rather than flying skill was required. How far Waldo is degraded by his encounter with show business is shown in a brief shot in which he appears in drag for a stunt. Again, Hill's ambivalent view of the crowd in a democracy is in tune with that of much literature and film. If we think of crowd scenes in *Huckleberry Finn*, for instance, we remember that Twain shows how mercurial and fickle the anonymous group can be. Huck, a puckish trickster figure and con artist himself, survives by his wits and by living on the fringes of acceptable society.

The film moves with a sense of inevitability toward Hollywood. Waldo tells Mary Beth that Valentino is not a real hero because he

is only "acting" in a film. But the only chance Waldo has for fulfilling his boyish fantasy is in the Dream Factory. There he finally meets
his idol, Ernst Kessler. After a series of funny bit parts as a stunt man
(they remind us of Gene Kelly in similar scenes in *Singin' in the Rain*),
Waldo is hired as a stunt pilot for a film in which Kessler is to reen-
act his famous dogfight.

Myth becomes reality as Waldo and Kessler talk. The spotlight passes
from Waldo to Kessler during this sequence—as it must, for it is Kessler that Waldo has tried to become. *Kessler is a hero*. But the truth
Waldo learns is that he is also a human being who has had a rough
personal life and who has been reduced to stunt flying for Hollywood
in an effort to pay off $40,000 in debts. The Pepper-Kessler talk is a
moving scene, one that Goldman feels is a personal favorite that pulls
all of the themes of the film together. As acted by Bo Brundin, Kessler
becomes a sympathetic character, much more so than Waldo, who is
engaging but limited in his stunted adolescence. Kessler has suffered,
made a kind of peace with himself, and kept on doing what he can
do best with as much dignity as possible in the crassly commercial
world of filmmaking. As he swigs from a bottle, Kessler explains to
Waldo and Axel: "All I can tell you is that life is clear for me up
there alone. In the sky I found, even in my enemies, courage and
honor and chivalry. . . . On the ground . . . only terrible confu-
sions."

On the misty morning of the reenacted aerial battle, Kessler re-
counts the actual historical battle for Waldo. "Were you scared?" Waldo
finally wishes to know.

"It makes no sense but I was happy. . . . it was exciting," explains
Kessler, adding that at the end of the fight he and his American opponent, Madden, saluted each other in recognition of their mutual
bravery.

In this confrontation and recognition scene, Waldo too is happy.
He is in the company of not only a true hero, but a master-father
figure. Again, as in so many of Hill's films, his main character has
built a father figure into his fantasy, a point that is important because
we are given almost nothing of Waldo's background and family life
except a brief scene with the girl he thinks he would like to marry

back home, played by Margot Kidder. Waldo is happy to hear the truth. What remains is for Waldo once and for all to turn myth into reality and be accepted as an equal by Kessler.

At this point Hill's penchant for satirizing Hollywood directors surfaces once again. Werfel, the effeminate director of the film, frets and fusses about the fight as Kessler and Waldo prepare. His thoughts are about the film and not about the safety of his pilots:

And make goddam sure it's flaming good before you get out. Then you jump, and I'll follow you down all the way. You can't open your chute too soon or you'll spoil the whole effect. I don't want to have to do this shot again, got it?

It is clear from the beginning of the fight, however, that Kessler and Waldo are their own men: they each toss away their parachutes. The dogfight is under way. In the air they ram each other, tail each other, and narrowly avoid disastrous crackups. Then they come at each other head on, appearing to have no way of avoiding a double explosion, when at the last second Kessler pulls off in one direction and Waldo another. Then Waldo is on top of Kessler, attempting to force him down when there is a frightening sound: Waldo's wheels fall off (a parallel to Axel's wheels dropping away earlier in the film as Waldo played a trick on the unsuspecting barnstormer). Like drivers in a demolition derby, they bump each other, knocking away props, damaging the Fokkers with each pass. Finally Waldo wins by almost managing to rip off Kessler's wing. Kessler is in serious trouble. But Waldo pulls alongside him and salutes. Kessler stares at him and returns the gesture but, as Goldman notes, "with a grave but slightly wry salute of his own."

The film ends with Waldo, dazed and in his own fantasy turning his plane heavenward and going up higher. The sound of his plane cuts out and the gentle, melancholic piano music of the beginning of the film returns. We then see Pepper in the scrapbook that opened the picture with his dates, 1895–1931. Waldo is fulfilled even though he will later die. Even more so than in *Butch Cassidy and the Sundance Kid*, where the outlaw duo are simply cut down, and *Slaughterhouse Five*, where Billy can only fulfill himself within his own imagination, Waldo manages to fuse myth and reality in one "climax." As a trickster–con figure, Waldo is also a romantic idol. But his infatuation with the idea of the hero means that even his erotic impulses must be satisfied through the romance of the sky. We end with a blissful Waldo, but his happiness is undercut by the scrapbook and our knowledge of his death. It is also lessened by the fact that his victory has come within the framework of a film and thus the manufacturing of illusions. It is still not "real" life outside the confines of the studio. Like Valentino in the Hollywood Sahara, Waldo in his California World War I is an actor reliving what cannot be recaptured.

*Freedom In The Sky.* The contrast between freedom in the sky and the restricted life on the ground was a favorite topic of another restless poet-adventurer during the 1920s and 1930s: Antoine de Saint Exupéry. In his *Wind, Sand and Stars* (1939), he writes to an imaginary bureaucrat living in Toulouse:

You are a petit bourgeois of Toulouse. Nobody grasped you by the shoulder while there was still time. Now the clay of which you were shaped has dried and hardened, and naught in you will ever again awaken the sleeping musician, the poet, the astronomer that possibly inhabited you in the beginning.

Waldo is never allowed the poetic and social insight that this French pilot who died in action expressed. But in *The Great Waldo Pepper*, George Roy Hill captures the joys of flying and perils of believing in the myth of heroism in a strongly American vein. "It's kid's stuff," says Axel when he realizes that the days of barnstorming are over. And so it is. But Hill managed in his ninth film to reach back into his own childhood and bring an era of kid's stuff alive once more with directness and excitement and humor.

## Slap Shot

*Right Back Where We Started From.*

"I went to a fight the other night and a hockey game broke out."—Rodney Dangerfield

There is a brief exchange in *Slap Shot* (1977) between Reggie (Paul Newman), an aging player-coach on a dying bush league hockey club, and a policeman who has just arrested the Hanson Brothers, a goonish mercenary version of the Three Stooges on skates, who have pulverized their opponents and beaten up a group of spectators. Newman protests their arrest: "They're folk heroes."

"They're criminals," returns the cop. *Slap Shot*, Hill's most violent and verbally abusive film, hovers between these two extremes as it unravels on the screen at the speed of a flying puck, backed up by the driving beat of the film's theme song, Maxine Nightingale's rock tune, "Right Back Where We Started From." *Slap Shot* is also Hill's most controversial film. Popular with audiences (it is still playing in theaters in Canada and Japan), the film seemed a radical departure from the sweet nostalgia of *Butch Cassidy and the Sundance Kid* and *The Sting*.

*Slap Shot* is *The Great Waldo Pepper* done darker, meaner, faster, and with the puck aimed below the belt. In both films what used to be an enjoyable sport becomes almost a gladiatorial event. In each film the blame for this corruption of sport falls on the owner-manager's greed for higher profits and the crowd's bottomless thirst for blood. And in both films Hill explores the tensions and conflicts that develop between public and private lives as men act as boys in their sporting lives and are puzzled when they are not accepted as men in their private lives.

Reggie embodies all of the contradictions of the film. Those who expected more of the same from a Newman-Hill collaboration were shocked.[8] Reggie is a single-minded bastard through-and-through. Believing that the ends justify the means, he skates his way to the championship (playing dirty hockey for the rabid amusement of the howling crowds) in a mad effort to save his team from being sold out from under him. To do so, he also skates over the lives and feelings of those around him. He has no regard for personal dignity, honor, or honesty. "I'm normal," he tells Lil, the dissatisfied young wife (whom he later seduces) of Ned Braden, a disgruntled college-educated player. "Then normal is fucked," she replies.

Scriptwriter Nancy Dowd *(Coming Home)* claims that her purpose in doing the script was, "To show that the level of violence we have in our entertainment is the thing that prevents people, especially men, from growing up."[9] The interplay of violence and immaturity is in the script, but it is not always clear which inspires which. What attracted Hill to the project was the originality of the subject and the liveliness of the script. Dowd had drawn upon the real experiences of her hockey-playing brother, Ned Dowd (who acted as an advisor on the film and who played the feared killer player, Oglethorp). He had taped hours of hockey-lockerroom patois and shipped the tapes to his sister, a UCLA Film School graduate, who fashioned a story from the material.

In *Slap Shot* Hill and Dowd have created a film that, like *Waldo Pepper*, uses a sport to suggest a wider perspective on American life styles.[10] Reggie is part folk hero and part criminal. "In a sense most of our folk heroes have been criminals," Hill comments referring to Jessie James, Bonnie and Clyde, and others. Reggie is no bank robber, nor is he a murderer; but within the sports arena he has come to feel that violence of language and action are acceptable norms. The underlying seriousness of each Hill film is here evident in the implications of Reggie's professional life for his personal life. The gap between the brightly lit action scenes on the ice and the drab motionless industrial landscape of Charlestown visually establishes the contradictions Reggie carries with him.

As Newman suggests, Reggie is a "born desperate loser" with charm, but he is a loser nevertheless. In many of Hill's films the main characters grow past their original fantasies and become wiser for their experiences. Reggie learns little, however. Joseph Campbell in his transcultural study, *The Hero with a Thousand Faces*, defines the adventure of a hero as a representation of a rite of passage which involves separation from society, initiation into a higher reality, and a return to his original society:

A hero ventures forth from the world of common day into a region of supernatural wonder: fabulous forces are there encountered and a decisive victory is won: the hero comes back from this mysterious adventure with the power to bestow boons on his fellow man.[11]

Campbell's definition suggests how far Reggie is from the self-knowledge and selfless service that a true hero performs. Despite the slapstick farce of many of the scenes and the bouyant striptease climax (to be discussed) the subtext of the film is disturbing: Reggie fails to grow as a person. As his ex-wife drives through the victory parade at the end of the film, towing her worldly possessions with her, Reggie still nurses the illusion that they may someday get together and that he will "make a fortune" playing for another team.

Butch Cassidy and the Sundance Kid lived out myths of themselves long after the West had changed, and Reggie similarly would like to be the star he once was. But *Slap Shot* is a finer role for Newman. His face, nearly a decade after *Butch Cassidy*, has become an almost perfect blend of Eternal Boyishness and the over-the-hill pro hockey player. "I was trying to imagine you when you're through with hockey and I couldn't," says his former wife.

For all of his Machiavellian bravado and deception, Reggie is still appealing.[12] He is the aging underdog, the kid who never grew up, and the man who never seems to learn. Hill comments that "all of my main characters are unlikable characters if you take their charm away. Reggie has enough charm so that he can get by trying to follow the American success formula." But he is too thick, too insensitive to understand why his wife leaves him (Newman also appears thicker, as Hill used a 25mm lens when shooting Newman to make him look more beat up).

Despite his charm, Reggie is manipulative of everyone around him. His chief means of manipulation is by sexual taunts. His affair with Lil is no exception. Ned is the butt of Lil's anger and Reggie's kidding for not making love. In his Hamlet-like pose, Ned becomes incapable of action. But Reggie taunts Ned enough for the young man to punch him out (Ned later appears on the local radio show ranting against Reggie's goon tactics). When Reggie learns the club is being dropped as a tax write-off, however, he tries to talk Ned into returning to the team. As Ned hides in the woods near his home, Reggie argues with him without luck. Finally Reggie resorts to a verbal slap shot: "Ned, Lily's been at my place. She's terrific. We've been having a helluva time."

In discussing *Waldo Pepper* we noted that Waldo had a double talent as a stunt pilot and as a storyteller caught up in his own myth. Reggie is of the same mold, but taken further: he can play rough hockey and he can make swearing and abusive language become his personal weapon. What gives Reggie more depth than Waldo is the glimpse Hill and Dowd allow us of a man whose sexual taunting of others masks his own inadequacies (shown with humor when Lil finally moves in and Reggie is clearly more interested in sleep than sex).

It is in this light that the foul language of the film is justified.[13] The swearing is a necessary parallel to the foul play in their profession. It is also an expression of impotence, of pent-up fear and frustration. Several critics have pointed out that *Slap Shot* owes as much to old Hollywood films, especially Disney's *The Absent Minded Professor*, as it does to the game of hockey. And as such the film could easily have settled for an R-rated Disney format: a bawdily chaotic sports farce.

On one level the lockerroom banter is justified because it is genuine. But the extended use of the language goes further to parallel and contrast the physical violence of the boy-men on ice. Some of the language is perhaps mildly shocking at first, but much of it is funny, and then, finally, monotonous. Behind the language and the laughter is the sense of the hollowness of their lives, spent speeding around the ice, bussing back and forth on highways between small cities, in and out of bars and motels. The speed, the lack of privacy, the absence of peace, the constant drone of television shows in the background (a motif that reaches a height when the players, congregating at a bar, critique a soap opera), and the continual den of jock bravado all work against their becoming mature individuals.

In such a world of sports camaraderie, the worst male fear is to be thought gay. Near the beginning we see the team members in a fashion show. One player protests because "the guys feel like fags." When Reggie complains to Joe, the general manager, that the Hansons spend their evenings with toy cars, Joe replies, "At least they don't play with themselves." When Susanne asks Reggie if he ever wanted to sleep with a man, he hastily (and nervously) replies "no," though the mood and Newman's delivery suggest that it's a more complex subject than he can possibly admit to himself. And when Reggie wants to blackmail Joe, he hints of some transvestite and "fag" behavior in Joe's past.

In sharp contrast to Reggie and his values is Ned Braden (Michael

Ontkean). Young, restless, bright, and unhappy with the goon-show direction professional hockey has taken, Ned is painfully caught in the middle: he wants to play hockey but not *that* kind of hockey, and he is under pressure from Lil (Lindsay Crouse) to get out. While Reggie's problem is that he is overly greared toward action, Ned remains what Pauline Kael called a brooding Hamlet on skates.[14] It is Ned who will ultimately suggest an alternative to the violence of hockey that will win his team the championship and bring his wife back to him.

But before Ned's last-minute triumph, the film mixes comedy and violence in large doses in both language and hockey action. The most violent scene, however, is reserved for a suburban living room. Despite his shortcomings, Reggie acts with seemingly limitless energy. Like all of Hill's protagonists, he has also created a fantasy world and proceeded to inhabit it. The story that Reggie has convinced his team to believe is that if they play well a deal will be concluded to sell the club to a Florida group and they will all live in the Sunbelt. In Florida the fortunes of the team will be reversed. Reggie is persuasive and so the team believes him. Only Reggie knows that the dream is a fabrication, for he doesn't even know who the owner of the club is. A climax thus becomes the showdown between Reggie and the owner who turns out to be a coldly efficient business woman, Anita Mc-Cambridge (Kathryn Walker).

Suddenly Reggie the con man is confronted with the truth. Reality turns out to be a dispassionate woman who does not allow her children to watch hockey on tv. Despite the bastard he has been, he has worked to save the team and his way of life. Anita McCambridge, however, is concerned only with profit and loss and therefore is closing down the team despite the club's current box office appeal. "My accountant tells me I'm better off folding the team and taking a tax loss." The scene closes with this exchange:

Reggie:
You're fucked.
    Anita (giggling):
What?
    Reggie:

You're totally fucked.
    (a beat)
You're garbage for letting all of us go down the drain.
        Anita:
Are you serious?
        Reggie:
You're screwed. You could sell us. We're hot. People go nuts for us. You could get a buyer.
        Anita:
I don't think you understand finance.
        Reggie
    (getting up to leave):
You know your oldest kid looks like a fag to me. You better get married again cuz he'll have somebody's cock in his mouth before you can say jack rabbit.
He slams the door behind him.
(Scene 122, in the March 11, 1976 version of the script)

One critic has called Reggie's last line, "The single most profane sentence ever uttered by a major American actor."[15]

Neither character is pure, but our sympathies go out to Reggie, who has the more admirable goal. The lockerroom language has led up to this startling moment. The contrast between Anita's sterile suburban life and Reggie's mill-town existence is great. Anita does not express anger, nor does she swear. But Reggie expresses his rage and his inability to do more than verbally abuse her with the worse insult he can think of: to accuse her son of being homosexual.

While our sympathies are more with Reggie than with Anita, the scene and the implications are nevertheless disturbing. Throughout the film we have seen men as boys. Furthermore, we have seen men who cannot establish lasting or meaningful relationships with women. And we are introduced to hockey wives who are driven to drink, loneliness, and, finally in the case of Susanne and others, to lesbian relationships as a substitute for the tenderness they cannot find with their men. The bed scene in which Susanne, a hockey wife, explains to Reggie how she became bisexual is moving. But it becomes a moment that Reggie shamelessly exploits in the lockerroom and on the ice as he calls her a "dyke" in front of her husband.

As the team plays for the championship with not a hope of surviving even if they win, Reggie, the shameless ham, pulls one last stunt: he decides to play "old time hockey," (this, as anyone who knows hockey will tell you, is also a joke since hockey has always been a violent game in the bush leagues).

At this point we again see Hill's ability to help improve an earlier version of a script. In the March 11, 1976, script, Reggie returns to the team before the championship game and makes up a story about the need to play old-time hockey because of the death of Ned Braden's mother. Reggie states (making it all up) that the death made him realize what "criminals" they had been. Hill (who annotates all the scripts he reads while they are in progress) has written in the margin, "What is powerful enough to motivate Reggie's final decision to play the game straight?"

In the revised script as it appears on screen, "what is powerful enough" turns out to be Reggie's feeling of having nothing to lose by telling the truth and playing on the feelings of his team to the hilt. Reggie enters the lockerroom after his confrontation with Ned in the woods. He is not suited up. Reggie confesses to all:

The Chiefs are history, guys. There is no Florida deal. I conned you guys. We were never nothing but a rich broad's tax writeoff. I'm ashamed of myself. Ned was right. Violence is killing this sport.

He urges them to go out and play a clean game, something they have never really done before.

Just how hypocritical Reggie has been in his "confession" becomes apparent during a break between periods when Joe McGrath announces that there are talent scouts in the audience. Reggie's face lights up with a smile and the fight is on. The team instantly regresses into its violent ways as the players begin to fight back against the imported goons on the opposing team.

In his fight scene, as in all of the on-the-ice scenes, Hill blends comedy and violence with a sure touch. Pauline Kael says Hill directs with dispatch and that, "You're aware of the seams and joints, but you can admire the proficiency."[16] And Stanley Kauffmann notes that "for the first hour it's fun."[17] What holds us is the zippy action of hockey that makes us ask why no other major hockey films have been made before.

In terms of comedy, The Hanson Brothers on ice represent some of Hill's most inspired comic work. Who can forget the three pimple-faced monsters in dark-rimmed glasses who enter the film destroying a Coke machine as a prelude for their specialty on ice? Hill gives us just enough of them with their gung-ho, gum-chewing, model-car-playing identities for us to enjoy Reggie's disbelief and the Brothers' sudden rise to fame as "folk heroes." The segment in which they hit the ice for the first time is irresistibly hilarious.[18] Hill's timing, Vic Kemper's cinematography, and Dede Allen's crisp editing juxtapose the comic mayhem on the ice with close-ups of the audience's excited approval.

Hill also obtains strong performances from the whole cast. Newman shines in one of his best performances, but we should not lose sight of how good the other performances are. Andy Duncan as the sportscaster turned out to be one of the few actors Hill has ever allowed to improvise on camera. Strother Martin as the Charlestown Chiefs business manager, Joe McGrath, is both tricky and sympathetic (he had played the mine foreman in *Butch Cassidy*). And all of the women, especially Lindsay Crouse as Lil, are well cast and sympathetically drawn.

If Reggie has been the motivating force behind the team reaching the championship, Ned finally drops his Hamlet-like indecision and wins an unexpected victory. While the two teams fight it out on the ice, Ned begins a slow striptease as he cruises the rink. He has had enough of the team's violent attitudes and enough of his wife's attempt to become a hockey wife as she sits with the other "girls" in the crowd wearing her hair in a beehive hairdo. In one simple action Ned both ridicules hockey and proves himself even more outrageous than Reggie. He circles the rink casting off his clothes until he is down to his jockstrap. The crowd cheers, but McCracken, the captain of the opposing team can't take it:

MCCRACKEN
This is a serious game. This isn't a freak show.

REF
What do you mean a serious game? Huh? What are you talking about? This is hockey!

The Chiefs win the championship by default as the other team leaves the ice in protest of Ned's show.

As always in Hill's films, winning is on a deeper plane a form of losing. Ned as a thinking man proves himself superior to Reggie's conscious degradation of hockey. With the striptease, sport becomes spectacle pure and simple. And yet the victory parade scene that follows, and which closes the film, pictures Ned, Lil, and Reggie sitting together on a car in the parade. The Chiefs will disband, but Ned has compromised himself by becoming one of the "boys" who will, we are led to believe, be farmed out to other bush-league teams. For all of his Hamlet-like posturing, he too could easily become another Reggie in twenty years with Lil playing the role of the hockey widow to perfection. Despite the sense of celebration in the parade, Ned's victory suggests he has lost his crusade for the preservation of hockey as a professional sport.

It is a fault of the script that Ned's character is not more adequately developed: we do not see enough of him to clearly understand his dissatisfaction with goon hockey and thus to comprehend his problems with Lil. But as given, Ned's compromise to join "them" instead of fighting them is finally more disturbing than Reggie's inability to learn from his experiences. Maxine Nightingale's tune "Right Back Where We Started From" is literally true for the lives of the protagonists. Despite the catchy beat of the tune, the words suggest the rut the characters, and by extension pro hockey, have gotten themselves into. The only relief to the bleakness of the ending is our attraction to Reggie, yet as his wife drives off leaving him behind, we too realize that charm alone can not lead to fulfillment.

Hill's films start light and end on a much darker note. The first half of *Slap Shot*, which uses verbal and visual comedy to capture the violence of hockey on and off the ice, is the best sustained light work Hill has done. The second half, the darker half, however, is not as successful. Because Ned's character is not drawn fully enough, his sudden striptease (itself highly derivative from other films, most par-

ticularly Gene Hackman's strip at the climax of *Scarecrow*) appears
more as a *deus ex machina* than as an integral part of the plot. And
finally the hinted-at effort of the film to explore the ambiguous territory of folk heroes who are criminals and vice versa remains only a
hint.

Robert Altman's *Nashville* used the world of country and western
music to explore a complex American social reality and as a provoc-
ative metaphor for the state of the nation on its two hundredth birth-
day. *Slap Shot* similarly points toward a larger film that uses the subject matter at hand—sports—as a means of suggesting larger American
concerns. While individual moments in the film cut emotionally deeper
than *The Great Waldo Pepper* (Newman sitting alone in his car by
the side of the road after his confrontation with Walker, for instance),
*Slap Shot* as a whole does not evoke a wide sense of North American
values beyond the sport in question, as does Hill's barnstorming film.
As it is, *Slap Shot* falls awkwardly into a gap between a sports film
(and thus a genre piece) and a more "open framed" realistic comic
drama.

# 10

## Innocence Revisited

"I haven't got the ruled account-book, I have none of the tax-gathering elements in my composition, I am not at all respectable, and I don't want to be. Odd perhaps, but so it is!"—Mr Skimpole in Charles Dickens' *Bleak House*

*A Little Romance* (1979) was both a departure and a return to familiar territory for Hill. For the first time in his film career, Hill chose a love story. But in doing so, he returned to the world of adolescence and childhood he had begun to explore in *The World of Henry Orient*. The result is a film that cuts emotionally deeper than the more frolicksome earlier effort. It is a work in which Hill's style and technique are well matched to the tone and content of the story. Though the movie never found a wide audience in its first run, *A Little Romance* is one of Hill's most satisfyingly complete projects.

*The Adaptation.* The film, scripted by Allan Burns, is based on a French novel, $E = MC^2$, *Mon Amour*, by Patrick Chauvin.[1] Hill was handed the French version and passed it on to Owens, one of his two daughters, to read. She enjoyed it; Hill had it translated, studied it, and finally decided to undertake the film.

There are striking similarities between the French novel and *The World of Henry Orient*. Both deal with two youngsters who create their own world apart from the confused world of their parents, and each film includes the affable con man (Peter Sellers as Henry Orient, Laurence Olivier as Julius) who becomes important to their fantasy.

And both films end at the point that the teenagers will have to face the more difficult compromises of growing up.

As usual in Hill's work, the adaptation he and scriptwriter Burns ended up with contains only the general outlines of the original novel. Both tell the story of the romance between Daniel, a young French son of a taxi driver, and Lauren, an American girl in Paris with her ITT executive father and socialite mother. The teenagers have genius IQ's (they enjoy reading Heidegger) and realize that "People don't exactly love bright kids." The romance that begins in Paris flowers on an adventuresome romp through Italy. Julius, who goes along, serves as a kind of fairy grandfather figure. Both film and novel end with the young couple being apprehended, returned home, and then separated as Lauren is shuffled off to America (Tucson in the book, Houston in the film).

The novel, however, is supposedly written by the two young lovers in alternating chapters and points of view. The book itself becomes a monument to love constructed by the couple and, finally, left incomplete by their separation. We come to know each character through their writing style. Daniel is a kind of young Jean-Paul Belmondo figure who writes in a clipped tough-guy argot heavily influenced by films, especially those starring Robert Redford: "I think I look like Robert Redford as a child," he says—thinking especially of *The Great Waldo Pepper* which he has seen five times in one week. Before the book is over, he has worshipped or identified with Burt Reynolds ("Bingo" is his favorite expression in the book and in the film), Marilyn Monroe, Jane Russell, Gary Cooper, Henry Fonda and many others.

Even the romantic adventure is an outgrowth of the influence of cinema. Daniel wins two round trip tickets to Venice by answering a Redford quiz question on a French radio show. But Venice is not the focal point of their dreams. Daniel and Lauren instead wish to travel to a Greek island.

The young lovers have distinct personalities. Lauren writes in a more flowing, easy-going style. She sees herself as "a sentimental romantic" who is a "hyper-gifted child." She imagines herself a beauty with a "large unused void" in her heart. She reads chunks of Racine and quotes French Symbolist poets. While everything relates to the cinema for Daniel ("He would be a Communist except for the poor quality of Soviet cinema"), Lauren sees the world through poetry and art. When she first meets Julius (Edmond-Julius Santorin) she notes that he "looks like an engraving in our French literature textbook."

Hill, however—who cuts away the literary superstructure—keeps Daniel's love of cinema but drops Lauren's literary pretensions. As in *The World of Henry Orient,* he has chosen to focus on the nonsexual aspects of romance and childhood. "I did not want to do a romantic love story," says Hill, "about two kids who want to make love. I wanted to have two kids who had a romantic ideal, who shared it, and who thus became close to each other. If there had been any sexual activity between them, and there probably was, I didn't want to show it as the reason for their relationship."

Sexuality is a strong theme in the book. Daniel loves the rear of the girl in front of him at school, and at age eleven has had sex with a girl named Leonore, an experience he described as "a form of tickling." Lauren is, of course, more subtle and poetic as she yearns for her "large unused void" to be filled. She states she was nearly raped once, quotes lines such as "come, come, handsome stranger" and agonizes over her virginity with her good friend, Natalie (she also appears in the film). During Christmas, the couple writes in a sex scene for their book, a scene which is, we suppose, an act of imagination rather than a document of their experiences. When they finally reach Venice, they have a mock wedding service, but there is no suggestion that the marriage is consummated. Hill cuts these scenes.

Hill also tightened the plot. He felt the adventure in Italy needed a stronger motive than in the novel and credits Bob Crawford, the producer of the film, with urging that the kiss at sunset under the Bridge of Sighs in Venice, which occurs in the novel as just a small scene of no particular importance, be used as the motivation behind the young couple's adventure. Thus in the film, the kiss became the goal Lauren and Daniel pursued. Additionally, Hill strengthens the role of Julius. In the novel he is a retired stationmaster who was never married, and his pretensions to be otherwise are known to Daniel but not to Lauren. In the film the role takes on immediate importance as portrayed by Laurence Olivier, who despite having serious problems with his health at the time obviously enjoyed playing the Maurice Chevalier figure. The screenplay makes him both more sympathetic as a character and more integral to the plot than in the novel. In the film it is Julius-the-pickpocket who makes the trip to Italy possible after the couple have lost their money at the races. And in the film, neither Daniel nor Lauren knows his true identity until Verona.

*A Little Romance* is a modern Romeo and Juliet, as Hill emphasizes by having them stop off in Verona before heading for the finale in Venice. The novel on the other hand moves from Venice first and then to Verona for no compelling reason.

Finally, Hill and Burns have given Lauren a family much like Val's in *The World of Henry Orient*. In both, according to Hill, "There is the tramp mother in love with the phony artist" (Henry Orient the pianist; the movie director George de Marco in *A Little Romance*). David Dukes, dressed in a Boy Scout shirt, becomes a wry continuation of Hill's satire of filmmaking so sharply depicted in *The Great Waldo Pepper*.[2] In fact, while Hill claims he had no one director in mind (and denies that George is self parody), many saw the figure as a spoof of director William Friedkin, a friend of Hill's who, like Hill, has had his share of battles with studio heads over budget restrictions ("A twelve million dollar picture and you mean I can't break one goddamn mirror" rants George de Marco in the film).

Hill also works in a dig at film critics. He says he and Burns used to argue about the strengths and weaknesses of Pauline Kael, a leading critic. Burns claimed he didn't always agree with that writer's point of view but enjoyed her style. Hill claimed playfully that even the style was unreadable because of the sentence structure. The night before they shot the party scene in which a French critic talks to George de Marco, Hill inserted a direct quote from Kael. When Burns read it the next morning, he said, "This doesn't make sense. It isn't even grammatical." Hill was delighted to point out the source of the quotation. The lines were used in the film.

*"You Really Are Smart, You Know That?"* Critic David Ansen calls the film, "a sophisticated fable about innocence and romantic hero-

ism battling to survive in a world that won't long tolerate such grand illusions."³ "Fable" because the story is contrived and removed from the everyday world of the average viewer. "Sophisticated" because of Hill's carefully controlled atmosphere and tone and because the young couple themselves are "geniuses" (when Daniel receives his first kiss from Lauren, she beams with admiration, "You really are smart, you know that?"). And concerned with innocence because Hill dramatizes a particular moment in their lives.

Part of the charm of A *Little Romance* is that, even more intensely than in *The World of Henry Orient*, Hill provides enough of the adult world for us to realize that this romance is a bright brief moment that will pass. "In my mind there's not a chance that the young couple will ever get back together again," says Hill about his ending.

To deal with adolescent love in the late 1970s without including sexual activity was, as suggested in the opening chapter, bold. But that Hill was able to do so without becoming sentimental is all the more remarkable. If *Slap Shot* rubbed our noses in the gritty reality of bush-league hockey, A *Little Romance* celebrates that spark of pure commitment between two youngsters before they change and become less innocent, less idealistic. They find each other, share love and a dream, and fulfill that dream before they separate. It is *Romeo and Juliet* with an ending that is bittersweet rather than tragic.

Vincent Canby belittled Hill for doing what the "Our Gang" comedies used to do: to have the "child actors ape not the behavior of children but of grownups."⁴ But Canby overlooks the fact that these are unusual children who are, in their own way, more adult than the adults around them who wander around in Boy Scout uniforms (George de Marco) or stay glued to television sets (Daniel's father). If anything, Hill has deemphasized the stylized format of the novel in favor of more direct expression of emotion and action.

The film belongs primarily to the two young principals: whether or not we accept the film depends on how we react to Daniel and Lauren. For writer John Skow the casting obviously worked. Calling the script "agreeable silliness," he goes on to speak of Diane Lane as Lauren and Thelonious Bernard as Daniel as "fresh and effective."⁵ As Skow notes, Lane brings a "braces-just-came-off prettiness" and natural poise to her performance. Bernard has a winning boyishness that is closer to a young Newman than to the Redford Daniel claims to admire. A non-actor (he did not know English when he was discovered in Paris)[6] Bernard was chosen after a difficult search by Marion Dougherty.

"There is an impulse in all of us for romantic love, but it's been messed up in the films by the obligatory sex scenes," wrote critic Tom Topor about the appealing freshness of A *Little Romance*.[7] Hill captures this romantic impulse in large part by downplaying the physical aspects of love. It is not that the film projects a Pollyanna viewpoint—far from it. We do see Lauren's mother acting out her affair with the movie director, and Lauren and Daniel even wind up at a porno flick (which they walk away from). It's rather that Hill allows us the luxury of remembering that there can be more to love than sex, and that as hardened as many people have become today, there is still a part of us that responds to some belief in innocence and idealism.

Their feelings are well expressed as they leave the porno show. Daniel, for all of his tough guy talk, admits that he has never been to one before. Lauren is crying. Daniel speaks gently saying, "It isn't love." As they walk along the Avenue de Ternes, Lauren speaks:

I used to think that maybe long ago, some time in the past . . . say in the time of the Pharoahs or Louis the Thirteenth . . . there was the one person who was really made to order for me.

Daniel nods uncertainly. Lauren continues:

I mean, when you think about it and consider that your feelings about love start when you're about ten and if you live to, say, seventy . . . well that's pretty limiting because you'll only be able to know those men who are also alive during your life span, you know?

Daniel replies:

I've thought the same thing. I mean, me, living in La Garenne, what if my perfect woman lived in California or India or Brazil? What chance is there that I'd meet her in my lifetime?

They hold hands. Lauren says, "It's incredible, isn't it?" and Daniel replies, "Absolutely. Incredible." And they walk on. Such a scene could easily have been overdone. But Hill finds a delicate balance between the depth and truth of the emotion and the unsentimental, clear-headed delivery of the lines. True, most young teenagers would never speak such thoughts; yet anyone who has ever read a book like *The Diary of Anne Frank* is aware how much insight the young often have.

Hill's ability to balance emotions is also seen in the juxtapositioning of scenes. The porno scene follows one of those comic moments that Hill delights in. Lauren is visiting the Louvre on a class trip. As the teacher babbles on about the glory of Greek art, Lauren and her friend Natalie stand transfixed by the genitalia of a Greek statue. The camera is at a high angle near the rear of the statue looking down at the girls as they gaze up in awe. While they stare, Lauren leads Natalie to believe that she and Daniel have "done it" many times, a fabrication that drives Natalie to distraction. Lauren later informs her friend that she was only joking. But the scene, besides being funny, shows Lauren as someone who can appreciate the thought of nudity and sex as presented through art but who is completely shaken by the "real thing" as presented on film.

Music and photography also contribute to the fable-like atmosphere of the film. There is original music, composed and conducted by Georges Delerue, who received an Academy Award for the film. But much of the music used is Vivaldi's, which adds a sprightly Baroque quality to the film. Pierre William Glenn's cinematography is lush and—especially in the French sections—brings out an Impressionistic feeling to Paris, as if these twentieth-century teenagers were living in a world designed by Renoir, Monet, and, most directly, Seurat. And in the Italian segments, Hill emphasizes Italian art's warm, mellow hues. That Hill was consciously thinking of painting in his own cinematic compositions is most apparent in the climax. As Lauren and Daniel kiss under the Bridge of Sighs, the rich sunset that is part of their dream is strikingly reminiscent of Turner's Venetian sunset paintings. A mark of Hill's maturity as a director of cinematic elements is that the photography and the music enhance the actions and emotions of the young lovers without calling attention to themselves as "special effects," as the camera tricks in *The World of Henry Orient* often did.

The playful side of a young romance is also seen in the conflict and juxtapositions of cultures, apparent throughout the film: a MacDonald's golden arch is seen with the Arc de Triomphe in the background; George, the loudly American director, is surrounded by an elegant chateau (filmed in the Ville De Comte, built for the finance minister under Louis XIV and located some 50 kilometers outside of Paris); a stereotyped American tourist couple is encountered in Verona (played with comic brio by Andrew Duncan and Claudette Sutherland). Most important, there is Daniel's love of American movies, an obsession that is reminiscent of the young Truffaut and his protagonist Antoine in *400 Blows*. Critics saw Hill's inclusion of clips of his own films as self-indulgent; but those references are in the original novel. In any case, these segments serve to introduce us immediately to the multicultural world the characters inhabit. We laugh seeing Butch Cassidy and the Sundance Kid, dubbed into French, joking with each other as they prepare for their leap off the ciff (Redford: "Je ne peux pas nager!" and Newman: "Bête, idiot, c'est la chute qui probablement va te tuer!").

*"Are Any of Us So Blameless?"* The romance belongs to Lauren and Daniel. But the motivation for their dream of becoming eternal lovers belongs to Julius. This most engaging old rogue, a pickpocket by profession ("I am a voleur-a-la-rite," he states with pride), he is an adventurer, a romantic and a lonely old man all at once. And he has all the charm of the Europe of another era. In Hill's gallery of con men, Julius quietly shines as the most flamboyant and yet the most compassionate of the lot.[8]

Together with the two teenagers, Julius completes a "family" structure that is more meaningful than the families Lauren and Daniel have left behind. Families do not succeed well in Hill's films (as we have noted) and the best his protagonists can hope for is friendship or the creation of a substitute family (the need for father figures in Hill's films fits in this category). Pauline Kael, who did not like the film as a whole, did appreciate the role of Julius and Olivier's performance. "Pickpocket or no, he would clearly make a much better parent than any one of the children's own parents do."[9] She notes that Olivier's vast knowledge of theater has served him well: "He endows this one [performance] with some of the debonair alertness he gives to Restoration comedy."

Clearly it is Lauren who is the most taken with Julius. As he treats the youngsters to hot chocolate near a park, he quotes from Elizabeth Barrett Browning while Lauren completes the poem. Daniel is bored. But Julius, grateful for the young company, swings immediately into his story of having lived in the Browning villa in Italy with his one true love, Emilienne. He then fires their romantic imaginations with the tale of the importance of a kiss under the Bridge of Sighs at sunset, concluding that "the legend is true."

In Verona the film moves toward the dénouement. As a small family of adventurers, the three share active imaginations, quick wits, and an ability to con. Each has in his own way "lied" to the others, and all of the truth surfaces as the threesome realize that their journey has become a chase: Lauren's parents and the American couple whom Julius has robbed have sent out alerts. After a hilarious interlude-escape during a bicycle race (a scene that reminds us of Hill's musical-bicycle interlude in *Butch Cassidy*) each confronts the other.

Julius is exposed as a pickpocket. But he explains he saved their journey by picking enough pockets at the horse races to make up for Daniel's failed scheme to beat the track with the help of computer analysis of percentages. Lauren confesses she is not going to visit a sick relative as she had told Julius. She simply wants to kiss under the Bridge of Sighs. Then she informs Daniel of the news she has withheld from him: she must return to the States with her family. Daniel is outraged at first, but Julius in his gentle voice asks, "Are any of us so blameless?" Julius softens the hurt as he explains that his story about Emilienne and the Browning cottage was also fabricated. He asks Daniel if his story has been less unreal than Daniel pretending to be Robert Redford. Julius, backed by the soft warm light of an Italian evening, tells them that Emilienne "was an attempt to bring a little romance into my life," a line that was modified from several suggestions originally made by Olivier himself.

If we are touched by the innocence of the young lovers, there is pathos in Julius' attempt at "a little romance." After being called a fraud by Daniel, Julius replies: "I may be an old fraud, Daniel, but I know this is true: something that two people in love create and share together against the impossible can hold them as one forever." So much of Hill's best work derives its power from counterpoint and balance. And in Julius' loving con, Hill plays off young love against the spirit of youth kept alive in Julius' imaginative actions. The resonance of the film is the awareness of each that they are separate (youth–old age) and that they are one in spirit (a substitute family). The reuniting of father and daughter in *The World of Henry Orient* is similar, but there is an even deeper tenderness to the bond formed between Lauren and Daniel and Julius because the old rogue is a substitute parent.

*"We're Different . . . and I'm glad."* A *Little Romance* is a comically romantic film rather than a romantic comedy. In Hill's film we follow the usual boy meets girl, loses girl, gets her back formula up to the ending; then we are denied the happily-ever-after conclusion. As in Hill's other films, the ending serves to remind us of the brevity of such innocent moments.

In A *Little Romance* Hill creates the comedy and pathos from the character of his three main protagonists. The plot keeps them in motion, building to a grand chase and finale, all executed with swift efficiency and effective cross-cutting. More important, however, is the fulfillment of the young lovers' romantic impulse, Julius' faithfulness to the couple (even under the pressure of torture at the hands of the Italian police), and the final goodbye as the young couple face the reality of their separation. The speed of the finale works as counterpoint to the depth of the feeling, keeping the film from becoming maudlin.

The final sequence begins in Paris when Lauren's current stepfather, Richard (Arthur Hill), finally takes action and tosses out director George de Marco, reclaims his faithless wife (Sally Kellerman), and heads for Venice to look for his daughter.

The Venice police have been alerted and are on the lookout for two teenagers and an old man. Julius sees the police coming and goes off with them without a struggle. The couple hide out in a cinema which just happens to be playing *The Sting* dubbed into Italian. Hill edits well as all three story elements begin to come together: Julius is tortured by the police, Lauren's parents arrive in Venice, the young lovers wake up in the cinema and rush to complete their dream in a gondola under the Bridge of Sighs.

In the police station, Laurence Olivier touches us with his battered face, his high, thin moan of pain, and his tattered dignity which he never lets fall. The parents arrive at the station, and Richard questions Julius as the bells of the cathedral ring in the background. Julius assures them that the children are safe. When Richard asks why Julius has been a part of this plot, Julius responds, "I'm not sure you'll understand, but for the first time in my life I am helping to make . . . a legend." Lauren and Daniel are hand-propelling their gondala along, having pushed the gondolier into the canal after haggling over the price. There is the sound of bells, a Turner sunset, a low-angle shot of the bridge, the kiss, a cut to bells ringing, and back to the kiss.

Between Olivier's broken voice and bruised face and the consummation of the long-desired kiss, the legend becomes reality. The scene is straightforwardly emotional and romantic. But the simple emotion of young love is made more complex and thus even more moving by its juxtaposition with Olivier's selfless suffering. His behavior is also an act of love, but on a level that only age and experience can bring. Finally, Hill's intercutting between the two scenes leaves us with an understanding of how strongly youth has needed age, and age has needed youth.

The closing scene is the moment of departure from Paris. The mood, tone, and rhythm of the scene is quiet and restrained, in marked contrast to the high emotion of Venice. Lauren's family is ready to leave in a large car, and Lauren and Daniel stand together for the last time. Lauren explains that she will probably be just "normal" if and when they meet again. Daniel, the tough guy who scoffed at legends, suddenly speaks about the need for illusion:

I don't want you to be like everybody else. I don't want to be like anybody else. We're not now . . . and I hope we never will be.

She nods, and he concludes, "We're different . . . and I'm glad." There are some more words, a kiss, and then Lauren notices that across the street, sitting on the bench, is Julius, poised, restrained, but *there*. She rushes across the street and throws herself into his arms. She then climbs into the car, and the car moves off. Daniel chases the car, as another car gets in his way. Daniel leaps into the air waving as the screen freezes with Daniel in mid-air. We leave him before he touches ground in every sense. He is still part of the romantic legend he has lived out with his true love. He is also in the open—on the street and not in a cinema. His love of images has become a love for a young woman.

There could be no more perfect ending for what has been a little romance.

# 11

## *The World According to Garp*

"We have, in short, been forced to admit that the absurd is more than ever inherent in human existence: that is, the irrational, the inexplicable, the surprising, the nonsensical, in other words, the comic."—Wilie Sypher, "The Meanings of Comedy" in *Comedy*

"Sometimes I wonder why I keep making films," Hill said during pre-production for *The World According to Garp*, his twelfth film. "Why keep going through so much anxiety and trouble?" He paused and smiled. "I guess it's because it feels so *good* when things do go well!" he concluded.[1]

Hill sees it as mere chance that he has been the one to film the major works of both Kurt Vonnegut and John Irving. But a closer look reveals that Irving's universe contains much of the chaos and humor associated with Vonnegut: for both authors the individual is bombarded by a bewildering combination of accidents, violence, cruelty, betrayal, and malice. Yet while Vonnegut's narrator adopts a purely cynical "And so it goes" attitude as Billy Pilgrim passively endures all, Irving's Garp lives creatively, facing the world with unending energy and emotion.

In his film, Hill channels Irving's creativity and Garp's energy into a cinematic narrative that is both a kind of anthology of themes and techniques he has been concerned with throughout his career, and a venture into more contemporary material demanding new approaches.

*Adapting Garp.* "All that is body is as coursing waters," writes eighteen-year-old Garp in John Irving's novel as he quotes Marcus Aurelius. What the would-be writer learns in his first full year as a writer in Vienna is that he has begun to know what kind of writing he does not like, to realize that in order to write something of value he must begin to have a personal *vision* (thus "The World According to . . . "), and to use his time wisely, since he feels men die young in his family.

John Irving's 1978 novel was not only a bestseller (it has gone on to sell more than five million copies), but also a cultural event. It is as important for its time as was J. D. Salinger's *Catcher in the Rye* for the 1950s and Vonnegut's work, especially *Slaughterhouse Five*, for the 1960s. A sprawling, almost plotless, novel of roughly 600 pages, *Garp* is held together by the comic-tragic misadventures of its central figure, whose life is chronicled from his ludicrous conception in 1943, when his mother, an army nurse who wished to have a baby but not a husband, seduced a dying tailgunner named T.S. Garp, to his absurd assassination in the late 1970s.

Thematically the novel is concerned with death (accidental or planned, and always untimely), violence, sex, feminism, and the difficulty of becoming a good novelist while also managing to live a full personal life. "We are all terminal cases," is the line that closes the book. And as Irving makes abundantly clear throughout his text (despite his spirited style and humorous moments) "There are no happy endings: death is horrible, final and frequently premature."[2]

In format and tone, Irving's work echoes both eighteenth- and nineteenth-century novels as well as numerous modern works of fiction. The womb-to-tomb personal epic structure of the book reminds us of such writers as Dickens and Balzac (complete with an ending that describes the fates of the large cast of characters). And Garp's inextinguishable zest for life, sex, and friendship puts this American protagonist in the company of Fielding's Tom Jones (as does Garp's preference for the country and small towns over the city). References are made within the book to such writers as Dostoyevsky and Joseph Conrad, but his black humor and sense of the absurd resemble the works of Kafka, Vonnegut, John Barth, and Günter Grass (all of whom he has stated he admires). Irving definitely creates his own world populated with his own characters and forged in his own style, but as a book about literature as much as it is about life, *Garp* proves to reflect a variety of influences and attempts to fuse an older literary tradition with a contemporary sensibility.

Such an ambitious scope and all-inclusive style has been both a strength and a weakness for the reception of the book. Many readers would agree with Marilyn French that, "Irving is able to juggle comedy, fantasy, the grotesque, the pathetic . . . with enough swiftness and grace that they cohere into a complete arc."[3] Others, however, have been highly critical of what they feel is an almost formless work. Pauline Kael felt that Irving "uses violence and morbidity the way a hack movie director does—to excite you, and maybe because he has nothing else on his mind,"[4] while another critic speaks of the book as, "an imitation-serious book, sentimental and chaotic at the core."[5] Yet despite these objections the novel remains popular.

At the center of all is Garp himself, who is a man of the 1970s. He is what feminist critics are calling "a male accommodator," a man who is sensitive to the needs of women and who is willing (though not always with great enthusiasm) to experiment with role modifications and altered responsibilities. Raised by his mother, Jenny Fields, without a father (the tailgunner died after Garp was conceived), Garp invests most of his nonwriting hours to being a house-husband for his English-professor wife, Helen, and a father to his sons, Walt and Duncan. When his eccentric mother becomes a feminist cult heroine with the publication of her autobiography *A Sexual Suspect* ("In this dirty-minded world you are either somebody's wife or somebody's whore—or fast on your way to becoming one or the other"), Garp does his best to cope with her new role. Jenny sets up a home for injured and troubled women at her late-parents' large estate, Dog's Head Harbor, and fulfills a contemporary Florence Nightingale role (Garp observes that she always thought of herself as a nurse, and in the film we always see her in her uniform). Such sympathy does not make Garp a feminist himself. And much is made in the novel of Garp's revulsion toward an extreme feminist group, The Ellen Jamesians, who cut out their tongues in sympathy for a young girl who was raped and who then had her tongue sliced out so that she could not describe her attacker (even Ellen James renounces the group).[6]

But Garp does show his toleration as he becomes good friends with the transexual Roberta, a former pro football player, who as Garp notes is perhaps the most level headed character he knows.

Above all, *The World According to Garp* celebrates the act of creation: imagination, literature, life. The sharp double vision Irving offers is a result of the strong "Undertoad" (Garp's son's mispronunciation of "undertow") of death, ignorance, and violence which work against the positive forces in the book. Despite the bleakness of this outlook, the tone remains sporting and playful because of Irving's delight in the art and craft of storytelling. While critics have attacked the book as a pop version of more serious works on the lives of writers (think of James Joyce's *Portrait of an Artist as a Young Man*, for instance), Irving nevertheless conveys a wide spectrum of ways in which stories are created and told.

There is Garp's first true story, "The Pension Grillparzer," in which Garp gives himself the family he has never had in real life. When he suffers his first case of writer's block in Vienna, it is his involvement with a dying whore, Charlotte, that gives him his first strong experience and thus the urge to complete his sad tale (almost everyone dies or becomes injured in one way or another in this tale, as in all of his tales). And perhaps with a nod toward Jorge Luis Borges and the movement of Latin American magical realism, Garp includes in this tale an acknowledgement of the transcendental power of the imagination. An old man in the pension is able to read the narrator's grandmother's mind and discover a recurrent and obsessive dream that has haunted her for years, a dream that is passed on to the narrator's mother when the grandmother dies. This endless hall of mirrors effect of fiction is also reflected in Garp's "God in the Alley," a story he creates for his son. We enjoy watching Garp at work, informally composing as he goes along, adding and subtracting elements at will to the degree that he has thoroughly confused his wife.

Finally, the whole book is constructed as a series of tales within tales. Beyond Garp's narratives there is the narrative voice which presents the novel we are reading, a voice which is aware from the beginning of the outcome. Thus the novel is a flashback, a recounting of events that have already transpired which the narrator (unidentified) brings to life, referring to future occurrences and by quoting from Garp's works. The triumph of fiction is realized: although Garp is already dead before the book begins, the narrator is nevertheless skillful enough to re-create Garp's life.

How could such a kaleidoscopic and labyrinthine novel be transformed into a two hour film? Screenwriter Steve Tesich laughs. "I have received letters from three film professors so far who say they have used *The World According to Garp* as an example of a novel that could *never* be turned into a movie," he stated while the film was being shot. The professors were not alone in their disbelief. In fact George Roy Hill put down the book after a hundred pages and turned down an offer from Warner Communications to film it.

Hill finally did finish the book, however. He liked it, but still harbored serious doubts about its cinematic potential. In the meantime the script assignment had been offered to several writers, including William Goldman. But Goldman backed off this time, claiming he could not figure out how to make the book visual enough for the screen. John Irving was also asked, but he declined without hesitation. He is the first to admit he doesn't think visually, and, as he put it, "I spent four years writing the book. The last thing I wanted to do was to have to go back over it and reduce it to a screenplay."

Academy Award-winning writer Tesich (*Breaking Away*) was then called in. Hill recalls, "I had great enthusiasm for the early version of *Breaking Away* and tried to produce and direct it, but we never got it off the ground." Hill was impressed with Tesich's sensitivity and ear for dialogue and asked him to have a shot at transforming *Garp*.

Tesich disappeared to East Hampton during the fall of 1979 and returned with the first draft of a screenplay that surprised and delighted Hill. *Garp* was under way.

"Normally I wouldn't do an adaptation," says Tesich. "But in the end, I really felt I was writing my autobiography. Like Garp, I was a wrestler who wanted to become a writer and who wanted to do so in New York. And like Garp I have a mother who is similar to Jenny in many ways." Tesich continued, "I've always wanted to write something that encompassed a man's entire life from the cradle to the grave."

That sweep is the scope of the book and the film. How did he meet the challenge? Simple, according to Tesich. He held on to the central concerns of the book, eliminated much, and wrote only those scenes that rang true to his experience. At the heart of all Tesich feels are Garp's three great loves: wrestling, being a family man, and writing. "It is really the epic of a family man," says Tesich. He and Hill both see *Garp* as a celebration of the simple joys and pleasures of life set against the chaos, violence, greed, and lust that threaten them constantly.

"*Garp* celebrates something so simple, so corny, that we tend to forget it: you have a life. Son-of-a-bitch, you have a life and before it's over, you can do wonderful things with it. It's the ultimate gift," remarks Tesich.

The script remains remarkably faithful to the *spirit* of Irving's bittersweet epic. And yet Tesich and Hill have made some substantial changes. In general the screenplay sharpens the focus on Garp's need for a father and his subsequent attraction to flying. Tesich has found an excellent image for the entire film which sets both the tone and theme: the film is framed at the begnning and end by an image of the baby Garp free-floating against a blue sky; the upbeat Beatles' tune "When I'm Sixty-Four" plays on the soundtrack for the opening and Nat King Cole's "There Will Never Be Another You" for the ending. The image is both pleasant and disorienting in the opening (we are up in the air whereas the rest of the film will be grounded in Garp's life) and disturbing at the close as Hill ends with a freeze-frame of the smiling baby's face. We respond to the innocence of the baby's smile, but we know that Garp is dying. Thus while Irving's book closes with the bleak line that "We are all terminal cases," Tesich and Hill have dropped the preaching tone and voted for an in-between mood of nostalgia for Garp's innocent years and a realization of the pain that he has suffered. Critics voiced unanimous appreciation for this framing device, well summarized by David Denby who wrote, "A baby floating in the blue sky doesn't have to mean anything—the image is satisfying without meaning."[7]

Tesich's opening image suggests how well he finds a cinematic equivalent for many scenes, themes, and characters in the novel. Both Hill and Tesich well understand that adaptation is more than simply transferring the text to the screen. It is, as one critic observed about the successful elements in the film, a matter of "providing enough subliminal subtext that we begin to *feel* more than we are told."[8] In the study of Hill's films we have seen how concerned Hill has been to build a tension between text and subtext in order to create a third text in the audience's mind, and working together with Tesich, he has even more successfully accomplished this goal in much of *Garp*.

The script tightens Garp's driving need to have a family and to be a writer, showing these elements as related to the sense of loss he feels in not having had a father (though a major point of both script and book is that Garp comes to realize Jenny has been both parents for him).

Another important alteration was the substitution of New York for Vienna in the scenes where Garp first sets out to be a writer. The switch was more than an aesthetic consideration; Irving has kept the rights to the story "The Pension Grillparzer" in case he decides to turn it into a film. Thus, since the Vienna segment of the novel would make little sense without the story and, more important, because New York proves a thematically more consistent choice as a goal for an aspiring American writer, Tesich made the switch. On a practical level, of course, this change also helped to keep the film within budget ($12 million).

Tesich had to condense and cut much in order to come up with a realistic script. In general little fault can be found with his choices, though quite obviously a fair amount of the novel's complexity of relationships disappears in the film, as a host of characters were left out— among them Irving's ever-present bears, Old Tinch (Garp's prep school English teacher), Charlotte (the Vienna prostitute who teaches Garp much more about the human heart and body than did Cushie), Mrs. Ralph (the aggressive but depressed mother of one of Garp's son's friends, who has been abandoned by her husband), and many others. While each reader may miss certain favorites (I would have included Mrs. Ralph somehow), the success of Tesich's script in preserving the spirit of the novel is a reminder of the truth that a film based on a novel must exist in its own right, presented in a way that will both reflect the concerns of the filmmakers and the capabilities and limitations of the medium.

Much the most difficult task was to present on screen the life of a *writer*. Tesich experimented with the idea of using animation to illustrate Garp's imagination as a child. As released, the film contains a segment of a minute and a half in which a dream pops out of twelve year-old Garp's mind as he sleeps after talking to Jenny about his father. John Canemaker's effective childlike images of a young Garp in a flyer's helmet sailing through the air with his father, pursued by enemy aircraft, and then by Death fill the screen. We are made to share the world according to a dreaming young Garp, a transformation by Tesich that is in keeping with the spirit of Irving's interest in dreams and dreamers (Garp, Walt, and the grandmother and mother within the Grillparzer story, for instance) and his technique of placing his readers within other fictional worlds as we read complete short stories.

The animated scene plays well as it now exists. But as written, Tesich used even more animation. In the final draft of the script (January 1981), Tesich begins the animation in the spot where it now occurs. But the scene is picked up again at the point that young Garp falls from the roof of the Steering School infirmary. In the film as it now plays we see a scene in which Jenny explains Garp's conception to old Dean Bodger while attending to the Dean's head wound (he was knocked out trying to help rescue Garp) as Garp listens on. In the script, however, Tesich cross-cuts between Jenny's account and Garp's animated fantasy of his conception. It plays as follows:

CLOSEUP OF GARP
During the above he listens, his mind racing. He sees the animated version of his father flying through the air surrounded by exploding flak and searchlights. The word ENEMY, encarnalized so that each letter represents a danger, comes after him. His father fires his machine gun that sounds like a typewriter and exes them out. A map of Germany with the name of GERMANY in the middle and a map of Japan with the name JAPAN, hurtle toward him. They hit him like great boxing gloves. He starts falling. He pulls a string and a parachute opens but a swastika turning like a buzzsaw cuts the

strings and he falls and falls and falls right into a bed in a hospital much to the shock of the animated version of JENNY the nurse. She quickly wraps him in bandages. He lies there all covered with bandages, a sheet on top of him. Only his mouth is exposed. Out of it comes one word: GARP. It appears like smoke letters and then rises and disappears. Suddenly his sheet rises up to right at crotch level. It's an erection by anyone's reckoning. JENNY tries to push it down but it comes back up. She tries to tie it down but it breaks the ropes and shoots up again. The word GARP comes out of his mouth again. The erection under the sheet is moving.

CLOSEUP OF THE DEAN

He was lying in a bed and now he jumps up.

DEAN

I see, that's . . . very interesting. I don't think I need to hear more. I'll just be going now . . .

JENNY

Not yet. You better rest. Anyway . . .

JENNY (continued)

where was I?

GARP

He kept having erections.

JENNY

Thanks. He was dying. I wanted a child. It seemed like a good way to have one without the bother of a husband hanging around who had legal rights to my body. So, one night when I was on duty and the wounded and maimed were all asleep, I went to him. He was asleep but his erection was still there. I removed my undergarments and got up on the bed on top of him. He woke up then and said the only word other than his name that I ever heard him utter. He said "good." . . . It didn't take very long and that once was all that was needed.

GARP'S VISION

As JENNY talks we see his animated version of JENNY entering the hospital room. His father is lying in bed. Out of his mouth comes first "ARP" and then only "AR." Out of Jenny's mouth come the missing letters. The two of them converse in this manner as JENNY takes off her uniform, lifts up his sheet and positions herself in place to conceive. As they make love they talk to each other. He saying "AR." She supplying the missing letter. The rhythm of this is the rhythm of making love. Together they make GARP. We are forced to abandon the animated fantasy by a sudden scream from the real world.

The scream is the old Dean shouting, "You raped him! You raped a dying man," as he rises and leaves the infirmary.

Animation is just one example of Tesich's imaginative use of film to convey what cannot be done on the printed page. In the above scene the juxtaposition of Garp's cartoon fantasies and Jenny's description of his conception sharpen both the comedy of the moment and our understanding of how young Garp's mind works. But after debating how much animation to use, Hill finally cut the animation from this scene and expanded the earlier sequence involving the sleeping and dreaming Garp. Hill felt the cartoon figures were effective to suggest the father Garp never knew, but he felt that turning Garp's conception into animation would cross that delicate balance he strove to reach between what is realistic (dramatic) and comic (absurd).

Irving was consulted frequently during the working out of the script, and though he had suggestions and even complaints to make about particular details and scenes, he nevertheless recognized the need for the film to be imaginative and selective. "I'm a narrative man," Irving commented, "And I see the main problem of the film as one of tone and narrative flow. Film is instant and two dimensional whereas in a novel there is the narrative voice that is a *presence* that directs you." Offering these remarks on the set, he concluded, "*Garp* is a domestic comedy that gets serious very quickly. The catch is to control the rhythm so that it doesn't move *too* fast."

The two-hour film moves quickly; Tesich tells Garp's life in a straightforward chronological order without the omniscient control of a "narrative voice," as Irving labels his unidentified narrator. We have seen that in all of his adaptations Hill has simplified the original materal and thus intensified the dramatic and comic impact. Tesich, whose *Breaking Away* is a straightforward story, has applied the same approach to Irving's novel. By cutting away levels of literary commentary he has lightened the tone of the film while intensifying the focus on Garp as a man rather than as a writer.

To show Garp as a writer, Tesich created the "Magic Gloves" story to replace "The Pension Grillparzer." Once again Tesich concisely exploits the visual possibilities of cinema to put the audience inside a writer's mind.[9] He cleverly has Garp stand in his New York apartment opening and closing his blinds as a means to begin a represenion of Garp's imagination. Each time the blinds are open we see a different scene from Garp's past. The audience is thus prepared for the growth of Garp's story from a street incident he witnesses in which a pianist and his lady friend (wife?) argue with each other. From this everyday occurrence we see Garp create a tale that "appears" on the screen as Garp expands and embellishes it to include Dean Bodger and an "ending" which clearly maintains Irving's double sense of comedy and tragedy: the pianist falls from his piano, which dangles outside his apartment window, but is saved by a large inflated net— only to be crushed almost immediately by the piano, which falls on top of him.[10]

In her review of the film in *The New York Times*, Janet Maslin spoke of the Tesich-Hill adaptation as "a very fair rendering of Mr. Irving's novel, with similar strengths and weaknesses."[11] Another critic who enjoyed the film observed that the task of adapting the novel was like trying to build the World Trade Center out of popsicle sticks. Maslin is correct: the script was an admirable accomplishment and a solid basis for Hill to begin filming with, and yet it could not avoid some of the serious difficulties of the novel. As Hill began shooting, he was aware of many of these problems which include how to pace and motivate the film, given the episodic and almost plotless structure of the novel (the screenplay is presented almost like a family photograph album complete with dates heading up each sequence); how to bring such exaggerated characters to the screen and make the audience care about them; how to balance the dramatic with the comic given the ease with which the film could fall into slapstick on the one hand and into television melodrama on the other (conflict is the basis of drama, and yet Irving's characters are maimed, injured, and killed by outsiders, sideline characters like Pooh, who murders Garp, and by accidents); and how to keep the film from becoming too light, since the narrative voice had been removed.

*Directed by George Roy Hill.* So far we have detailed the nature of Irving's work and Tesich's adaptation. What remains to be discussed is how Hill as director (and uncredited script collaborator, as usual) built on this base to make *The World According to Garp* his most mature work to date.

Hill is not an autobiographical director in a readily open way like a Jean-Luc Godard or a Woody Allen, but he does personalize each of his projects in terms of style, theme, characterization, and tone so that they become clearly his films. How much of the script belongs to Hill is impossible for either Tesich or Hill to say, since they worked so closely together on it once Tesich completed a first draft. But other elements belong unmistakably to Hill. Take, for instance, the early scene when Garp meets Helen in the stadium and talks to her about writing as she reads. In both the novel and the original screenplay Helen is noted as simply reading a book, title unknown. Hill puts James Joyce's *Ulysses* into her hands and adds an exuberant rambling monologue for Garp about Joyce's short career as a tenor in singing competitions as he and Helen walk off across a very green campus into the distance. This addition is a minor one, but it is indicative of Hill's attention to the kind of detail that adds up to the overall tone and impression of the film. This touch is personal because it quite obviously comes from his own fascination with Joyce and music (his abandoned Ph.D. thesis in Dublin). But rather than coming off as a private joke or a stroke of self-indulgent whimsy, Hill's addition helps further characterize both Helen and Garp: Helen is not just *a* reader in the film, but a serious one; and Garp is no longer just another jock dreaming of becoming something or someone else, but a fellow who has somehow exposed himself not only to serious literature but to the fascinating trivia that surrounds it. The tone established is basically romantic, as in the novel and script, but this added touch helps to add depth to Garp's playfulness and awkward flirtation.

A more significant contribution by Hill was the handling of "accident" which causes so much destruction for the Garp family. As all readers of the novel know, the accident scene in which Walt dies and Helen's graduate-school lover, Michael Milton, loses his penis is the climax of Irving's penchant for the vividly violent and bizarre. How to portray this scene on film? As Irving points out, there is a vast difference between what can be written about and what is shown on the screen. "The novel can be more explicit because of the narrative voice that controls what you *see*. But you can't bleed just a little bit on screen; you *bleed!*" When Tesich was stumped as to how to handle the scene, Hill stepped in with the solution. Garp sails down the road with his sons in his old Volvo, "flying" with the lights and the engine off as he has done on countless occasions before. This time, however, Helen is performing fellatio on her lover (whom Garp has told her to abandon) while he is parked in the driveway. There is a collision.

At the moment of impact, the screen freeze-frames on Walt's lovely face in close up as the sound of the accident continues. This is followed by a slow fade out of picture and sound. Hill thus draws our attention away from the bizarre horror of Milton's sexual dismemberment (in fact, those who have not read the book do not learn of this detail until later on, when Roberta comments on it to Jenny), and focuses on Walt, who is to die. Walt's death is tragic and untimely, but even more important, it is a blow to Garp's desire for security within family life. Hill always works to have a scene suggest at least two forces in operation (often expressed as the tension between text and subtext). Here in a single image, in conjunction with the soundtrack, Hill is able to suggest the horror of the accident (sound) and its most damaging consequence (the image of Walt). As throughout the film, Hill handles the tone of the scene carefully, so that what could easily have become pure sensationalism in the hands of another director (imagine the slow-motion dismemberment of Michael Milton with cross-cutting to his terrorized expression, for instance), becomes toned down so that we can more clearly experience the *consequences* of the disasters. The assassination of Jenny and of Garp are handled with similar precision, with the same results.

Hill's interpretation of *Garp* is most readily felt in the casting and handling of Garp and Jenny. In almost every way they contrast with each other, even though they are mother and son. The story details Garp's entire life, but we never come to understand why and how Jenny became the eccentric mother she did. As given, Jenny, with her obsessive intolerance of human sexuality, her driven aversion to close relationships beyond the rather stiff one with her son, and her inability to cast herself in any other role than that of a nurse, is less a character than a two-dimensional persona. Garp, on the other hand, longs to be everything his mother is not: a sharing lover, parent, husband, friend (Jenny's first aid to broken bodies and lost souls does not appear as an act of sharing so much as a matriarchal dispensing of help that reflects her power). She writes autobiography; he struggles with fiction. She has created an open-ended female society at Dog's Head Harbor (did Irving have Aristophanes' *Lysistrata* in mind?); he attempts to make the traditional nuclear family work through new variations (role reversals).

Glenn Close as Jenny and Robin Williams as Garp establish this dichotomy but with important differences that Hill accentuates. Virtually the only unanimous agreement among critics was that Glenn Close brought a great deal to the role in this her first film.[12] Close conveys both strength and warmth through a particular East Coast aristocratic bearing that suggests her well-bred wealthy background and a certain sense of style and grace that can easily turn to sincere concern and charm (Pauline Kael described Close's readings of her lines as "reminiscent of Katharine Hepburn's cadences filtered through Meryl Streep"). In scene after scene her dignity and warmth do not clarify the mystery of her personality, but they do help us accept her for who she is rather than dismiss her as a caricature.

The casting of Robin Williams as Garp was more controversial.[13] Certainly Williams differs in numerous ways with Garp in the novel. Most obviously, Irving's Garp is a more literary figure who spends much more time at writing than does Hill's Garp. But such differences do not demonstrate a fault of the film; rather, they point to the differences in concept between the character in the book and in the film. In casting Robin Williams against his usual image of Mork-from-outer-space Hill was purposely lightening up the character of Garp while simultaneously holding Williams down from his usual comic antics and drawing forth from him a performance with substance. Casting against type means to take risks when an actor has an established screen identity. Hill managed the opposite effect—casting a basically serious actor in a comic role in order to give it more depth—when he cast Paul Newman as Butch Cassidy and Lawrence Olivier as Julius in A *Little Romance*.)

Williams' entry into the film is carefully prepared for. We have covered all of Garp's youth and roughly a half hour of screen time before we meet him: Garp is thus already a character in our minds, and Williams fits right in. The swift pacing of this first part of the film is handled with the same ability to capture a youthful zest for life that we have seen in *The World of Henry Orient* and *A Little Romance*. When we do meet Williams, he is a teenage wrestler encountering Helen, his wife-to-be, for the first time. Hill builds on Williams' shyness and slight awkwardness to make this scene work as a smooth transition from childhood to young adulthood and from a child actor (James McCall) to Robin Williams. Williams' clipped speech, his impish and wholesome expressions, and his constantly erupting nervous energy are in sharp contrast to Glenn Close's powerful but controlled performance as Jenny.

What Williams lacks in range he more than makes up for in spontaneity and childlike integrity. Throughout the filming Hill was concerned that audiences not take Williams for Mork. One of the ads for the film, for instance, stated that Garp was "the most human being you'll ever meet." But whether Hill was ever conscious of it or not, the audience's memory of Williams as Mork is important to the success of the role, because in name, conception, and situation, Garp is virtually from another world. That world is, however, a *human* world and so the subliminal transformation of Williams from Mork to Garp helps the audience realize that Garp is different and to accept him as the "average" fellow he longs to be (except for being a writer, Garp wants a rather typical middle class existence). Furthermore, the childlike quality that Williams possesses closely resembles that element of childlike fantasy and nostalgia we have observed in all of Hill's films. Garp in the novel is playful, but Williams as Garp remains an overgrown kid who will die before he grows old.

Hill darkens the film and slows the pace after the frolicsome dangers of childhood to allow the more serious tone of the novel and script to emerge. While there is no narrative voice as such in the film, the pacing of sequences and the length of time devoted to individual scenes serve to help convey emotional changes. Similarly Hill directs Williams' performance carefully so that the moments of strongest emotion work effectively for the film. The first such moment is Garp's reconciliation with Helen after the accident. Hill lightens the emotional devistation in the scenes immediately after the accident by having Williams wear a neck brace contraption that makes him look comic while forcing him into the ironic position of having to write out messages (the device prevents him from speaking) in the same manner as the Ellen Jamesians—the tongueless feminists Garp so vehemently opposes. The reconciliation is brief, and often audiences chuckle when Williams delivers his "I mishhhh you" line, still suffering from the effects of the accident. But below the level of amusement Williams is successful in portraying a man who has made some internal re-evaluations of himself, and has realized his love of Helen and family is stronger than his anger and hurt. Because Garp is so childlike to begin with, we sense all the more how much a moment of growth this reconciliation has been.

Hill mixes humor and pathos in this scene as we have seen him do in so many. But Hill goes beyond the bittersweet in a later scene after Jenny's death as Garp makes a decision to attend the feminist funeral that is being held in Jenny's honor. Hill has stated how uncomfortable he feels with straight dramatic moments, but in this scene he directs Williams through a remarkably strong speech which follows the efforts of Roberta and his publisher to dissuade him from attending the funeral. Without a trace of humor Williams states:

I want my mother alive again, but since I can't, and since I miss her terribly, I want to be around people who feel the same way as I do. The more the better. I'll mourn her death alone for the rest of my life, but for the moment I want to share it with as many people as I can.[14]

Williams touches a depth with this speech that echoes backward across the film and stays with the viewer for the brief time before the finish. At the heart of Hill's Garp is an intense need to care and to share. That Williams succeeds in making this moment work affects us even more strongly than if the role had been assigned to one of the actors who would more conventionally fit in with many viewers' conception of Garp (Dustin Hoffman, though too old for the part, was frequently mentioned by fans of the novel).

That this scene is effective means the film as a whole is complete. I began this section by claiming that *The World According to Garp* is Hill's most mature work. It is also his most integrated. In *Garp* many of Hill's major themes and techniques (the freeze-frame, for instance) are even more fully integrated than in previous films. The image of a child floating in the sky, which he had toyed with earlier, is used brilliantly in *Garp*. Hill's movement in his films from bright to dark and comic to bittersweet is even more extreme in *Garp*, building to the above-quoted speech which touches an emotional level Hill has implied but not stated before. And in *Garp* the sense of isolation that plays so great a role in many of his films gives way to an extended web of friendships which includes Garp's immediate family and extends to the sympathetic companionship of Roberta and the quietly supportive presence of John Wolf, Garp's editor, not to mention the strong central love-friendship with his mother (that he must also harbor some ill feelings about her as well which are never brought to the surface in either the book or film only increases the complexity of his relationship: in a real sense Garp never seems to outgrow the Oedipal conflict). The sense of myth-making is also central to the public and private images of Jenny and Garp. As with Butch and Sundance and Waldo Pepper it is the myth that is created around Garp by his mother's sudden public visibility that brings about so much destruction from the outside.[15] The public vs private dialectic is all the more noticeable in *Garp* because it is the first film in which the family and a sense of roots becomes of overriding importance for a Hill protagonist.

What Hill has managed to capture in his version of *Garp* even more convincingly than in Irving's novel is the intensity between the security Garp seeks and the flux and danger of the world and society around him. Hill views himself as an entertainer, and no one would deny that his career has involved the creation of memorable entertaining films. But beyond this level, as we have seen, can be found the tension between the dreams of his characters and the shortcomings of their realities. In many ways, because his films have dealt with various American locations, periods and institutions, the gap between the illusions and realities of his characters mirrors a similar gap in much of American culture.

Within this framework, *Garp* is valuable as a film that reflects the fantasies and frustrations of many Americans of the late 1970s. Gone are the 1960s and a belief that society can either be ignored or swiftly changed. Gone also is the pure ego and instant gratification of the Me Generation. Garp (particularly as realized by Robin Williams) emerges as a figure comically and painfully caught in the middle of yet further social upheavals. He is desperately committed to family, monogamy (despite his moments of weakness), home, a safe neighborhood, respect for property, and a general apolitical approach to life. He is, in short, trying to uphold all of the institutions and beliefs that are rapidly changing and crumbling around and beneath him.

The poignancy of Garp as a character and as a film is that he lives in a time when the coursing waters Marcus Aurelius spoke of have become floods. The world according to Garp is drowned out by other worlds pressing in on the environment he would like to stake out and inhabit.

# Conclusion

"My way is to conjure you."—Rosalind in the Epilogue to Shakespeare's *As You Like It*

As I finish, George Roy Hill is completing the shooting of his thirteenth feature, *The Little Drummer Girl*. As has often happened during Hill's more than twenty years in Hollywood filmmaking, many were surprised at his choice for a project to follow *The World According to Garp*. But after a dozen films covering a variety of genres, Hill's maverick approach to picking films should be no surprise at all. In fact, *The Little Drummer Girl* based on John le Carré's richly textured contemporary political thriller about terrorism and anti-terrorism between warring Palestinian and Israeli factions, is both a summation of Hill's career to date and a hint of new directions he may choose to explore in the future.

The differences between le Carré's novel and Hill's films are readily apparent. Le Carré is a master of a finely tuned Baroque prose in which subtle elaboration of the psychology of characters is even more important than the Byzantine labyrinths of intrigue through which his characters move. Hill, in contrast, is a defender of the primacy of a strong story-line developing from a tight script. Le Carré has made his mark as a writer of contemporary existential espionage novels while Hill has never ventured into the political thriller area. And while Hill has always been able to find genuine comic touches in even the most tragic situations, le Carré depicts characters who endure the betrayals and horrors they encounter with a world-weary fatalism.

Yet beyond these contrasts, it is not difficult to detect elements in le Carré's work that correspond to Hill's interests and concerns. Overall, there is the focus in *The Little Drummer Girl* on what the Israeli anti-terrorist agent Kurtz refers to as the "theatre of the real." As agents and counteragents, le Carré's protagonists are necessarily forced to live dangerous lives which consist of roles within roles, identities within identities, all assumed and cast off in the pursuit of pressing political goals. Within this true-life improvisational theater, le Carré casts Charlie, a young, bright, creative, and romantic British actress who finds herself suddenly forced to play the role of her lifetime as her romantic interests lead her into a deadly crossfire between Palestinian terrorists and Israeli agents out to destroy each other in the "theatre of the real."

"My way is to conjure you" states Charlie towards the end of the filmscript by Loring Mandel as she speaks the lines of Shakespeare's Rosalind in *As You Like It*. And as actress within the play who has been a double agent in real life, Charlie represents the kind of character that has always fascinated Hill: one who creates his or her own world and then begins to live within it.

*The Little Drummer Girl* is thus a Big Con of a complexity and of a contemporary significance far beyond that of the primarily entertainment framework of a film such as *The Sting*. Charlie understands the nature of acting when she explains that "theatre's a con trick, Michel. Do you know what that means? Con trick? You've been deceived!" as she speaks (in the film script) to her Israeli agent romantic interest who is at that moment pretending to be a Palestinian terrorist wanted by the authorities. Le Carré's novel becomes both a personal odyssey of a young woman's journey of self-discovery and an international political fable about the tragic and often cold-blooded violence perpetrated by both Palestinians and Israelis in their unyielding struggle to claim the same territory as their homeland. The novel and film center on the confusion that ensues when Charlie finds herself conned and deceived by the agents of both nations who, in the theatre of the real, play a no-holds-barred drama she has never had to confront before. In this sense *The Little Drummer Girl* reflects Hill's interest in going even further than in *The World According to Garp* to suggest a contemporary reality that crushes individual dreams and "worlds."

And while Hill has not made a thriller before, he has, especially in his early television work, shown an interest and a talent for handling personal dramas woven around dangerous historical events ("A Night to Remember," "Child of Our Time," "Judgment at Nuremberg"). *Slaughterhouse Five*, while mixing black humor with historical reality (the fire bombing of Dresden), also emerges as a work that foreshadows his most recent project in presenting a complicated narrative structure to parallel the complexity of the times. Hill has also considered scripts in the past which were based on contemporary political events, including an ironic tale written by Gary Trudeau, the creator of Doonesbury, about Jimmy Carter's visit to Poland. Thus, while Hill has gained a reputation as a director concerned with a nostalgic American past, he is as much interested in finding scripts that use present-day historical and political concerns as a framework for stories about individuals pursuing their own goals.

We have seen how a deep sense of irony—the awareness of the gap between a character's actions and his asperations—is a major element in Hill's work. For this reason, the many ironic levels of le Carré's novel are surely appealing to Hill. Both the Israelis and the Palestinians wish to live in peace, and yet each has resorted to sanctioned violence to try and obtain that peace. Irony, often bitter, permeates the entire novel, including the final reuniting of Charlie and her lover. Such a reunion should be the signal for a "happy ever after" effect, but after the murder, betrayal, and manipulation of people and events that they have participated in, we are left with an uneasy hollow feeling that romance has been stained by blood and that, in fact, love may not be enough to raise these protagonists beyond their troubled pasts. Such a double ending is definitely in keeping with the endings of Hill's previous films.

Loring Mandel's screenplay remains faithful to the spirit of le Carré's novel while also reflecting Hill's concern for telling a strong story as directly as possible (as usual, Hill has been an important contributor to the script). As with *Slaughterhouse Five* and *The World According to Garp*, Hill has had his screenwriter hone down complicated texts to intensify the main themes and characters. One factor, in this sense, that makes *The Little Drummer Girl* unlike Hill's previous work is that le Carré's novel has a woman, Charlie, as the central figure (she is, after all, the little drummer girl of the title). Even more so than in the novel, Charlie is given center stage in the film. Much of what has been cut from the book has to do with subplots and minor characters not directly in touch with Charlie, and so, by omission as well, she stands out in the script in stronger relief.

Part of the pleasure of le Carré's novel is the deliberately and painstakingly long opening he provides as a background and framework for the development of Charlie's story. But in a feature film of two hours, Hill is aware of the need to get into the tale much more speedily. The opening of the film is a good example of Hill's consistent refinement of material he has adapted for the screen. The book concerns itself at first only with the explosion of a Palestinian terrorist bomb in an Israeli diplomat's home in Germany and its subsequent investigation. Mandel in the script, in contrast, opens with the bombing and cross cuts several times to Charlie participating in leftist activities in England. Hill is thus able to create an immediate tension between two seemingly unrelated worlds which will soon collide.

Hill has always combined careful planning with taking advantage of luck and unforseen obstacles. *The Little Drummer Girl* is no exception. Charlie is played by Diane Keaton, and at first she was to be a British actress, as written in le Carré's novel. Keaton was uncomfortable trying to find an acceptable British accent early on in the project, however, so Hill called for a script rewrite with Charlie as an American actress who has lived for years in England. As her role appears in the August 17, 1983, version of the script, such a switch enhances the character of Charlie. As an American expatriate, she is just that much more out of beat with any particular culture or social group. Furthermore, by making her from Iowa, Charlie emerges as yet another Hill protagonist with an American past but with no particular roots.

Careful and creative casting under the experienced guidance of Marion Dougherty is once again important for Hill's new film. Ironically, popular German actor Klaus Kinski plays the significant role of Kurtz, the Israeli anti-terrorist specialist who is much more at home in the field on assignment than in his native country where he must contend with inefficient and egotistical bureaucrats and politicians. Hollywood has always had foreign nationals played by whomever the studio heads found acceptable (Anthony Quinn as *Zorba the Greek*, for instance). But in a film that concerns the Mideast today, the use of a German actor portraying an Israeli suggests yet another level of role playing in Kurtz's "theatre of the real." Likewise Hill and Dougherty have used a number of foreign actors in other roles but playing nationalities other than their own (there are, however, a number of Israeli actors in minor roles playing Israelis). The Israeli agent Joseph is played by Greek actor Yorgo Voyagis, the Greek figure Dimitri is realized by Israeli actor Ben Levin, the most wanted Palestinian terrorist Khalil is acted by French actor Sami Frey, and Austrian terrorist Mesterbein is portrayed by British actor David Suchet. The overall effect should be to heighten the terrorist and anti-terrorist con: nothing is as it appears to be, and no one is what they pretend to be. As in many of Hill's other works, especially *The Sting*, the final con remains the film itself, which has made use of an old convention— using actors to pretend to be foreign protagonists—for a contemporary effect: in a film about terrorism and deception, most of the actors are *foreigners*, which adds a ring of authenticity at the same time that we come to realize these actors are cast against their home countries.

Part of what is new about Hill's *The Little Drummer Girl* is that at this point in his career he is setting himself ever more difficult and controversial tasks to perform. There are any number of scripts about that concern agents and double agents, terrorists and anti-terrorists, and Hill could have chosen any of them for his debut in the genre of political thriller. It is therefore significant that he chose one that uses the framework of the troubled Mideast, the topic of pressing and continuous concern to everyone concerned with a desire for world peace. Hill does not consider himself a political person and does not see *The Little Drummer Girl* as a political film. Such a position is, of course, in and of itself political. But what he means is that he is not concerned with using cinema for a blatantly partisan cause as have directors such as Costa-Gavras, Jean-Luc Godard, and Gillo Pontecorvo (whose 1965 film *The Battle of Algiers* depicted the personal horror of the death and suffering caused by terrorism but which suggests that such violence may in fact be a necessary phase in the liberation of a people from an occupying nation). Le Carré's novel refuses to take sides in the Palestinian-Israeli struggle. The screenplay likewise takes a noncommitted point of view, choosing even more so than the novel to focus on how such intense politics and personalities affect a Western outsider: Charlie.

If the film is successful, Hill will have managed to portray the drama of an individual caught up in contemporary events that are beyond her control. The blending of drama and such a complicated political reality, however, has the built in danger that the political issues will be oversimplified to the point of manipulation. Many critics have found Costa-Gavras' film, *Hanna K.* about a woman (Jill Clayburgh) caught between her love for an Israeli and a Palestinian as an example of such a film that in its effort to be fair becomes obscure and simplistic. That Hill is willing to take such risks is, I feel, an indication of a new maturity as an artist.

Hill continues. He is one of the few directors who has been fortunate enough because of his successes to be able to choose his projects carefully and, since *Butch Cassidy and the Sundance Kid*, to have a controlling say over every aspect of the filmmaking process. Rather than merely repeat himself, furthermore, he has continually searched for new subjects, new genres, new techniques with which to represent these projects. It would have been possible to play the sequel game with films such as his two popular Newman-Redford works. But instead he has opted for a widening and deepening of his style and of his subject matter. From the troubled comedy of middle class American marriage in the 1950s represented in *Period of Adjustment*, he has enlarged his scope in *The Little Drummer Girl* to include global terrorism and drifting loners without families or true friends.

What lies ahead? It is not unfair to expect another half dozen films before Hill hangs up his clapboard. Which projects he chooses will, as always, be subject to his own particular and eclectic tastes. Certainly many possibilities exist including the film he has shied away from since his Dublin days: *The Ginger Man*. And, then, it just may happen that he could turn to a small-scale project (as he did with *A Little Romance*) and shoot an adaptation he has always wanted to make: Sean O'Casey's play about the Irish revolution of the 1920s, *A Shadow of a Gunman*. Like many artists, it would be only fitting for Hill to return in the latter part of his career to his early interests and present them with the distance and fondness that age can bestow.

# Filmography

| | |
|---|---|
| *Period of Adjustment* | 1962 |
| Producer: | Larry Weingarten |
| Script: | Isobel Lennart from the play by Tennessee Williams |
| Photography: | Paul G. Vogel |
| Editor: | Frederic Steinkamp |
| Cast: | Jane Fonda (Isabel Haverstick) |
| | Jim Hutton (George Haverstick) |
| | Tony Franciosa (Ralph Bates) |
| | Lois Nettleton (Dorothea Bates) |
| Time: | 112 min. (Black & White) |
| Studio: | M-G-M |
| 16 mm Distributor: | Films, Inc. |

| | |
|---|---|
| *Toys in the Attic* | 1963 |
| Producer: | Walter Mirisch |
| Script: | James Poe from the play by Lillian Hellman |
| Photography: | Joseph Biroc |
| Editor: | Stuart Gilmore |
| Music: | George Duning |
| Cast: | Dean Martin (Julian Berniers) |
| | Yvette Mimieux (Lily Prine Berniers) |
| | Gene Tierney (Albertine Prine) |
| | Geraldine Page (Carrie Berniers) |
| | Wendy Hiller (Anna Berniers) |
| Time: | 90 min. (Black & White) |
| Studio: | United Artists |
| 16 mm Distributor: | United Artists 16 |

*The World of Henry Orient*                 1964

Producer:                 Jerome Hellman
Script:                   Nora and Nunnally Johnson from the novel
                          by Nora Johnson
Photography:              Boris Kaufman and Arthur Ornitz
Editor:                   Stuart Gilmore
Music:                    Elmer Bernstein
Cast:                     Merrie Spaeth (Marian Gilbert)
                          Tippy Walker (Valerie Boyd)
                          Peter Sellers (Henry Orient)
                          Angela Lansbury (Isabel Boyd)
                          Paula Prentiss (Stella)
                          Tom Bosley (Frank Boyd)
                          Phyllis Thaxter (Mrs. Gilbert)
Time:                     106 min. (Color)
Studio:                   United Artists
16 mm Distributor         United Artists 16


*Hawaii*                                    1966

Producer:                 Walter Mirisch
Screenplay:               Dalton Trumbo, based on the novel by
                          James A. Michener
Photography:              Russell Harlan
Editor:                   Stuart Gilmore
Music:                    Elmer Bernstein
Cast:                     Max von Sydow (Abner Hale)
                          Julie Andrews (Jerusha Bramely)
                          Jocelyne LaGarde (Queen Malama)
                          Manu Tupou (Prince Keoki)
                          Richard Harris (Rafer Hoxworth)
                          Gene Hackman (Rev. John Whipple)
Time:                     161 min. (Color)
Studio:                   United Artists
16 mm Distributor:        Twyman, Swank


*Thoroughly Modern Millie*                  1967

Producer:                 Ross Hunter
Script:                   Richard Morris

| | |
|---|---|
| Photography: | Russell Metty |
| Editor: | Stuart Gilmore |
| Music: | Elmer Bernstein and Andre Previn "Thoroughly Modern Millie" and "Tapioca" by James Van Heusen and Sammy Cahn |
| Choreography: | Joe Layton |
| Production Manager: | Ernest B. Wehmeyer |
| Cast: | Julie Andrews (Millie Dillmount) |
| | Mary Tyler Moore (Dorothy Brown) |
| | James Fox (Jimmy Smith) |
| | John Gavin (Trevor Graydon) |
| | Carol Channing (Muzzy Van Hossmere) |
| | Beatrice Lillie (Mrs. Meers) |
| Time: | 138 min. (Color) |
| Studio: | Universal |
| 16 mm Distributor: | Twyman, Swank |

| | |
|---|---|
| *Butch Cassidy and the Sundance Kid* | 1969 |
| Producers: | John Forman |
| Executive Producer: | Paul Monash |
| Script: | William Goldman |
| Photography: | Conrad Hall |
| Editor: | John Howard |
| Music: | Burt Bacharach |
| Cast: | Paul Newman (Robert Parker, "Butch Cassidy") |
| | Robert Redford (Harry Longabaugh, "Sundance Kid") |
| | Katharine Ross (Etta Place) |
| | Strother Martin (mining operator) |
| | Jeff Corey (old sheriff) |
| Time: | 112 min. (Color) |
| Studio: | 20th Century Fox |
| 16 mm Distributor: | Films, Inc. |

| | |
|---|---|
| *Slaughterhouse Five* | 1972 |
| Producer: | Paul Monash |
| Screenplay: | Stephen Geller from the novel by Kurt Vonnegut, Jr. |

| | |
|---|---|
| Photography: | Mirislov Ondricek |
| Editor: | Dede Allen |
| Production designer: | Henry Bumstead |
| Music: | J. S. Bach, adapted by Glenn Gould |
| Cast: | Michael Sacks (Billy Pilgrim) |
| | Ron Leibman (Paul Lazzaro) |
| | Valerie Perrine (Montana Wildhack) |
| | Eugene Roche (Edgar Derby) |
| | Sharon Gans (Billy's wife) |
| | Friedrich Ledebur (German officer) |
| Time: | 104 min. (Color) |
| Studio: | Universal |
| 16 mm Distributor: | Universal 16, Twyman, Clem Williams Films |

*The Sting*   1973

| | |
|---|---|
| Producer: | Tony Bill and Julia and Michael Phillips |
| Screenplay: | David S. Ward |
| Photography: | Robert Surtees |
| Editor: | William Reynolds |
| Production designer: | Henry Bumstead |
| Music: | Marvin Hamlisch, arranged from the music of Scott Joplin |
| Cast: | Robert Redford (Johnny Hooker) |
| | Paul Newman (Henry Gondorff) |
| | Robert Shaw (Doyle Lonnegan) |
| | Charles Durning (Lt. Snyder) |
| | Ray Watson (Singleton) |
| | Eileen Brennan (Billie) |
| | Harold Gould (Kid Twist) |
| Time: | 129 min. (Color) |
| Studio: | Universal |
| 16 mm Distributor: | Clem Williams Films, Twyman Films, Swank |

*The Great Waldo Pepper*   1975

| | |
|---|---|
| Producer: | George Roy Hill |
| Script: | William Goldman from a story by George Roy Hill |

| | |
|---|---|
| Photography: | Robert Surtees |
| Editor: | William Reynolds |
| Music: | Henry Mancini |
| Production designer: | Henry Bumstead |
| Cast: | Robert Redford (Waldo Pepper) |
| | Bo Svenson (Capt. Axel Olsson) |
| | Susan Sarandon (Mary Beth) |
| | Bo Brundin (Ernst Kessler) |
| | Ed Herrmann (Ezra Sykes) |
| | Philip Bruns (Doc Dillhoefer) |
| Aerial sequences advised by: | Frank Tallman |
| Time: | 107 min. (Color) |
| 16 mm Distributor: | Universal |
| | Clem Williams, Films, Twyman, Swank |


*Slapshot*　　　　　　　　　　1977

| | |
|---|---|
| Producer: | Robert J. Wunsch and Stephen Friedman |
| Script: | Nancy Dowd |
| Photography: | Vic Kemper |
| Editor: | Dede Allen |
| Music: | Supervised by Elmer Bernstein: Songs by Fleetwood Mac, Elton John, and Maxine Nightingale. |
| Cast: | Paul Newman (Reggie) |
| | Michael Ontkean (Ned Braden) |
| | Lindsay Crouse (Lily Braden) |
| | Jennifer Warren (Francine) |
| | Jerry Houser (Killer) |
| | Strother Martin (Joe McGrath) |
| | Ned Dowd (Oglethorp) |
| | Andy Duncan (Jim Cost) |
| Time: | 121 min. (Color) |
| Studio: | Universal |
| Distributor: | Universal 16, Twyman, Clem Williams Films |


*A Little Romance*　　　　　　1979

| | |
|---|---|
| Producer: | Yves Rousset-Rouard and Robert L. Crawford |

| | |
|---|---|
| Script: | Allen Burns from the novel $E = MC^2$, *Mon Amour* by Patrick Chauvin |
| Photography: | Pierre William Glenn |
| Editor: | William Reynolds |
| Music: | Georges Delerue |
| Cast: | Laurence Olivier (Julius) |
| | Diane Lane (Lauren King) |
| | Thelonious Bernard (Daniel Michon) |
| | Arthur Hill (Richard King) |
| | Sally Kellerman (Kay King) |
| | Broderick Crawford as (himself) |
| | David Dukes (George de Marco) |
| Time: | 108 min. (Color) |
| Studio: | An Orion film through Warner Bros. |
| 16 mm Distributor: | Films, Inc. |

*The World According to Garp*    1982

| | |
|---|---|
| Producer: | Robert Crawford |
| Script: | Steve Tesich from the novel by John Irving |
| Photography: | Mirislov Ondricek |
| Editor: | Stephen A. Rotter |
| Music: | Adapted by David Shire including "When I'm Sixty-Four" by The Beatles and "There Will Never Be Another You" by Nat King Cole |
| Production designer: | Henry Bumstead |
| Cast: | Robin Williams (Garp) |
| | Glenn Close (Jenny Fields) |
| | Mary Beth Hurt (Helen) |
| | John Lithgow (Roberta Muldoon) |
| | Hume Cronyn (Mr. Fields) |
| | Jessica Tandy (Mrs. Fields) |
| | Swoosie Kurtz (The Hooker) |
| Studio: | Warner Bros. |
| Time: | 128 min. (Color) |
| 16 mm. Distributor: | Swank |

*The Little Drummer Girl*    1984

| | |
|---|---|
| Producer: | George Roy Hill and Robert Crawford for Pan Arts; Pat Kelley, executive producer |

| | |
|---|---|
| Script: | Loring Mandel from the novel by John le Carré |
| Photography: | Wolfgang Treu |
| Editor: | Bill Reynolds |
| Production Design: | Henry Bumstead |
| Cast: | Diane Keaton (Charlie) |
| | Klaus Kinski (Kurtz/Gold) |
| | Yorgo Voyagis (Joseph) |
| | Sami Frey (Khalil) |
| | Eli Danker (Litvak) |
| | Moti Shirin (Michel) |
| | Kerstin De Ahna (Helga) |
| | David Suchet (Mesterbein) |
| | Ben Levin (Dimitri) |
| Studio: | Pan Arts for Warner Bros. |

# Notes

## 1. Creating an Environment

1. Henry Mitchell, "Bettelheim: Films, Fairy Tales and the Affirmation of Life," *The Washington Post*, February 6, 1981, p. C-10. Bettelheim's book, *The Uses of Enchantment* (New York: Knopf, 1976), while dealing with fairy tales, has a number of implications for cinema.

2. Bill Davidson, "The Entertainer," *New York Times Magazine*. (March 16, 1975), p. 19.

3. Robin Wood, *Hitchcock's Films*. (New York: A. S. Barnes, 1965), p. 19.

4. Edward Shores, *George Roy Hill*. (Boston: Twayne, 1983).

5. Northrop Frye, *Anatomy of Criticism* (Princeton: Princeton University Press, 1957), p. 180.

6. Andrew Horton, "Creating a Reality That Doesn't Exist: An Interview with Louis Malle," *Literature/Film Quarterly* (1979), 7 (2):88.

7. Christian Metz, *The Imaginary Signifier*, trans. by Celia Britton et al. (Bloomington: Indiana University Press, 1982), p. 4.

8. All script quotations are taken from George Roy Hill's copies of his scripts and are used with permission.

9. Erik Erikson, for example, writes, "But the survival value of the ritualizing patterning of interplay can only become clear if we fully realize the stark probability that playfulness throughout life *is* liveliness, and that the lack of it causes a specific form of deadliness." *Toys and Reasons* (New York: Norton, 1977), p. 58.

## 3. A Period of Adjustment

1. *Period of Adjustment* was well received as a film. Brendan Gill in his *New Yorker* review called it "a pleasant surprise," complimenting Hill for directing with "unembarrassed broadness," and stating that "unlikely as it sounds, in some uncanny fashion, the scene works" (Gill refers to the mixture of farce and pathos in the closing scene). Arthur Knight praised the screenplay for being better than Williams' play.

2. Signi Falk, *Tennessee Williams* (Boston: Twayne, 1961; 2d ed. 1978), chapter on the play.

3. *Period of Adjustment* opened on Nov. 10, 1960, produced by Cheryl Crawford, and starring James Daly as Ralph, Barbara Baxley as Isabel, and Robert Webber as George. Elia Kazan was slated to direct the play but pulled out because of other commitments. Hill accepted the assignment when Williams personally chose him on the strength of his direction of *Greenwillow*, a production that Williams much admired. Unhappy with the casting of the play, which was already in production, Hill nevertheless did his best.

4. It is an interesting minor note that Hill used Hutton in his first film; eighteen years later Robert Redford, one of Hill's best-known stars, used Hutton's son in *Ordinary People*, his first effort as a director.

5. The strong influence of film on Williams' conception of drama is well documented in Maurice Yacowar's book, *Tennessee Williams and Film* (New York: Ungar, 1977). As a script writer he is the uncredited author of Visconti's *Senso* (1954) and specifically wrote *Baby Doll* for the screen. As a playwright, film influenced him to avoid using "acts," to emphasize naturalistic dialogue, and to believe in a fluid, plastic use of theater.

6. Other ironic and comic bits added by Hill and Lennart include the use of "Jingle Bells" as a musical motif that begins as a typical rendition and becomes ludicrously "Southern" by the time the couple reaches Ralph's place. Hill also handles the café scene along the road with a deft comic touch. The beer-bellied rednecks at the bar become a local Greek chorus as they watch Fonda shake rice out of her shoe and order milk while George has moonshine, and as both get into their first fight.

7. *Time.* (Aug. 9th, 1963) p. 73. The reviewer goes on to say, "But something is terribly wrong with this picture. It is cold, mechanical, dead."

## 4. New Directions

1. Many directors shy away from working with children and teenagers. But Hill had already proved his ability to bring out the best in young actors in his television work, especially as he directed Robert Crawford in *A Child of Our Times*. Val's line about "BEING somebody else" reflects for Hill a child's ability to *act*. "Children," Hill says, "are able sometimes much better than adults to put themselves into imaginary roles. Even the word MAKE BELIEVE is the greatest instruction you can gave because you want to make someone believe you are somebody else. That illusion of being somebody else is the actor's craft." Brendan Gill in his review best captured the delicate balance that Hill created in the film when he said it was a movie "that will suit the milkshake set and, miraculously, will not give offense to oldsters of twenty or thirty." Brendan Gill, *The New Yorker*, March 28, 1964, p. 144.

2. *The World of Henry Orient* was later produced at the Place Theater in New York, beginning on October 23, 1967, as a musical comedy, adapted by Bob Merrill.

3. Again, casting was significant. There was some pressure on Hill to choose Joseph Cotten for the role of the father. But he felt strongly that he "wanted someone who was not so attractive on the outside, but who was very warm as a person." As Hill explains, her father is a businessman and "those men who are successful do not look like the fellows in cigarette ads. They're often tough little guys who have struggled to get where they are." Tom Bosley captured this toughness and yet responsive inner life extremely well.

4. For a fascinating study of how frequently the father-daughter relationship occurs as an ambiguous image in American literature and film, see Ruth Prigozy, "From Griffith's Girls to Daddy's Girl: The Masks of Innocence in *Tender Is the Night*," *Twentieth Century Literature* (Summer 1980) 26(2):189–221. (Prigozy is writing about the novel.)

5. Slow motion had been used in other feature films, but almost always for purely slapstick effect, even when the film itself was more serious. Take for example Rouben Mamoulian's *Love Me Tonight* (1932), which includes a hunting sequence complete with mounted hunters romping in slow motion just after Maurice Chevalier has taken off in fast motion on a wild stallion named Solitude.

6. Hill may have had an event in his own childhood in mind when directing the scene. He states that when he was young, he was asked to play a cruel trick on an aunt. The trick was set up by his uncle, who had just had a fight with his wife. He had Hill come in and say that her favorite dog had run away and that he couldn't find it. "I came in and cried, and I was so convincing that my uncle thought it had actually happened. I was so able to *make believe* that I was able to make him believe it had happened too!"

7. John Simon, *Private Screenings* (New York: Macmillan, 1967), p. 115. Simon, in fact,

dismissed the whole film as a "clean, happy, dishonest little picture that is wonderful anti-intellectual fun for the entire family," a point of view that seems a willful distortion of what actually appears on the screen.

8. Long before Woody Allen's *Manhattan*, Hill's film was in many ways a personal celebration of New York. The personal quality needs to be stressed. Hill captured New York in all seasons and shot on locations that he was fond of. Gil's house was done in the studio in New York, but it is a model of his own house at the time in New York, with certain modifications.

## 5. Who's in Control?

1. Pauline Kael, *Kiss Kiss Bang Bang* (Boston: Little Brown, 1968) p. 166. She also comments about Hill, that he, "compensates for his inexperience in the medium by developing strong characterizations that succeed in binding the material." Other critics were most unkind. Vincent Canby in the *New York Times* (October 11, 1966) called the film, "as big and familiar as Diamond Head and ultimately almost as heavy." Archer Winsten, however, in the *New York Post* (October 31, 1966) sums up the feeling of many who have seen the film, "How can people not admire Abner Hale? I admire him without agreeing with a damn thing he believes."

2. To search out a queen, Marion Dougherty, Hill's casting director, travelled to Pango-Pango, Fiji, Western Samoa, and Tonga where they considered the Queen of Tonga but finally settled on LaGarde. Wherever possible, Dougherty cast Polynesian natives, and Hill claims that the natives accepted La Garde as a real Queen even though she was from a different island.

3. Kael speaks of LaGarde as "sublime as the sacred queen of the island, a warm mountain of flesh that is balanced against von Sydow's scarecrow of spirit."

4. Hill states that both he and Mary Tyler Moore were conned by Hunter: Moore felt she was wrong for the part as did Hill, but Hunter insisted; Hill and Moore agreed to make the most of it. Though he still feels she was miscast, he thinks "she's a hell of an actress: I grew very fond of her as a person."

5. Compare the parody and wit and speed of *Millie* with Lucas' *Raiders of the Lost Ark*: *Raiders* goes in for slightly more character plausibility and depth, but the plot is held by a thrill a moment, all of which spoof some film or cliché, much as *Millie* blends romance, music and farce.

6. Hollis Alpert, *Saturday Review* (April 15, 1967), p. 45. His review is very positive, though he finds Channing boring because of "her never-varying style."

7. Brendan Gill, *New Yorker* (April 1, 1967), p. 94. Gill complains of the intermission and length of the film, but speaks of the "urgency and light touch of Hill who knows thin ice when he sees it." He is displeased with Julie Andrews (with her "strenuous winningness') but finds Carol Channing "a wonder."

## 6. "Just So We Come Out Ahead"

1. Goldman claims that the blowing up of a railroad car with the money in it is a true incident.

2. William Goldman, *Butch Cassidy and the Sundance Kid*. Final version: July 15, 1968.

3. There is much speculation and little fact about the lives of Butch and Sundance, especially during the South American years. Perhaps the best reasoned account occurs, strangely enough, in a book about a walking tour, Bruce Chatwin's *In Patagonia* (New York: Summit Books, 1978). According to Chatwin's sources "the family of three" sailed from New York to Buenos Aires and purchased 12,000 acres of land in Cholila, Argentina in 1901. The film's version of their deaths in Bolivia belongs to an account set down by Arthur Chapman in *Elk's Magazine* in 1930. But President Rene Barrientos of Bolivia investigated the story, dug up corpses

in the cemetery, and "concluded that the whole thing was a fabrication." Chatwin looked up Butch's sister with these results: "She has no doubts: her brother came back and ate blueberry pie with the family at Circleville (Utah) in the fall of 1925. She believes he died of pneumonia in Washington State in the late 1930's. Another version puts his death in an Eastern city, a retired railroad engineer with two married daughters (p. 50)."

4. Goldman sold it when he did because Sam Peckinpah was set to use some of the same material in *The Wild Bunch*. Actually the films remain quite different in tone and scope, and in fact there is no Butch in Peckinpah's film, though the role of William Holden follows Butch somewhat. The main similarity is a sense of the closing in of the frontier.

5. Hollis Alpert, *Saturday Review* (September 27, 1969), p. 39.

6. Lévi-Strauss, *Structural Anthropology* (New York: Basic Books, 1963), p. 226.

7. John Simon, for instance, found it a comic *Bonnie and Clyde* and Pauline Kael spoke of it as a "glorified vacuum" and a "facetious Western."

8. Goldman claims he was not really thinking of the "times" when he wrote the script, but he is fascinated that many young people saw the superposse as a metaphor for the United States government, especially as it related to the draft, drugs, and Vietnam: "It was relentless and would hunt you down," students told him.

9. It is worth noting that 1969 was the year for two other male duo films. *Easy Rider*, with Peter Fonda as the detached "Captain America" and Dennis Hopper as the hip, spaced-out sidekick, became peculiarly American prototypes for future cycle odysseys of contemporary Don Quixotes and Sancho Panzas. *Midnight Cowboy*, on the other hand, filmed in the urban landscape of New York, dealt with the city's glamorous and seedy sides. Dustin Hoffman as Ratso and John Voight as the naïve cowboy who wishes to take the city by storm but who ends up being taken himself, provided a moving glance at male friendship as a means of survival.

10. Just before the less than daring duo jump off the cliff, Butch replies to Sundance's memorable line that he can't swim, with "You stupid fool, the fall'll probably kill you." And yet they plunge together just as they will leap to their deaths in Bolivia together.

## 7. Unstuck in Time

1. Crawford's documentary is every bit as captivating as his earlier *The Making of Butch Cassidy and the Sundance Kid*, though it has, unfortunately, not been released because of legal and union difficulties. It is an excellent behind-the-scenes film that provides insight not only into George Roy Hill's direction, but also into the work of his whole group, most especially the production design by Henry Bumstead.

2. Kurt Vonnegut, Jr., *Slaughterhouse Five or The Children's Crusade* (New York: Dial Press, 1969), p. 19.

3. Kurt Vonnegut, Jr. as interviewed by David Standish in *Playboy* (July 1973) 20:66.

4. Stephen Dimeo, "Novel into Film: So It Goes," in Gerald Perry and Roger Shatzkin, eds., *The Modern American Novel and the Movies*, pp. 282–92 (New York: Ungar, 1978).

5. Penelope Gilliatt, *The New Yorker*, April 1, 1972, p. 93.

6. Edward Shores, *George Roy Hill* (Boston: Twayne, 1983), p. 57.

7. Both *Being There* and *Slaughterhouse Five* are interesting books that improved as films. There are several reasons why this is so, but I am most concerned with the fact that on film the abstract (Chance, Billy Pilgrim) becomes concrete, and so, more realistic. Billy Pilgrim is still a symbolic figure, but he is also an actor and a personality, albeit limited!

8. Michael Sacks has not become a well-known star, but this film did lead to a modest career in such films as *Sugarland Express*, *Hanover Street*, and *The Amityville Horror*.

9. On-location designing can have its large headaches, however. Bumstead remembers that it was a dry winter that year, and it seemed as if they would not be able to film the snow

sequence in Europe. At the last minute though, there was a snowstorm and all was saved. Bumstead is capable of working efficiently and swiftly. One morning they were supposed to film in a small city where a large part of the downtown section was to be destroyed by the local officials because coal was to be mined underneath (the film crew was lucky to get permission from the officials to hold up the demolition until they were ready to shoot). Hill looked over the shelters that had been constructed for the shot and asked for four times as many to be constructed. By 1:00 P.M. that same day, Bumstead had put together a makeshift set that worked well in the film. What might have taken another designer days or weeks to do, Bumstead had done in a few hours.

10. Stanley Kauffmann, *National Review*, August 12, 1972, p. 35. Kauffmann speaks of Vonnegut's book as, "facile wryness, sophomoric rue, mousetrack implications of cosmic mysteries," but feels the "film supplies what he doesn't."

## 8. *The Big Con*

1. Hill decided on Joplin's music after he heard a nephew playing some of his tunes one evening after Hill had already begun shooting the film. Redford feels the choice of Joplin's ragtime tunes helped Hill understand the tone of the whole film. "When I hear this music," Hill said, "I sort of see the film in my head," he once told Redford.

2. Production designer Henry Bumstead explains that finding a Joliet location was the most difficult task for him on the film. Bumstead recalls with humor that Hill likes to shoot on location and enjoys getting away from Hollywood. After reading the script he had to explain to Hill at a planning session, "You're going to be mad, but most of this film is going to have to be done on the lot here in California." Hill good naturedly responded, "I didn't call you down here from Mono Lake (where Bumstead had been working on Clint Eastwood's *High Plains Drifter*) just to tell me we're going to shoot this on the lot because I hate the lot!" Bumstead looked at many towns for Joliet, but finally found a street in Pasadena as he was driving to work one day. The buildings have since been torn down for new construction.

3. Hill added the shot of Newman's hand exposing the four threes. All three versions of the script I have read simply cut from Lonnegan's four nines to Gondorff's four jacks. Either way we know Newman has pulled a fast one, but Hill's addition makes it that much funnier since we realize he must have worked with lightning speed.

4. Think of Tony (Paul Muni) in *Scarface*, for instance, who is shown to have a strong Italian background complete with a worried mother and a sister he treats more like a lover than a sister. There is also Poppy, the vamp, who becomes one of the "objects" Tony craves. As several critics have noted, by the time the gangster genre reached Francis Ford Coppola's *Godfather I* and *II*, "family" becomes the central concern of the story. Hill, on the other hand, opts for keeping the focus on the male world of conning and camaraderie.

5. Paul Newman comments on the Gondorff–Hooker relationship: "One thing that is really overlooked about *The Sting* is that it is about the transfer of the crown from the King to the Prince."

6. For a thorough discussion of American con men, see: Gary Lindberg, *The Confidence Man in American Literature* (New York: Oxford University Press, 1982). Commenting on the King and the Duke in *Huckleberry Finn*, Lindberg states, "As they prey on others, they illustrate not what energy and diligence but what spunk and audacity will do in a protean society." Such a description works well for Hooker and Gondorff as well, not to mention many of Hill's other protagonists.

7. Jay Cocks *Time*, December 31, 1973, p. 50. Cocks goes on to criticize the film further for not being a social documentary on the Depression: "It lacks the elements that could have given it true drive: a sense of urban underworld, or the Depression that sucked so many people

into it, an understanding of the con man's pathology that goes beyond surface style and patter—a story that depends not on plot twists but on character." Once again, it appears clear that the reviewer has not recognized the importance of the theme of initiation in the film and its obvious intention to be an entertainment rather than a historical or politically aware drama.

8. Pauline Kael, *Reeling* (Boston: Little, Brown, 1976), p. 333. Kael perhaps suggests more about herself than about the film when she compares it to *Butch Cassidy* saying, "They were darling desperadoes in their last match: now they're hearty hoods. I would much rather see a picture about two homosexual men in love than see two romantic actors going through a routine whose point is that they're so adorably smiley butch that they can pretend to be in love and it's all innocent." How to respond to a remark that goes so far beyond observing the actual workings of the film? As discussed in the introduction and in chapter 6, Hill and similar directors seem to be haunted by those critics who cannot accept male friendship for its own sake without its becoming sexual.

9. Newman, Redford, and Hill would like to work together in the future. But they all agree thay do not wish to repeat themselves, and they have been unable to locate a script that lives up to their standards and desire to break new territory for their talents. Though David S. Ward wrote the script for *The Sting II*, none of the three felt the material was strong enough to merit taking on.


## 9. The Corruption of Sport

1. Andrew Britton, "The Great Waldo Pepper," *Movie* (Winter 80/Spring 81), 27/28:66–70. Britton's article is a perceptive one that turns to Norman O. Brown's discussion of the trickster in *Hermes the Thief* (New York: Vintage Books, 1969).

2. George Roy Hill now lives in New York, but when he lived in California, some of his best friends were stunt pilots. The most daring of them all was Frank Tallman, who died when he ran into a mountain in a storm. With these pilots and most especially with Tallman, Hill was able to keep alive his lifelong interest in flying. "Tallman and I talked for over ten years about doing a film in which we would do all the stunts done by all the aviators I had known and collected in my scrapbook in my youth," says Hill. He wished to re-create the glory of such pilots as Paul Mant, who was killed flying a stunt for Robert Aldrich's *The Flight of the Phoenix* (1966) and Frank Clark who died later while playing a practical joke on a friend. The friend had bought an old mine somewhere up in the Northwest, and Clark decided to fly up and dump manure on his house. To do so, he had to fly his plane upside down, and could not straighten it out afterward. That was the last of Frank Clark.

3. *Newsweek* (Mark 17, 1974), p. 93.

4. It's a fascinating fact of script-writing that must have been devised to drive film scholars crazy that there are often many "final" versions of a script. The three *Waldo Pepper* scripts I have studied are marked "First Final Rewrite" (Feb. 15, 1973), "Absolutely Final Rewrite, But One" (October 1973), and the final one that only says "October 31, 1973."

5. In early versions of the script, Waldo calls himself third best, and something is made of the number 2 pilot, but in the interest of brevity and plot directness, number 2 was dropped. Originally Ezra was the best pilot, and Paul Newman was interested in playing the role.

6. Bruce Dern had been considered for the role but Bo Svenson was, according to Goldman, less expensive.

7. Andrew Britton, "The Great Waldo Pepper," p. 66. "The trickster," Britton notes, paraphrasing Norman O. Brown, "may evolve into any one of such contrasting figures as a benevolent culture-hero nearly indistinguishable from the Supreme God, a demiurge in strong opposition to the heavenly powers, a kind of devil counter-acting the creator in every possible way, a messenger and mediator between gods and men, or merely a Puckish figure, the hero of comical stories."

8. *New York Daily News*, January 21, 1981. Paul Newman says of his role as Reggie, "It may not have been the best movie I ever made, but it was the most original role I'd played in years. The funny thing is, when I did it I knew I'd make a lot of enemies," he says gleefully referring to his character's spicy language. "I got one letter from a woman in Indianapolis who said I raced at her track in 1967 and this was the high point of her life. But she said, 'last night I saw *Slapshot* and if you ever set foot on my property I'll set the dogs on you.' "

Hill had also considered Jack Nicholson for the role of Reggie, and Nick Nolte had wanted the role so much that he devoted two weeks to trying to learn, unsuccessfully, to skate. Newman does his own skating and a double is used only in two scenes.

9. Nancy Dowd quoted in M. J. Sobran Jr.'s review in *National Review*, April 1, 1977, p. 392.

10. Hill worked hard on the script, pulling it together and trying to delineate the story more clearly. Because of a tight shooting schedule caused by the brief availability of the rinks they chose to use (in Johnstown, Pennsylvania, Hamilton and Syracuse, New York), much of the script was rewritten on the run, and in fact Dowd did much writing on the set as it was in production. The film reflects both the freshness and the haste of its production.

11. Joseph Campbell, *The Hero With A Thousand Faces*, 2d ed. (Princeton: Princeton University Press, 1968), p. 30.

12. Newman laughs when he thinks of Reggie. "I like Reggie more than any character I have played in ten years," he says. "I look back on him with such incredible affection." But what about the way he rolls over people's feelings? "You can't be called a bastard," Newman replies, "If you simply manipulate a bunch of urchins and clowns. Reggie is at the end of his strap; he's the eternal optimist, a born desperate loser who will scrap for the last piece of hamburger on the plate."

See also Pauline Kael, *New Yorker* (March 7, 1977) p. 91. She praises Newman as a "casual American star—acting at its peak." She finds that Newman has matured well and yet, "He makes boyishness seem magically attractive." Kael also singles out his healthy enjoyment of sex in the scene with Susanne in which Newman displays a "luscious infantile carnality."

13. In one sense, Dowd and Hill have taken the trend toward more startling language in American film to its extreme. But they have done so within a particular context, much as Hal Ashby's *The Last Detail* gave Jack Nicholson the chance to bring sailor talk on screen for the first time. In both cases the abusive language points to the immaturity and impotency of the male characters.

14. *The New Yorker*, March 7, 1977, pg. 92.

15. Jack Kroll, *Newsweek*, March 7, 1977, p. 68.

16. Pauline Kael, *New Yorker*, March 7, 1977, p. 92.

17. *New Republic*, March 19, 1977, p. 20.

18. The Hansons are not pure fantasy. Hill explains that there were three Carlson brothers on the Johnson Jets and that two of them play the Hansons in the film. What the Hansons do on screen is thus not far removed from what actually happened with the Jets. Hill is quick to note that many people attacked the film as being pure exaggeration. "But these are people that don't know hockey," he says, "because that is the way it is. For instance, players really do go up into the stands and fight with crowds!"

## 10. Innocence Revisited

1. The original novel was published by Editions Jean-Claude Lattes in Paris, 1977. The English translation for Hill was done by Pierre Sauvage. The novel was to be released as a tie-in with the film, but Hill refused to have a picture from the film on the cover since he felt (rightfully) that the film was too different from the novel to make such publicity fair.

2. The Boy Scout shirt was screenwriter Burns' idea. Hill was dubious about such an outfit,

but Burns showed up one day carrying one and Hill gave the go-ahead for David Dukes to wear it.

3. *Newsweek*, April 30, 1979, p. 81.

4. The *New York Times*, April 27, 1979, p. C–16. Oddly enough, while Canby disliked *A Little Romance* ("a movie that seems to have melted the minds of everyone of any stature connected with it"), he enjoyed *The World of Henry Orient*, which he labels as "still charming."

5. *Time*, August 13, 1979, p. 64. He quotes Hill on how he managed to get them to act so naturally in a romantic story. "I made them hold hands and not break eye contact for ten minutes. Soon they started giggling, then arguing, and then breaking into gales of laughter," says Hill.

6. To teach him English, Hill's daughter Owens spent several months working with him in California. Thelo has gone on to French films and television.

7. Tom Topor, *New York Post*, May 4, 1979.

8. Hill admits that Olivier became such a shameless ham in some of the scenes that it was difficult not to sit back and enjoy letting him take the role wherever he wished. "He's so entertaining that I became enraptured with his warmth and his exaggerated character," says Hill.

9. *New Yorker*, May 7, 1979, p. 141.

## 11. The World According to Garp

1. For a behind the scenes glance at the filming of *Garp*, see Andrew Horton, "Getting a Hold on Garp," *American Film* (July–August 1982) 7(9):38–45.

2. Thomas Williams, "Talk With John Irving," *New York Times Book Review*, October 19, 1978, p. 26.

3. Marilyn French, "The *Garp* Phenomenon, *MS*, September 1982, p. 15.

4. Pauline Kael, *The New Yorker*, August 23, 1982, p. 15.

5. David Denby, *New York*, August 2, 1982, p. 46.

6. Marilyn French ("Garp Phenomenon") clearly maps out the feminist criticism of Irving's novel and also the film. She feels that instead of proving to be sensitive to women's issues, Irving portrays feminists as villains. According to French, "One may not complain that Irving omits, ignores the power world with its male domination, its oppression and exploitation of women, minorities, and the poor; its injustice; its criminal practices; its poisoning of the earth, air, and water; its heaped up profits for the few. But one may complain that he disregards the effect of these things on ordinary people in their small domestic sphere."

7. David Denby, *New York*, August 2, 1982, p. 46.

8. Joseph Gelmis, *Newsday*, July 25, 1982, p. 35.

9. The scene as it appears in the final draft is given below. The changes between this text and what actually appears on the screen can be largely attributed to Hill. In brief, Hill has used the venetian blinds to expand on earlier scenes from Garp's life, including the surf at Dog's Head Harbor and the pages of Garp's short story blowing in the wind (but expanded from incident as filmed to include hundreds of pages blowing in the football stadium).

EXT: GREENWICH VILLAGE—DAY

GARP is walking on University Place. He looks dejected. A couple get out of a parked car ahead of him. The couple are having an argument. Both are carrying suitcases.

STEPHEN

Oh, c'mon, Rachel.

RACHEL

Don't Rachel me, Stephen. Just don't Rachel me. I told you we should've stayed in Chicago.

She hurries away. He hurries after her dropping a pair of gloves on the sidewalk. GARP picks up the gloves and wants to give them back but the couple have entered a building. He looks at the gloves . . . seems ready to throw them in a trash can but doesn't.

As HE CROSSES A STREET he sees a moving van and movers with ropes looking up. He looks up and sees a piano being hoisted into the eighth story window of a nine story building. GARP stops. He looks at the window. He plays with the gloves. He's thinking. He hears a siren. We don't know if he's imagining it or if it's a real siren in the city.

GARP looks up again at the window and the piano and STEPHEN. The man who dropped the gloves, pops into the scene. GARP is obviously now imagining the scene. He doesn't like the fact that the man is dressed just as he was in the street so he pops him into the scene again dressed in a tuxedo. STEPHEN is standing on the ledge, leaning on the piano, looking down.

A CROWD POPS INTO THE SCENE.

A POLICE CAR arrives and a woman runs out of the car. It is RACHEL. She's in tears.

FIREMEN are spreading inflated mattresses on the street to catch the man should he fall.

DEAN BODGER. For a split second GARP pops DEAN BODGER into the scene and then takes him out again. GARP heads toward the scene looking up at STEPHEN.

    STEPHEN

RACHEL! RACHEL!

    RACHEL

STEPHEN

    STEPHEN

Rachel, I can't live without you. No-can-live. Cannot. No-can-do.

The firemen are getting their high ladder into the act. The cop is trying to talk to RACHEL. She's crying.

    STEPHEN—THE PIANIST:

I LOVE YOU, RACHEL!

    RACHEL

STOP IT!

    STEPHEN

ADORE YOU! REMEMBER CHICAGO. DO YOU? REMEMBER THESE, RACHEL?

He takes out a pair of gloves. He clutches them to his bosom and then he shows them to her . . . making them dance in the air.

    STEPHEN

DO YOU? I DON'T WANT THEM ANYMORE.

He throws them down. The gloves fall not far from GARP. He picks them up. He wants to give them to the woman but the cop is taking the woman toward the building. As she's heading toward the door STEPHEN starts to play. He sings.

    STEPHEN:

Sings lyric to "There Will Never Be Another You"

He's crying. He either slips or falls off his ledge on purpose.

The crowd screams. The woman stops. STEPHEN falls into the inflated mattress. The woman is ready to run to him. And then another scream is heard. GARP and the others look up. The piano ropes have snapped. The piano starts to fall. The piano falls right on top of him obliterating him from view. The sound of the vibrating piano wires fill the air.

Closeup of GARP

Gloves in hand he turns away from the sight. He still would like to give the gloves to RACHEL but she's being led away by the police. GARP starts walking away from the scene. He's looking st the gloves and thinking.

Closeup of a typewriter page

Letters appear: *The Magic Gloves* by T. S. GARP

In the film Hill has tightened this scene further by beginning it in Garp's room (after he has witnessed the argument between Rachel and Stephen) beginning to write the story. Across the street in another room is a man playing a melancholy sax: the tune is "There Will Never Be Another You." We cut to an ever-embellished version of the story with cross-cuts to reaction shots of Garp typing. When he finishes we close with the sax player still playing across the street. The experience has come full circle, and a short story has been completed. Garp smiles with satisfaction.

10. Steve Tesich smiles and refuses to explain the personal meaning of "Magic Gloves" but

clearly it is autobiographical. The male character *is* named Stephen and Rachel speaks of their old home in Chicago where Tesich grew up.

11. Janet Maslin, *The New York Times*, July 23, 1982, p. C–13. Maslin also felt the film was much lighter in a healthy way than the novel. She appreciated the fact that the film by-passed the "self congratulatory streak" in the novel.

12. Maslin, p. C–13. Close is complimented on her ability to perform "miracles with the toughest of the story's many difficult roles." And among many other favorable reviews of her acting, Gary Arnold in the *Washington Post* wrote of her as "regally handsome and self possessed" (July 23, 1982), p. D–6.

13. In her negative review Pauline Kael stated that, "The difference between Irving's face and Williams's face is comparable to the difference between *Garp* as a novel and *Garp* as a movie." Gary Arnold states that, "Williams, looking like a cross between the young Red Skelton and Rod Taylor, always seems puppyish and overmatched in her [Jenny's] presence." David Denby in *New York*, August 2, 1982, p. 46, is even less kind: "Robin Williams is completely at sea. This isn't acting; it's ingratiation."

14. This important speech belongs to Tesich. It does not occur in the novel. What it succeeds in doing is to suggest how strongly Garp has taken control of what he wishes to do. Tesich dramatizes more clearly than the book a depth of human feeling at this point and also provides yet another example of how much Garp follows his own path.

15. Garp is murdered by Pooh, wearing a nurse's uniform that reminds us of Jenny. While technically we cannot consider her an outside force, since her motives are in part personal (we have watched her watching Garp throughout the film), she is deeply affected by a warped perception of feminism. She too becomes an Ellen Jamesian.

# Index